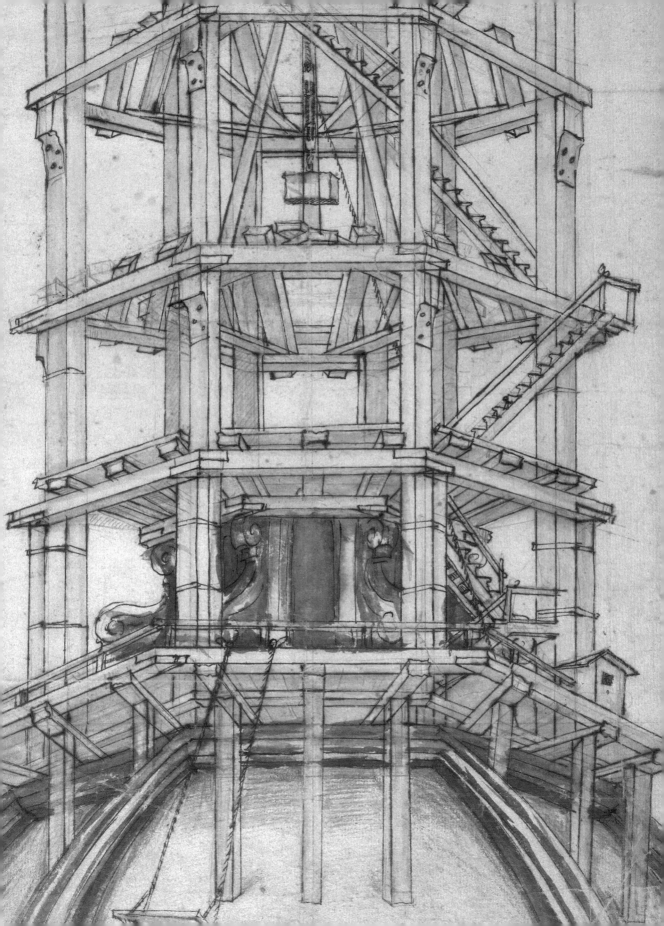

EDITED BY KENNETH POWELL

The Great Builders

Thames & Hudson

CONTENTS

ACKNOWLEDGMENTS
My greatest debt as editor is to the band of authors from around the world who expertly condensed their profound knowledge of their respective subjects into succinct and scholarly texts for this book. Among those who provided invaluable advice are Mosette Broderick, Francesco Garofalo, Martin Meade, Thomas Muirhead, David Peyceré and John Zukowsky. I should also like to thank everyone at Thames & Hudson for their help and encouragement during the preparation of this volume.

HALF-TITLE *Filippo Brunelleschi's lantern on the dome of Florence Cathedral, under restoration in 1601 following lightning damage. Drawing attributed to Gherardo Mechini.*

TITLE PAGE *John Fowler's Forth Railway Bridge under construction, Scotland, 1890.*

Sinan translated from the Turkish by Gülay Eskikaya
Giuseppe Mengoni translated from the Italian by Grace Crerar-Bromelow
Konstantin Melnikov translated from the Russian by Christine Barnard

First published in 2011 in hardcover in the United States of America by Thames & Hudson Inc., 500 Fifth Avenue, New York, New York 10110

thamesandhudsonusa.com

Library of Congress Catalog Card Number 2011922601

ISBN 978-0-500-25179-9

Printed and bound in China by C&C Offset Printing Co., Ltd

INTRODUCTION

THE GREAT BUILDERS OF HISTORY WERE INNOVATORS AND VISIONARIES.
Brunelleschi's dome in Florence amazed his contemporaries. It became the
prime landmark of Florence, just as the concrete poetry of Utzon's Sydney Opera
House is a symbol of Australian identity, the Eiffel Tower a universally recognized Parisian icon, and the Taj Mahal a key image of India. Building has been
a fundamental human activity since the dawn of civilization: the first structures recognizable as buildings, rather than primitive shelters, probably
appeared in the Near East around 9000 BC. Civilization means life in cities,
and the worlds' earliest cities grew up in the Near East, in a swathe of territory extending from Anatolia in modern Turkey to the Nile Delta. By the
second millennium BC the sophisticated civilization of China was generating its own ways of building. Here were the roots of technologies,
styles and forms that were to underpin the subsequent development of
building in Japan, India, the Islamic world and the Mediterranean. And
from this remote era we have, for the first time, the names of a few individuals who designed buildings – for example, the pyramid-building high
priest of Egypt, Imhotep (*fl. c.* 2780 BC), alleged inventor of the column,
who has also been claimed as the father of medical science.

ARTISTS, SCIENTISTS AND RULERS

The earliest builders did not style themselves 'architects' or 'engineers'
– professions that emerged only relatively recently. They might
be artists (such as Giotto or Brunelleschi), scientists (like
Wren) or even monarchs: the great Mughal emperor

OPPOSITE *To-ji lecture hall, Kyoto, rebuilt in 1491:*
a classic example of Japanese timber roof construction.
RIGHT *Imhotep, the designer of the Step Pyramid at*
Sakkara, Egypt, the world's first large-scale masonry
structure. It was completed around 2780 BC.

PREVIOUS PAGES *Shah Jahan, emperor and architect, before the Red Fort in Delhi, painted in the early 19th century.* **ABOVE** *Roof boss from Canterbury Cathedral bearing a portrait of the master mason Henry Yevele (c. 1320–1400), designer of the cathedral's nave.*

Shah Jahan, the greatest builder of his age in India, was far more than a passive client. The era that this book covers begins in the early 15th century, when artists were first emerging as personalities in their own right; in the West, Giorgio Vasari's *Lives of the Artists* (published in 1550), in which Brunelleschi features, was a landmark in this direction. Building itself was identified as an art. Contemporary with Brunelleschi, Tamerlane's architect Qavam al-Din Shirazi was afforded celebrity status, although he was still content to describe himself as a mason. In contrast, the builders of the great cathedrals of France and England remain largely anonymous figures categorized as 'master masons', with only the exceptional individual emerging from the shadows, such as the Englishman Henry Yevele, who was given the title King's Deviser of Masonry in 1360. Goethe, writing in 1772, presented Erwin von Steinbach (d. 1318) – whom he erroneously believed to be the sole architect of Strasbourg Cathedral – as a superhuman genius. Other writers of the Romantic period imagined abbeys designed and built by monks, and the great 14th-century English bishop William of Wykeham as the designer (as well as the founder) of New College, Oxford, and Winchester College.

In reality, the respective contributions of the medieval mason–architect and client are hard to disentangle. Was the early 12th-century Abbot Suger, of the abbey of St-Denis near Paris, actually a visionary pioneer of Gothic or just a progressive patron? In the medieval period, as ever, building was indelibly linked to power: Edward I's castles in Wales, for instance – designed by the late 13th-century Savoyard James of St George, who was described as an 'engineer' as well as a mason – were the mightiest of their age. Sébastien Vauban's fortifications, in their turn, expressed the territorial ambitions of Louis XIV's France: the Sun King was a phenomenal builder and founded the French Académie Royale d'Architecture in 1671, which was later incorporated into the Académie des Beaux-Arts.

The work of Wren, in contrast, reflected the cultural and political ethos of a monarchy that was no longer absolute (no Versailles for Charles II). Wren was essentially a gentleman–architect, a scholar at heart, whereas Vauban was a professional soldier and military engineer who became a Marshal of France. The tradition of the gentleman–amateur continued into the 18th century: the Englishman Richard Boyle,

Joseph Paxton's Crystal Palace, the spectacular structure that housed the Great Exhibition of 1851 in London and a landmark in the development of iron and glass building.

3rd Earl of Burlington, was a classic example. It was the 19th century that saw the formal emergence of the professions of architect and engineer, traditionally entered through a system of apprenticeship. The Architectural Association (founded in London in 1847) began to provide part-time courses, followed by the establishment of a full-time school. The Royal Institute of British Architects was set up in 1834, and the American Institute of Architects in 1857. The first American school of architecture, at the Massachusetts Institute of Technology in Cambridge, enrolled its initial students in 1867. The engineers were quicker off the mark in advancing the cause of professionalism: the Institution of Civil Engineers had been founded in London in 1818.

From the mid-18th century onwards, the torch of innovation passed to the West, as the Industrial Revolution produced a new world of canals, railways, warehouses and factories. Thomas Telford, John Rennie, Joseph Paxton, Isambard Kingdom Brunel, Victor Baltard and James Bogardus utilized 'new' materials – iron and glass, for the first time produced in large quantities – to create the icons of a new age. Mechanized brick manufacture, with the finished product transported by canal or railway, provided another new raw material, and local traditions of building were displaced by new technologies (British brick production doubled between 1820 and 1840). Terracotta and glazed faience also lent themselves to mass production and became widely used, both as a structural component and for decorative purposes. The response of the Romantic movement was to forge new boundaries between 'art' and 'building' (John Ruskin, for instance, referred to Paxton's 1851 Crystal Palace as a 'crystal humbug'). The distinction was telling, but essentially false: Neoclassical architects such as Karl Friedrich

BELOW *Transverse section of the Birmingham Canal, re-engineered by Thomas Telford in the 1820s.* OPPOSITE *Exploded view analysing the springing point of a typical 13th-century arch, published by Eugène-Emmanuel Viollet-le-Duc in 1859.*

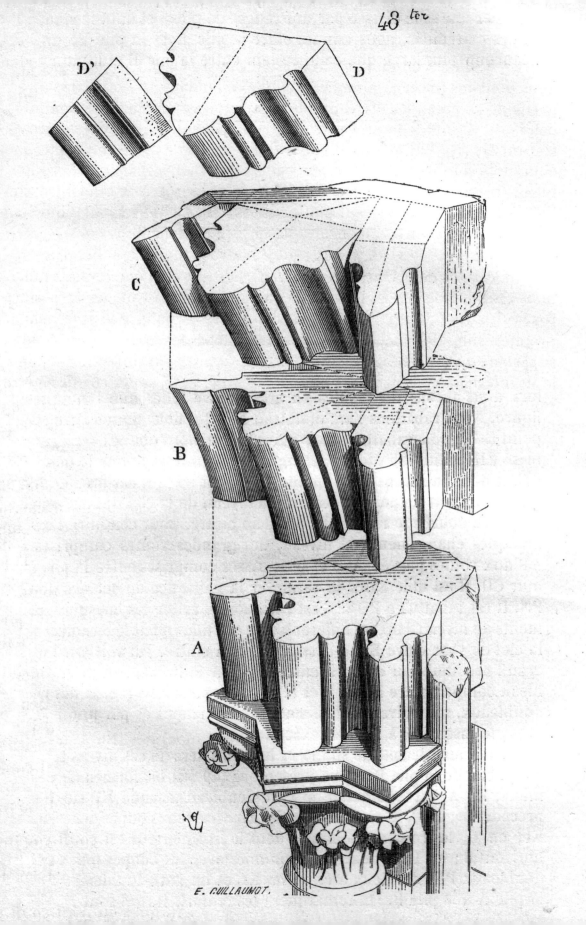

48 ter

D'   D

C

B

A

E. GUILLAUMOT.

The Gage Building in Chicago, part of a group designed by Holabird & Roche. The right-hand section features a decorated façade by Louis Sullivan (1898–99) while the adjacent frontages remain rigorously functional in appearance.

Schinkel, and Gothic Revivalists including George Gilbert Scott, also made free use of iron in their buildings. In the 20th century, Modernist critics would describe engineering structures such as the Crystal Palace as the 'real architecture' of the 19th century.

At the same time the great theorists of the Gothic Revival, A. W. N. Pugin and Eugène-Emmanuel Viollet-le-Duc, set out theories of rational construction that were to influence the pioneers of Modernism, although Pugin's writings, notably *Contrasts* (1836), reflected his doubts about the benefits of industrialism that would feed into the philosophy of the Arts and Crafts movement. (His frenetic career was, in fact, dependent on the use of the railway system – he described himself as 'a locomotive being' –

and he even sketched ideas for railway structures in Gothic mode.) The search for
new materials and technologies continued relentlessly throughout the 19th century:
steel, which gradually displaced cast and wrought iron, launched the skyscraper on its
global trajectory (even if the Eiffel Tower in Paris was, as late as 1889, fabricated using
a form of wrought iron). In the second half of the 19th century the torch of architectural progress passed from Europe to the United States, as William Le Baron Jenney,
John Wellborn Root and Louis Sullivan developed the theory and practice of the tall
building in Chicago. Equally, the modern skyscraper was made possible only by the
development of the elevator, a device perfected in the 1850s by the American Elisha
Otis and quickly adopted in other Western countries. The 19th century also saw the
development of building services – central heating, plumbing and ventilation – that
were similarly fundamental to the evolution of modern ways of building. By the 1880s
electric lighting was being widely introduced, both in buildings and to illuminate city
streets, after the incandescent light bulb was perfected by Joseph Wilson Swan in
England and Thomas Edison in the US.

THE MODERN WORLD OF REINFORCED CONCRETE

Along with steel, the material that made possible the building of the modern world
was reinforced concrete. The Romans had, of course, made extensive use of concrete –
in the dome of the Pantheon, for example – but in succeeding centuries the material
was little employed until interest in its possibilities was rekindled in the 19th century.
Early experiments in reinforcement took place
in Britain and America, but it was the work of
the Belgian-born engineer–entrepreneur François
Hennebique that made reinforced concrete a
medium in which every sort of structure, from
bridges and textile mills to mansions, could
be designed and built. As with iron and steel,
concrete challenged the inventive powers of engineers and architects. The Catalan Antoni Gaudí
made surprisingly little use of it, given its potential
for creating sculptural forms (realized to fine

Frank Lloyd Wright experimented with 'textile blocks'
of concrete as the basic material for a number of
his buildings, such as the Storer House, Los Angeles
(1923–24).

effect in the church of St-Jean in the Montmartre district of Paris, designed by Anatole de Baudot and completed in 1904). Frank Lloyd Wright used monolithic in-situ concrete for the Unity Temple at Oak Park, near Chicago (1908), and a reinforced-concrete frame for the Imperial Hotel in Japan (1914–22), but the precast concrete 'textile blocks' he came to favour were used as a cladding, masking the structure in the same way other architects used bricks or terracotta. The work of Wright's near contemporary Auguste Perret was rooted in the French rationalist tradition; he developed a distinctive new language for the use of concrete and applied it to a wide variety of structures, from warehouses and factories to churches and theatres. Perret continued working into the postwar years, but his influence waned as that of his sometime pupil the Swiss-born Le Corbusier became dominant in France.

Indeed, Le Corbusier can be seen as the 20th century's most influential architect worldwide, as he moved on from his early, essentially rationalist work to a poetic, sculptural approach in his later buildings, such as the chapel of Notre Dame du Haut at Ronchamp (1950–55), which baffled some of his followers. Rivalling Le Corbusier as an influence on modern architecture internationally was Mies van der Rohe, who trained in Berlin with the progressive German classicist Peter Behrens. Mies's work was clearly rooted in classicism, and after his emigration to the US in 1938 he became the prime exponent of the International Style associated with the Bauhaus. His approach, intensely rational, eschewing the romanticism of late Le Corbusier, was in tune with the American tradition of high-rise building in steel: his finest example, the Seagram Building (1954–58) in New York, inspired many imitations. The work of the great American partnership of Skidmore, Owings & Merrill developed in a broadly Miesian mould and was characterized by a close integration of architecture and engineering: Fazlur Khan, who joined the firm in 1955 and was responsible, with the architect Bruce Graham, for the John Hancock Tower (1969) in Chicago, was one of the great structural engineers of the 20th century.

The more expressive mode associated with Le Corbusier's late work found strong voice in the work of the Italian architect–engineer Pier Luigi Nervi, who took the application of reinforced concrete to new heights of delicacy, and equally in that of the Brazilian master Oscar Niemeyer, whose sculptural use of concrete is seen to dramatic effect in the country's new capital, Brasília (Modern architecture blossomed in Brazil during the interwar years, and the influence of Le Corbusier was strong). Louis

The Seagram Building (1954–58) on New York's Fifth Avenue is one of the masterpieces of the International Style, notable for its sleek aesthetic and its structural innovation. Here, Mies van der Rohe (left) inspects the installation of its curtain-walled façade, July 1956.

Kahn injected a new force into the American architectural scene with a series of works of immense poetic resonance, beginning in the early 1950s with his first significant project, the Yale University Art Gallery in New Haven. Kahn's influence on the so-called High-Tech architects, including Richard Rogers, Norman Foster and Renzo Piano (who worked for a time in his office), derives from his definition of 'served and servant spaces'; Rogers and Piano's Pompidou Centre in Paris (1971–77) reflects the influence of his thinking.

THE REINTEGRATION OF ENGINEERING AND ARCHITECTURE

In the 20th century the impetus for new ways of building came from the engineers and their expression from the architects, but some individuals cannot be categorized easily: Nervi, for example, and Jean Prouvé, who was content to style himself a 'constructor'; R. Buckminster Fuller, best known for geodesic domes but actually the supreme prophet of sustainable design; and Frei Otto, who took building into new territory with his exploration of tensile and membrane structures. The Spanish Santiago Calatrava, both architect and engineer, has demonstrated through his own career the irrelevance of such professional divides. The absolute integration of engineering and architecture espoused by Ove Arup has underpinned late 20th-century developments in building – the work of Norman Foster, for instance, and that of Frank Gehry, for whom the use of the computer made possible forms that would have been inconceivable a generation earlier. The 20th century was the age of globalism and universalism, yet some of the greatest builders of the age – Kenzo Tange in Japan, for example, and Niemeyer in Brazil – were notable for creating buildings that strongly reflected their distinct national cultures. Japan became a fertile territory for the evolution of a modern architecture of place. Whereas Tange's work was, in the end, strongly Corbusian, that of Kengo Kuma, a leading present-day Japanese architect, is clearly rooted in an exploration of traditional forms and materials. The history of building over many centuries is about the efforts of men (women were excluded from careers as architects or engineers until well into the 20th century) to dominate nature and to impose a new pattern on the world. Today, the world suddenly seems a fragile place, and the priority is to ensure that human life remains sustainable in centuries to come. Architects and engineers have a vital part to play, in that the buildings they create must contribute to protecting our planet from irreversible environmental damage.

Hoshakuji Station in Takanezawa, Tochigi Prefecture (2006). Kengo Kuma employed timber as well as steel and glass to create a modern building that incorporates themes from traditional Japanese architecture.

PIONEERS OF
STRUCTURE

Centuries before the roles of architect and engineer were formally defined by professional codes and legal prescriptions, the great builders of history were – necessarily – polymaths. That description could certainly be applied to Filippo Brunelleschi, who was part of the spectacularly creative artistic world of 15th-century Florence, a friend of painters and sculptors but equally an extraordinary technician, whose proposal for roofing the crossing of the city's cathedral was so innovative that some derided it as sheer madness. Brunelleschi's initial training was as a goldsmith and sculptor, and his career embraced everything from designing theatre machinery to building ships and city walls. By devising novel ways of constructing the Florence dome with a minimum of scaffolding, he significantly reduced the cost of the project. Brunelleschi's genius, like that of his contemporary the Persian architect Qavam al-Din Shirazi – the first celebrity architect of the Islamic world – lay in the dramatic enclosure of space and the development of the dome, achieved by both through a remarkable degree of structural inventiveness. Contemporaries praised the extent of Qavam-al-Din's knowledge and skill as engineer, draughtsman and constructor, but he simply called himself a mason, the term generally applied to the largely anonymous medieval architects of Europe.

Great buildings have always reflected the support of determined and enlightened patrons. The great Turkish architect and engineer Sinan served a succession of Ottoman rulers, reputedly designing nearly five hundred buildings. Trained as a soldier, he was an expert designer of fortifications but is best known for some of the greatest mosques of the Islamic world. The son of a mason and carpenter, Sinan achieved social status through his place at the court of the sultans. Giuliano da Sangallo was the favoured designer of the Medici, and when they fell from power in Florence he courted the papacy. A member of a notable woodworking family, Sangallo was able to adapt his skills to a wide range of projects, ranging from military fortifications to churches and the design of tombs. The life of Shah Jahan, creator of the Taj Mahal and a transforming influence on the development of Indian architecture, demonstrates the degree to which a client could be much more than the inspiration for a great building project: like those great European rulers Louis XIV of France and Frederick the Great of Prussia, Shah Jahan considered building the greatest expression of royal power (and he personally oversaw his own academy of architects and constructors). The idea of the ruler as architect was not new – it can be traced back to ancient Mesopotamia – but Shah Jahan's role was unusually active. Under Louis XIV, who claimed no skills as an architect, France entered an era of expansion that generated not only the château of Versailles, but also the fortifications of Dunkirk, Metz, Lille and other French border cities. Vauban's skills as a military engineer were honed during his career as a soldier: conducting sieges, he began to consider ways in which cities could be made impregnable. The extraordinary range of Vauban's interests, including livestock breeding, statistics and economics, makes him one of the most fascinating figures of this golden age of France.

In contrast, Christopher Wren was a scholar – a mathematician called upon to serve a restored monarchy that no longer wielded absolute power and to apply his geometrical expertise to the design of buildings. Wren's masterpiece, St Paul's Cathedral in London, was his own creation, but he assembled a team of designers to organize the rebuilding of the city's parish churches after the Great Fire in 1666, and the genius of one of his assistants, Nicholas Hawksmoor, arguably outshone even that of his master. Wren was the classic gentleman–architect, with connections to the court, the Church of England and the universities. He never travelled farther than Paris, yet was familiar with Italian sources and equally able to work in harmony with older buildings (as at Christ Church, Oxford). His career gives lie to the notion that a great genius must be at odds with the establishment of the time. Gradually the idea emerged later in the 18th century of the architect as an independent figure, standing apart from the world of mere construction, and this notion helped to set the stage for the age of Romanticism in Europe.

FILIPPO BRUNELLESCHI

The father of Renaissance architecture

1377–1446

FILIPPO DI SER BRUNELLESCO, better known to us as Filippo Brunelleschi, was born in Florence and educated as a sculptor in the goldsmith's guild. His most celebrated work, the construction of the dome of the cathedral of Santa Maria del Fiore in Florence, is among the world's most important buildings, both for its technical achievements and for its artistic, cultural and urban impact. Brunelleschi is also recognized as the inventor of linear perspective, a representational system that changed the course of Western art. His contemporaries admired his knowledge of mathematics, science, literature and classical architecture, and the government employed his expertise not only to build fortresses, develop mining and divert rivers but also to construct a range of projects including theatrical machines and amphibious boats. Brunelleschi worked in a city with a clearly defined and complex identity. In 1377, the year of his birth, finishing touches were still being applied to monuments and urban spaces planned almost a century before. Most were part of an overall urban plan developed to incorporate into the city's fabric the political project of the young communal government. What is remarkable is that Brunelleschi was able to make both formal and spatial interventions that further developed this vision and also opened the culture of Florence to a new era of architectural and artistic exploration.

TECHNOLOGICAL AND ARTISTIC DEVELOPMENTS

Brunelleschi's best-known work is the dome of Santa Maria del Fiore (1420–36). The original project of 1296 by Arnolfo di Cambio had already been under construction for almost a century, but the dome, 42 metres (138 feet) across, although anticipated in the project, had not been realized. Its construction posed a significant challenge: there was no obvious precedent for building what would effectively have been the largest dome in Europe at the time. In 1418 a competition was launched to find an answer to this technical problem. Given the condition of the existing church structure, earlier examples such as the Pantheon in Rome that required massive walls or traditional Gothic buildings with their exterior buttresses, were not viable. A new and

Brunelleschi's dome for Florence Cathedral has dominated the cityscape for over five hundred years. This coloured woodcut, the so-called 'Pianta della Catena', dates from c. 1472.

innovative solution was needed. Brunelleschi's proposal did not require an armature to support the dome, nor could it have been successful without a number of additional technical inventions, including designs for the scaffolding as well as the machinery necessary to haul up the building materials – a major feat when one considers that the top of the dome is 90 metres (nearly 300 feet) from the ground. Brunelleschi's unique idea, probably inspired by the Baptistery, was to construct the dome as a double shell: the interior shell is thicker than the exterior one, and the space between them is large enough to accommodate stairs to climb to the top of the dome and the lantern. The elements are tied together in such a way as to avoid the need for exterior buttresses, and the eight major and sixteen minor ribs that form the main structure distribute the stresses so that the existing walls and piers can support it.

Although Brunelleschi won the competition, for reasons that are not completely clear he was asked to collaborate with Lorenzo Ghiberti, who had won the 1401

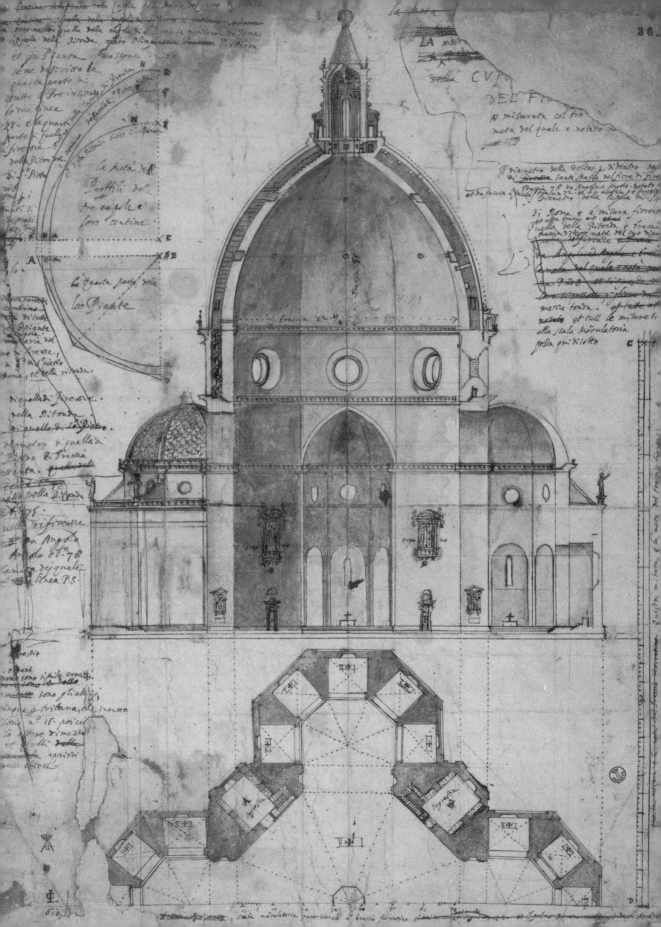

competition for the decoration of the Baptistery doors. As well as the actual dome, the project also included both the construction of the lantern at the top and the raising of the base of the dome structure itself. The lantern, built according to Brunelleschi's design, plays a structural role in holding together the ribs of the dome; the lantern is also important in the formal logic of the dome's geometry, emphasizing the vertical thrust. Brunelleschi raised the level of the base of the dome by building the octagonal drum higher than anticipated by Arnolfo, giving it an even more impressive presence above the city landscape. The urban and symbolic role of the dome was best expressed by Alberti in the next century, who described it in one of his treatises as 'covering under its shadow all the Tuscan people'.

BRUNELLESCHI'S IDEAS OF MODULAR CONSTRUCTION

Brunelleschi's design for the Ospedale degli Innocenti (1419–24) uses a loggia to define the façade and the relationship of the building to the urban space in front of it. Such public arcades were built in Florence in previous centuries, but there are important differences in the way Brunelleschi defines the loggia as a spatial and structural element. His arcade of slender classical columns and broad arches is raised above ground level by a set of stairs, creating an overall effect that is at once theatrical and profoundly urban. The architectural language is based on the components of a single bay: each is a square both in plan and elevation, covered by a semicircular dome.

This unit defines a precise modular system in which repetition is the organizational principle – an innovation that can also be seen in Brunelleschi's later work. His arcaded elevation was later imitated on two other sides of the Piazza SS. Annunziata: over the next century two new loggias were built, and the result is one of the most impressive urban spaces of the Renaissance.

Brunelleschi's other projects also had a fundamental impact on the city of Florence. The churches of San Lorenzo (begun 1421) and Santo Spirito (commissioned 1436) reflect his continuing architectural research based on the concepts of measure, repetition and perspective. Both buildings are related in scale and plan to the churches built by the mendicant orders in the 13th century, particularly Santa Croce (designed by Arnolfo) and Santa Maria Novella, and they have a similarly strong connection to the public piazzas in front. The Old Sacristy of San Lorenzo, commissioned in 1419 and finished *c.* 1428, was built before the church was reconstructed and exemplifies Brunelleschi's modular system based on mathematical proportions and his use of classical forms. In Santo Spirito his ideas are developed in a fuller and more accomplished manner. The plan of the church respects the traditional layout of the Latin cross, but again it is the individual bay that becomes the theme and organizational principle of the entire building, creating ambiguity within the traditional hierarchy of nave, transept and apse through the effect of an implied infinite space. Brunelleschi accomplishes this by literally wrapping the space with small semicircular chapels that run without interruption along the side of the nave, the transept and the aisle. In fact these were supposed to have gone around the front of the church as well, creating the need for another architectural invention: four doors at the front of the church, as opposed to the traditional three, with their implied hierarchy of centre and sides. His original solution of bays and four doors was never built, leaving Brunelleschi's project incomplete, and the church was not completed until long after his death.

Together with the Palazzo Medici, the church of San Lorenzo became the centre of an area identified with the powerful family. There are accounts of Brunelleschi's proposal for the Medici palace suggesting that he wanted it to be built right across the front façade of the church, creating a unified urban ensemble. His proposal was not accepted, probably for political reasons. For Santo Spirito, his original plan was for the church to be reoriented by 180 degrees towards the river, a simple but powerful move that would have redefined the city's relationship to the river as a public space. Although his wish to rotate the church was not fulfilled, the idea of the river as a public space would later catch the collective imagination in such projects as Giorgio Vasari's Palazzo degli Uffizi, begun in 1560.

Brunelleschi's designs, built and unbuilt, were profoundly influential both in his own time and for generations to come, not only for other architects and theorists like Alberti, but also for artists including his friends Donatello and Masaccio. From a modern perspective, Brunelleschi's life and work present us with important questions. Of all his projects, we can only be certain that two were carried out strictly to his plans: the cathedral dome and the Old Sacristy. The original plan for the Ospedale was enlarged and many details were changed after he was no longer in charge of the construction project, and San Lorenzo was only partially completed while he was alive. In 1446, the year of Brunelleschi's death, only one column had been erected in the church of Santo Spirito. But by defining architectural discourse in a new way and establishing a fresh set of principles, techniques and instruments, Brunelleschi made it possible for the works to continue with an integrity and cultural dimension independent of specific motives or solutions. The idea of a rationalized space based on geometry and the measurements of elements and components, organized or brought together in response to a multiplicity of factors, marked a sharp departure from established practice. This is all the more significant since Brunelleschi has been credited as the first example of the modern architect, as opposed to the traditional master mason working in a collective system of decision making. He may, indeed, have constructed not only the concept of the architect as a sole creator, but also the idea of design as an intellectual discipline.

LINEAR PERSPECTIVE

Brunelleschi's major contribution to the history of architecture and art was the invention of linear perspective. It is known that he constructed two panels that represented precise perspective, one of the Baptistery seen from the cathedral and the other showing the Piazza della Signoria. Unfortunately neither of these panels has survived. For centuries, thinkers from Ptolemy and Euclid to Muslim and Western medieval scholars had pursued an interest in perspective as a form of knowledge based on optics, mathematics and physiology. In this context the studies of Alhazen (Ibn al-Haytham, *c.* 965–1039) are fundamental, and have been credited as the basis of our modern concept of the scientific method of investigation. Alhazen's work deals with the mechanism of perception through experimental methods. Texts by Alhazen were translated from Arabic into Italian and are known to have circulated in Florence in Brunelleschi's time. Tracing the influence of Alhazen's work in the intellectual milieu of Florence during the early 15th century opens a window not only into possible relationships in Brunelleschi's work, but more broadly into the humanist culture that was emerging in Florence from the 12th century onwards, which came to fruition in what we now call the Renaissance. The fascinating flow of ideas between cultures in this period reflects the connections between the humanists and antiquity via Islam, even as some channels closed with the fall of Constantinople in 1453. Brunelleschi's legacy as a great builder is not only demonstrated by his admirable works of architecture but also through the part he played in this wider intellectual process, with his own contribution affecting the history of architecture and art for centuries.

QAVAM AL-DIN SHIRAZI

Architect to the House of Tamerlane

fl. 1410–1438

Q AVAM AL-DIN SHIRAZI WAS ARGUABLY THE FIRST of the great architects in the Islamic world to acquire celebrity status. Despite the public expression of humility in choosing to associate his name with the professional title of *tayyan* (plaster mason), he developed a style so distinctive in its architectural and engineering ingenuity that it inspired, in his lifetime, an extraordinary wealth of literary commentary. Given how little we know about architects in the history of Islam prior to the 16th century, his visibility testifies to his greatness. Qavam al-Din worked almost exclusively for the family of Shah Rokh (r. 1405–47), the son of Timur (Tamerlane, r. 1370–1405) who succeeded his father as ruler of the Timurid dynasty (1370–1506) with a dominion that extended over the vast Persianate cultural area of present-day Iran, Afghanistan and Central Asia. The architect's most astonishing inventions issued from an especially auspicious working rapport he seems to have struck with his other royal patron – the remarkable Gauhar Shad (1377–1457), the influential wife of Shah Rokh and an accomplished woman in her own right. It was for her foundations in Mashhad and Herat that Qavam al-Din erected monuments of such scale and architectural significance that they eclipsed anything built by her male contemporaries, including her husband.

LUMINARY OF THE COURT

Qavam al-Din's epithet 'Shirazi' indicates that he (or his family) came from the city of Shiraz in south-central Iran, where during his campaigns of conquest Timur had gathered noted architects and other building professionals for export to his capital of Samarqand. According to the Timurid historian Daulatshah al-Samarqandi, Qavam al-Din was one of the four luminaries of the court, a master in *mohandessi* (engineering or geometry), *tarrahi* (design or drawing) and *mi'mari* (architecture or building). In the words of Khwandamir, the early 16th-century historian, 'Master Qavam al-Din the Shirazi architect [was] the exemplar of the engineers of the age and the reference point for the architects of the epoch.'

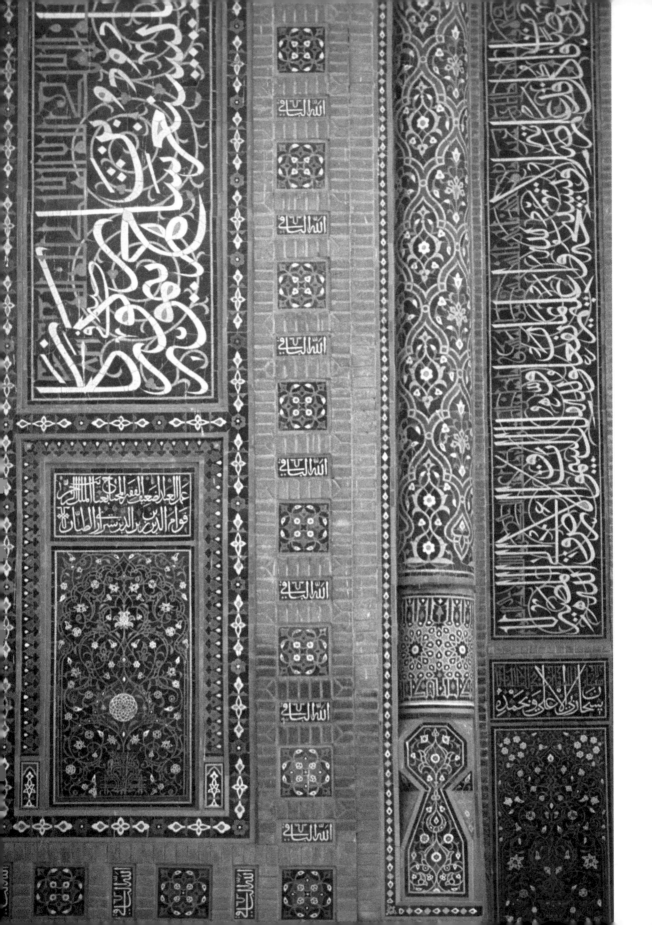

Five structures or ensembles of buildings (datable from 1410 to 1442, since they include a posthumously completed project) are securely attributed to Qavam al-Din. His earliest surviving edifice, completed in 1418, is the mosque of Gauhar Shad at the shrine of Imam Reza (d. 818), the eighth Shiite imam, whose martyrdom had given his burial site the status of a *mashhad*, hence the city of Mashhad in the north-eastern Iranian province of Khorasan. Here he devised a creative solution to the problem of integrating a large congregational mosque into a pre-existing tomb without eclipsing the main attraction of the site. Located on the south side of the tomb (elaborated since the 16th century), the mosque was focused on its large courtyard where each of its two-storey arcaded sides was pierced by a monumental ayvan (Arabic *iwan*), a vaulted space enclosed at sides and back but open on the courtyard side. In such mosques, the south ayvan ordinarily led through a screen into a sanctuary consisting of a domed chamber where the mihrab niche would mark the qibla, the direction of Mecca, towards which Muslim prayer is orientated. Instead, Qavam al-Din replaced the formula of screen and domed chamber with an unencumbered space that extended from the façade of the south ayvan, through a nested inner arch and a transitional domed space filled with stalactite net pendentives on four massive piers,

OPPOSITE *The mosque of Gauhar Shad, Mashhad, completed 1418. The architect's signature appears on the qibla ayvan, in a rectangular panel (far left, centre) directly beneath the royal foundation inscription.* BELOW *The mosque of Gauhar Shad: Qavam al-Din's blue-tiled dome and qibla ayvan can be seen behind the golden dome of the shrine of Imam Reza.*

towards the mihrab wall of the sanctuary. This unusually open vista was accompanied by an equally impressive framing of the ayvan with two attached minarets and the sheathing of all the surfaces with high-quality tilework and inventive designs. The effect is to transform the south façade into a monumental mihrab, while tempering the external profile of the dome so that it is invisible, despite its massive size, from the vantage point of the pilgrim standing in the courtyard. Qavam al-Din's only signature appears in a panel at eye level, just below the main foundation inscription that frames the ayvan.

NEW THEATRICS OF ARCHITECTURE

That Qavam al-Din's genius was recognized and rewarded can be measured by the scale of his subsequent commissions and the availability of resources allowing him to develop his architectural imagination. Twenty years in the making, with no costs spared, his next project was again for Gauhar Shad: a mosque–madrasa complex in Herat (1417–37) also known as the Musalla (mostly destroyed in 1885, on the instigation of the British). Notwithstanding the superb tilework on its sole remaining minaret, a further step in Qavam al-Din's mastery of chromatic revetment schemes, it is the domed chamber on the west side of the ruined madrasa that stands as his masterwork and one of the greatest feats of Islamic architecture. On its exterior, the ribbed bulbous dome with a high drum recalls the earlier mausoleum of Timur in Samarqand. Unlike such earlier domes, however, this one is engineered on the basis of a quadruple-dome structure: an intermediary, low-rise dome accommodates the weight of the outer shell by transferring that weight through quarter domes placed over the recesses of the four great arches that mark the boundaries of the central space. In this way the inner side of the intermediate dome, the space that vaults the interior, is left free to carry a complex network of arches, ribs and pendentives that rise unencumbered from the floor to the apex of the inner vault. Stalactites in relief or in painted form conclude the apex of each pendentive, contributing to the astonishing web-like vault. This kind of arch-rib system was not only better suited to withstand earthquakes: more spectacularly, the net of sequential pendentives in the vaulting enhanced the visual effect of soaring height. Qavam al-Din's architectural and architectonic solutions for this structure were in tune with its intended function as a dynastic mausoleum for Gauhar Shad and her son Prince Baysunghur.

Qavam al-Din's last project was the equally impressive madrasa of Ghiyasiyya in Khargird (Khorasan), completed after his death. Luminous with extraordinarily beautiful mosaic faience tiles that cover all the courtyard surfaces, the building is based on

Vaulted lecture hall of the madrasa of Ghiyasiyya, Khargird, showing Qavam al-Din's arch-rib system, here leading into pendentive nets and an eight-sided lantern.

a four-ayvan plan with strict bilateral symmetry from the portal to the row of domed chambers before the qibla wall. In the domed lecture hall, intersecting arches and articulated pendentive nets rise into a vault that achieves a new degree of lightness with the placement of an eight-sided lantern above its smaller inner dome. Qavam al-Din's nuanced interventions into established architectural forms and methods of vaulting and surface-sheathing are punctuated by his bold inventions at all levels of conceptualizing buildings. In its measured theatricality, development of bilateral symmetry and commitment to solidity of architectural designs and solutions, his work is a precursor to 16th-century and later developments in the Persianate world of the Safavids in Iran and the Mughals in South Asia.

GIULIANO DA SANGALLO

Wood sculptor, architect and student of antiquity

c. 1443–1516

BORN IN FLORENCE, GIULIANO GIAMBERTI was trained as a wood sculptor by his father, Francesco, and by Francesco di Giovanni (Francione), a military engineer. Around 1465 he began to study antiquity in Rome, probably guided by Leon Battista Alberti. Some of the drawings from his *Taccuino senese* ('Sienese sketchbook') and the *Libro piccolo* ('little book') of the Barberini Codex in the Vatican Library may date back to these years. During his lifetime these studies had a constant influence on his work, and today his collected drawings constitute a rich archive. Together with the drawings of architectural projects conserved in the Gabinetto dei Disegni e delle Stampe at the Uffizi in Florence, they give an idea of Giuliano's planning methods and their evolution.

LORENZO DE' MEDICI

Thanks to the patronage of Lorenzo de' Medici, Giuliano designed churches and domestic architecture in Florence in the manner of the ancients. The 'theatrical motifs' in the small courtyard of the palazzo of Bartolomeo Scala (1472–73) combine pillared

arches and a columnar order used in Roman amphitheatres and evoke the ancient Roman house. Around 1480 Giuliano experimented with more complex rhythms at Palazzo Cocchi, using pillared arcades combined with orders of twin pilasters. The Medici villa at Poggio a Caiano near Florence, planned around 1485, represents the first large-scale attempt to reconstruct the ancient *domus*. The arcaded terrace platform derives from the Roman *podium villae*, the pedimented Ionic entrance loggia from the *vestibulum*, and the barrel-vaulted sala follows Vitruvius's description of the atrium. In 1488, for the palace of the king of Naples he proposed an even more precise philological reconstruction, which also included a peristyle, *cavaedium* (central court) and basilica.

ABOVE *Santa Maria delle Carceri, Prato, 1484: a Greek cross design capped with a dome over the crossing. The interior and cupola reflect Brunelleschi's influence, while the exterior is inspired by Alberti.* OPPOSITE *Giuliano da Sangallo, in a portrait by Piero di Cosimo, c. 1485.*

In 1484 at Santa Maria delle Carceri in Prato, Giuliano varied the language of Brunelleschi in a more normative vocabulary. In the plan he combined the domed crossing of Brunelleschi's Santo Spirito with a Greek cross plan, while the orders and the marble revetment of the exterior are more classicizing than such Florentine models as the Baptistery and Alberti's façade of Santa Maria Novella. In Florence he built the Palazzo Gondi (1490–1501), a skilful variation of the Palazzo Medici, and in 1489 he made a wooden model for the Palazzo Strozzi. In the sacristy of Santo Spirito (1489–95), executed in collaboration with Cronaca, the octagonal cella is inspired by the Baptistery, the presumed temple of Mars, and by a Roman ruin near Viterbo that Giuliano had surveyed. The vestibule is covered by a barrel vault and supported by a

Giuliano's wooden model for the Palazzo Strozzi, Florence, 1489. In the palazzo as built, the upper two storeys are much taller.

vigorous composite colonnade. In 1492 Giuliano repeated this system in the Madonna dell'Umilità in Pistoia. In the same year he followed the typology of a cloister with the Ionic atrium of Santa Maria Maddalena dei Pazzi, but here under the influence of Brunelleschi's Pazzi Chapel. Surviving views of ideal cities show his command of perspective, as attested by Vasari: a panel in Urbino is dominated by a round church, according to Alberti's preference, while in another panel (now in Baltimore) the central space is empty and orientated on a triumphal arch and an amphitheatre.

GIULIANO DELLA ROVERE

The golden age of Giuliano's career suddenly came to a stop with Lorenzo's death in 1492 and the expulsion of the Medici from Florence two years later. He immediately found an equally charismatic patron and passionate builder in Giuliano della Rovere, but the cardinal's political situation did not allow him to complete great projects: he was an enemy of the new Borgia pope, Alexander VI, and went into exile from 1494 to 1503. In 1495 Giuliano started a huge palace for his new patron in his native Savona, but only five bays of the ground floor of the façade up to the architrave seem to follow his design. In 1496 Giuliano went with the cardinal to France. In Lyon he presented a model of a palace to King Charles VIII and executed surveys of antique ruins in southern France. Thanks to Giuliano della Rovere, he was commissioned to complete the cupola of the basilica of Santa Maria at Loreto (1499–1500), where he had limited leeway to change a project that had probably been started by Giuliano da Maiano. Hidden behind the name of his younger brother (Antonio the Elder), the architect of Alexander VI, he succeeded in collaborating with him in Rome on the marvellous wooden ceiling of Santa Maria Maggiore (*c.* 1492) and the completion of the courtyard of Cardinal Raffaele Riario's Cancelleria (1489). He may have designed the chapel of the Succorpo (1497), under the cathedral of Naples, for Cardinal Óliviero Carafa, where three aisles are reminiscent of the atrium he planned for the palace of the king of Naples.

When Giuliano della Rovere was elected pope in 1503, taking the name of Julius II, he made Bramante his chief architect and commissioned the reconstruction of St Peter's and the Belvedere courtyard. Giuliano was asked only to give his opinion on St Peter's: in his project he reinforces the pillars and criticizes the structural weakness of Bramante's famous parchment project. While Bramante revolutionized European architecture, Giuliano had to be satisfied with modest commissions such as the little Doric loggia of Castel Sant'Angelo (1505) and a design for the loggia for the papal trumpet players, in which he followed the triumphal prototype to the smallest detail. In his designs for the restructuring of the pope's hunting lodge at Villa Magliana, Giuliano added three new wings to the existing building. The solution that was executed consists of only one wing with a comfortable papal apartment, furnished

Cappella Gondi, Santa Maria Novella, Florence, 1509. The altar wall is dominated by a triumphal arch of the kind recorded by Giuliano in the Barberini Codex.

by broad arcades with theatrical motifs and an order of Tuscan pilasters. In 1508 Giuliano probably designed the Palazzo della Valle, where he played on his original design for the courtyard of the Cancelleria. In the irregular and slightly curved façade he combined the typology of the Palazzo Venezia in Rome with Ionic windows.

Giuliano's first attempts to deal with Bramante's highly plastic articulation of the wall and his dynamic rhythms can be seen in a project for an ephemeral building with secular Virtues designed around 1507–8, and in two slightly later projects for a church façade. In spring 1509 he returned disappointed to Florence. There he concentrated on his *Libro* and the Barberini Codex, and copied earlier projects and drawings of antique monuments from his Sienese sketchbook and probably others. Thanks to his experience in the field of military architecture in Poggio Imperiale near Poggibonsi and, in partnership with his brother Antonio, in Arezzo (1502–3), Borgo San Sepolcro (1502–5) and Nettuno (1501–3), Giuliano was engaged for the fortress in Pisa (1509–12). Probably only in 1509 he executed Giovanni Gondi's chapel in Santa Maria Novella in Florence. Its altar is distinguished by a triumphal arch that reflects his studies in the *Libro degli archi* ('book of arches') of the Barberini Codex. The contemporary marble altar of Santa Maria delle Carceri is inspired by the aediculae of the Pantheon.

GIOVANNI DE' MEDICI

A new phase of Giuliano's career began with the ascent of Giovanni de' Medici, the son of Lorenzo, to the papal throne in the spring of 1513, but in the event he was only appointed second architect of St Peter's. Nevertheless, the three preserved plans from his hand are among the most important evidence about the planning process of the basilica from 1513 to 1515. By the time he returned to Florence in 1515, the late works of Bramante and those of Raphael had exerted a strong influence on him. One of his drawings for centralized churches was inspired by Bramante's round conclave chapel and may have been for San Giovanni dei Fiorentini. The most beautiful designs of Giuliano's last years are those for the façade of San Lorenzo in Florence, in which he rules out the arcades of the triumphal arches that did not correspond to Vitruvian architecture, and tops the vestibule with a balustrade.

The designs for a papal palace in Piazza Navona, dated 1 July 1513, and the slightly later plan for a Medici residence in Via Laura in Florence reveal how much he remained faithful to Quattrocento tradition. His difficulties in dealing with High Renaissance principles and forms are also visible in the drawing of the revetment of the Torre Borgia in the Vatican, characterized by giant pilasters and, above them, smaller twin pilasters. Around 1513 Giuliano may have designed for Cardinal Egidio da Viterbo the great cloister of SS. Trinità in Viterbo, one of the rare examples of a monumental colonnade with straight entablature. He seems also to be the author of Alfonsina Orsini's Palazzo Medici-Lante near Sant'Eustachio in Rome, begun 1514–15. The three storeys articulated only by aedicule and string courses are reminiscent of Palazzo della Valle, while the corner columns in the courtyard link the palace to Florentine tradition. The change in Giuliano's language can also be seen in his late surveys of huge antique monuments in the Barberini Codex and in his more rational and precise method of orthogonal presentation. The evolution of his studies of the antique went hand in hand with that of his architecture, each improving the other.

Project for a church façade, c. 1508–9. Combining a basilican section with a triumphal arch, the design's three-dimensional qualities reveal the influence of Bramante.

SINAN

–·–·–·–·–

Master architect of the Ottoman Empire

1494?–1588

S INAN WAS BORN IN KAYSERI IN CENTRAL ANATOLIA to a Christian family. Recruited into the Janissary corps in 1512, he became an army engineer and was able to study a wide variety of structures during military campaigns. In 1539 he was appointed chief architect of the Ottoman court, and, when Sultan Süleyman commissioned a mosque for his heir to the throne, who had died young, Sinan exceeded the great iconic Byzantine church Hagia Sophia by placing the dome on a square base and flanking it with an additional four half-domes. Particularly after the construction of his Süleymaniye Mosque (1557), the dome as an architectural element was no longer simply a semi-sphere positioned on top of a prism. Support elements transferred the weight directly to the ground, opened up the architectural space like a pyramid and became an integral part of it. The dome at the apex of the building became the most expressive element of an organic whole. The façades increasingly took on the form and dimensions of residential buildings and were therefore closer to human scale. A portico with eaves was added to the domed entrance to the mosque – a practice unique to Sinan.

THE IMPORTANCE OF FOUNDATIONS

The organization of a building site in Sinan's time required a systematic plan, with strict adherence to such matters as completion when the Sultan demanded. Everything had to be rationally based, and inessential jobs shunned. Unwritten rules thus meant that structural components became standardized, space for ornamentation was restricted, the structure's interior was reflected on the exterior, and there was no room for false domes or ostentation. The function and structure directed what needed to be done, and so a pure and minimal architecture was achieved. And yet these buildings had to endure for centuries. Sinan had used foundations made of

The main aisle of the Süleymaniye Mosque, Istanbul, 1557. The dome and two semi-domes supported by four broad arches create an impression of monumentality.

In the Mağlova Aqueduct (1560?) Sinan transformed load-bearing and functional elements into an aesthetically harmonious whole.

stakes for building bridges during his time in the army. When a Roman bridge at Büyük Çekmece, along the route of the European campaigns, collapsed during a flood, Sinan inspected the site and rejected the original location for a sandy section of land. His ensuing report to the sultan gives us an important illustration of Sinan's knowledge of foundations. When an aqueduct he constructed collapsed after some years owing to flooding, his sense of failure propelled his design of the Mağlova Aqueduct (1560?), an extraordinary structure and a work of art. His calculations in hydraulics, experiments and erections to meet Istanbul's water needs secured the confidence of the sultan, who placed him in charge of all building work. The endless requests for buildings – Sinan built over four hundred structures during his fifty-year tenure as chief architect – obliged him to design constantly. He may also have compiled notebooks of designs that he could make use of when the time came.

INSPIRATION FROM THE PAST

Moving on from the form of a dome on a square plan with additional half-domes, his search for a new plan took him to the model of a dome placed on top of a hexagon executed in Edirne eighty years previously. This was a different shape from that of Hagia Sophia. He liked the hexagonal plan and tried it out several times until he created the Kadirga Sokollu Mosque (1572), a building of crystalline purity. When he wished to return to the square plan, he came up with a completely different structure. The piers of the four arches carrying the dome were moved to the exterior so that the dome seemed to float in the air. Windows embedded in the arches allowed light to flood in. Edirnekapi Mihrimah Mosque (1570?) is the product of just such a daring design and structural form. In Sinan's works the structure is not a separate system with the sole aim of carrying the building, but a unity of components that define the space. The simple 'stacking-up' style of construction had made way for a framework system. Sinan's returns to the past always yielded magnificent results. The multi-domed and multi-columned old style of mosque building had not been used for many years, but a beautiful example of how Sinan took and developed this idea is the mosque he built for Fleet Admiral Piyale Pasha (1573?). Sinan was capable of creating new designs while remaining within the bounds of tradition. All were the product of serious research, trial and development, and this fastidiousness can be witnessed in all his works, from the loftiest to the smallest.

During Sinan's long life it fell to him to build the mausoleums of two sultans – buildings that have since taken their place in the history of world architecture with their distinctive design and structural forms. When Selim II, the third sultan under whom Sinan served, commissioned a mosque from him, it is possible that he already had in mind the design he wished to pursue. Unusually, this mosque was built in the old capital of Edirne. Once again Sinan had found the opportunity to compete with

Selimiye Mosque, Edirne, 1574. Subsidiary elements, such as the eight central arches, are reined in, allowing the dome's massive span to completely dominate the interior.

the Hagia Sophia, which still fascinated him and which he always tried to surpass in size. With its dome measuring over 30 metres (nearly 100 feet) in diameter, it was equal to the Hagia Sophia, but Sinan's years of experience obliged him to be prudent. An octagonal base supported the dome, which structurally gave great confidence. Because there were no other large architectural elements competing with the size of the dome, it dominated the whole space. The central space, created by the shorter arches of the octagonal form, brought the dimensions closer to human scale. After the Selimiye Mosque (1574), Hagia Sophia was no longer the iconic building it had once been: the narrative of the monumental had changed. God had been surpassed by his servants, and for that reason we must see Sinan as an artist of the Renaissance.

Following this significant achievement Sinan continued to design until his death, producing his plans from his mind or his notebook according to the commission. His long life allowed him to satisfy his passion for endless research, and no other architect has given the world so many creations. However famous he might be now, he had no official position within the state protocol and so official history did not mention him. He compiled an inventory of his works and wrote down his experiences without exaggeration or arrogance. As he was approaching his hundredth year, he passed quietly away in his mansion opposite his beloved Süleymaniye Mosque. His last wish was that those who gazed upon his buildings should acknowledge the seriousness and industry that lay behind his endeavours and remember him with a prayer of blessing.

The outlines of the Süleymaniye Mosque resemble the profile of a pyramid. This effect, achieved through the gradual massing of semi-domes, cupolas and buttresses from apex down to ground level, not only diffuses the structural burden, but also allows the eye to rest.

SHAH JAHAN

Mughal emperor and builder

1592–1666

SHAH JAHAN (r. 1628–58), FIFTH RULER OF THE MUGHAL DYNASTY in India, was the perfect embodiment of the ruler as architect, an idea that can be traced back to ancient Mesopotamia. In his endeavour to explore and refine architecture as an imperial statement, Shah Jahan employed a whole team of architects and advisers with whom he personally developed his building projects and established principles of construction. He went so far as to suppress the names of his architects so as to take sole credit for his buildings. Shah Jahan represented himself as the supreme architect of the Mughal Empire: any architects he employed were merely agents who realized his designs. His greatest creation was the Taj Mahal, which earned him immortal fame as a builder.

'KING OF THE WORLD'

Shah Jahan ('King of the World') was born in Lahore on 15 January 1592, during the reign of his grandfather Akbar (r. 1556–1605); he was the third son of Akbar's son Salim, later the emperor Jahangir (r. 1605–27). He was named Khurram ('Joyous') and given his title, Shah Jahan, in 1617 for successfully campaigning in the Deccan for his father. 'Baba Khurram', as Jahangir affectionately called him, received a very careful education that began, according to custom, after his circumcision, when he was a little over four years old. Distinguished scholars were selected as his teachers, and poets and Sufi mystics as well as the eminent scholar and physician Hakim ʿAli Gilani were part of the circle. The prince was not only educated by 'the masters of the pen', to use the Mughal expression, but also by the 'masters of the sword', to which he seems to have been more inclined. He became a proficient swordsman, passionate hunter and excellent shot. Shah Jahan spoke Persian, the official language of the Mughal Empire, and Hindavi, the language of North India. In 1612 he was married to Ajumand Banu Begam, daughter of an Iranian family with great influence at the Mughal court. He loved her dearly and gave her the title Mumtaz Mahal ('Chosen of the Palace'). When she died in childbirth in 1631, he built the Taj

Mahal as her mausoleum, an earthly realization of her house in the Koranic garden of Paradise.

Shah Jahan's interest in architecture manifested itself early. Kanbo, one of his historians, says that while still a prince 'he was exceedingly fond of laying out gardens and founding buildings'. At fifteen he earned his father's praise by building a pleasure house in the Urta Bagh, an imperial garden at Kabul that dated from the time of his ancestor Babur, the founder of the Mughal dynasty and a great garden builder. He built a riverfront palace garden as his residence at Agra, and pleasure houses and palaces in central India where he was campaigning. Realizing his son's talent for architecture, Jahangir entrusted him with imperial projects and in 1620 ordered him to lay out the Shalimar gardens on the Dal Lake in Kashmir.

Allegorical portrait of Shah Jahan as a universal ruler whose authority is sanctioned by the heavens; painted by Hashim, 1629.

When Shah Jahan came to the throne in 1628 the Mughal Empire experienced its period of greatest prosperity and stability. His was the classical phase of Mughal rule, and as early as the 18th century the historian Khafi Khan looked back to it as a golden age. Shah Jahan brought the centralization of the administration to its peak, and systematized court life and the arts for the purpose of imperial self-representation. Pomp and show, architecture and the arts were emphasized as indispensable instruments of rulership. This conformed to prevailing ideas about patronage in the Islamic world, where architecture and the arts had long been considered the immediate expression of the ruler.

CLOSE IMPERIAL CONTROL

Using the political role assigned to the arts to lend force to his authority while assuming the functions of supreme administrator of his court-led state, Shah Jahan sought to assert as close control over his artists as over his court and administration. Mughal art was never as regulated as under Shah Jahan. All his historians agree that Shah Jahan made the personal overseeing of his artists a fixed part of his daily routine, thereby acting – with characteristic perfectionism – as his own artistic director. Most important were the daily planning sessions with his architects, but these figures had to remain anonymous, and only occasionally do their names appear. Mir ᶜAbdul Karim Maᶜmur Khan ('Lord Architect'), the chief architect of Jahangir's reign, is mentioned only as supervisor of the Taj Mahal, together with Makramat Khan, a high-ranking administrator; other names include Ustad Ahmad Lahauri and Ustad Hamid, who laid the foundations of the emperor's new city of Shahjahanabad at Delhi. We can only guess at their contribution.

To represent Shah Jahan as being above all involved in the creation of architecture certainly reflects his personal interest, but it also accorded with the view of building as the most appropriate artistic form of expression for a ruler. As the most prestigious and useful art, it had the capacity to represent the ruler and his state in the eyes of a wider public, and to provide an everlasting memorial to his fame. So systematically do the buildings and formal gardens of Shah Jahan express the theories to which they owe their appearance that we can derive the theories directly from their forms. They speak to us 'with mute eloquence', as the chief historian Lahauri puts it in his account of the emperor's daily meetings with his architects: 'The mind [of the emperor], illustrious like the sun, pays great attention to lofty edifices and strong buildings, which according to the saying "Verily our monuments will tell of us" speak for a long time with mute eloquence of their master's high aspiration and sublime authority, and for ages to come are memorials of his love of land development, spreading of ornamentation and nourishing of purity ... In this peaceful reign the work of building has reached such a point that it astonishes even the world traveller who is hard to please and the magical masters of this incomparable art.'

Shah Jahan's approach stands out in its systematic use of highly aestheticized form as an expression of his specific state ideology, in which centralized authority and hierarchy bring about balance and harmony. After Akbar, Shah Jahan was the most tireless builder of the Mughal dynasty. He rebuilt, from 1628 onwards, the palace complexes of the Agra Fort and the Lahore Fort, and raised a new palace and city called Shahjahanabad in the old Delhi of the sultans (1639–48). He also established a great number of suburban palaces, country houses and hunting palaces, as well as large formal gardens of which the most famous are the three Shalimar gardens: in Kashmir (1620 and 1634), Lahore (1641–42) and Delhi (1646–50), sponsored by Akbarabadi Mahal, the favourite consort of his later years. Shah Jahan commissioned or initiated the construction of more mosques than any other Mughal emperor before him. The largest is the Jamiᶜ Masjid at Shahjahanabad (1650–56), and the most beautiful is the Moti Masjid in the Agra Fort (1647–53). The emperor's enormous building programme also encompassed a number of mausoleums: for instance, he raised a tomb for his father Jahangir at Lahore (1628–38), which was supervised by Jahangir's wife, Nur Jahan. However, his most ambitious mausoleum project was the Taj Mahal (1632–48).

THE TAJ MAHAL

Shah Jahan conceived the Taj Mahal as a universal building of eternal fame and the culmination of Mughal architecture – a creative blending of Central Asian, Indian, Persian and European architectural traditions. The design epitomizes his architectural principles on a monumental scale, not least in its symmetry and strictly rational geometry. Its hierarchy is expressed through a studied grading of material, forms and colour down to the most minute ornamental detail (particularly striking is the use of white marble and red sandstone). Also characteristic are the proportional relationships and the uniformity of building types and elements ordered by hierarchical accents. In addition there is a sensuous attention to detail, expressed in a sophisticated architectural decor of carved marble, sandstone relief and the new stone intarsia with semi-precious stones (*pietra dura*). The selective use of naturalism is expressed through an organic florid vocabulary, and finally there is the symbolism, in which the plans and architectural forms express the meaning of the building.

Where the emperor led the way, the court was bound to follow. The imperial family and the great nobles of the empire were expected to respond to Shah Jahan's taste for architecture, and members of the family were employed in imperial building projects – in particular Mumtaz's father, Asaf Khan, who had to write out directions to the builders according to Shah Jahan's orders. The emperor's daughter Jahanara fully shared her father's passion for building, thus extending the Mughal tradition of female patronage of architecture that had earlier been represented by builders such as Jahangir's mother, Maryam-az-Zamani, and his wife, Nur Jahan. Not only sponsoring, but also designing, buildings appears to have been a regular fashion at court. Jahanara and the emperor's favourite son, Dara Shikoh, designed buildings in Kashmir under the guidance of their spiritual teacher, the Sufi mystic Mullah Shah Badakhshi.

Baluster column in the Shah Burj (Royal Tower), Red Fort, Delhi, 1648. The 'cypress shape', as the Mughals termed it, is characteristic of Shah Jahan's new organic architecture.

Taj Mahal, Agra, 1632–48. Built by Shah Jahan for his favourite wife, Mumtaz Mahal, it was conceived as an earthly replica of her house in Paradise and as the ultimate memorial to his rule.

The important position of architecture was reflected in detailed accounts of the imperial building projects by the court historians in the official chronicles of Shah Jahan and in the descriptive and interpretative eulogies composed by the court poets. Shah Jahan personally supervised the writing of his history, so this sudden appearance of the recording of buildings, unparalleled in exactness and consistent terminology in the entire Persian-speaking world, could only have occurred by the emperor's order. In no other period of Mughal history is such a singularly rich body of surviving monuments matched by detailed written descriptions. Theory and symbolism were expressed through the buildings themselves, while the historical and poetical texts provide information about dates, architectural terminology, forms, types, function and clues to the meanings of buildings.

By the time of his death Shah Jahan had thoroughly transformed the architectural landscape of India. His new curvilinear and florid vocabulary with its characteristic forms – the bulbous dome, the up-curved *bangla* roof, multi-cusped arches, baluster-shaped supports and naturalistic plant decoration – became a hallmark of later Mughal architecture and led to the formation of a pan-Indian style.

CHRISTOPHER WREN

Scientist, architect and engineer

1632–1723

ANYONE PASSING BY ST PAUL'S CATHEDRAL in the early years of the 18th century might have been surprised to see an elderly man being winched in a basket into the upper parts of the building to inspect the stonework. They would have been even more astonished had they realized that he was Sir Christopher Wren – the surveyor of the cathedral, a founder of the Royal Society and one of the most prominent men of his age. Today he is considered England's most famous architect, yet nothing in his early career had suggested that he would ever achieve anything in architecture. Critics endlessly discuss his comparative

Design for a weather-clock, 1663 – one of the pieces of apparatus that Wren designed and built to carry out experiments for discussion in the Royal Society.

merit as an architect on the global stage, but his most profound contributions to the history of building go largely unnoticed.

Wren's early academic career reflected his family background. He was born in East Knoyle in Wiltshire, where his father, a former Fellow of St John's College, Oxford, was the rector, and from 1634 dean of Windsor. The young Wren's early childhood was divided between the Deanery at Windsor Castle and the rectory at Knoyle. He was a sickly child, the only surviving son, doted on by six sisters and taught by a series of talented private tutors. He went up to Wadham College, Oxford, in 1650 and quickly became involved with a group of scientific researchers who would later form the nucleus of the Royal Society, including John Wilkins, Charles Scarburgh, Robert Boyle, John Wallis and Lawrence Rooke. It was under Scarburgh's direction that Wren made the first intravenous injections. He also assisted the anatomist in dissections and made models to demonstrate the workings of muscles for his lectures. Wren's extraordinary abilities first became evident in these early exercises in the manufacture of apparatus and in the preparation of illustrative drawings that accompanied them. As lists of his discoveries show, his interests were not limited to anatomy but spread over the whole range of scientific exploration and mathematics. His intelligence was widely noted and he seemed destined for a great academic career. He graduated with a BA in 1651 and received his MA in 1653, when he was made a Fellow of All Souls. In 1657 he became Professor of Astronomy at Gresham College in London and after the Restoration he succeeded Seth Ward as Savilian Professor of Astronomy at Oxford in 1661. The Royal Society was founded after one of his lectures at Gresham College, and he later became its president. As the great architectural historian John Summerson observed, had Wren died before the age of thirty-five he would still have warranted an entry in the *Dictionary of National Biography*, but it would have been as a scientist. Little, if any, mention would have been made of architecture.

FROM SCIENCE TO ARCHITECTURE

Wren's switch from science to architecture would have seemed less abrupt in 17th-century England than it does today. Book and library catalogues from the period show that architecture was considered a branch of applied mathematics. Thus it was not so unnatural for a talented young mathematician to be consulted on architectural matters and even considered to oversee building projects, particularly if he showed an

Wren's dramatic domed design for rebuilding the tower of old St Paul's Cathedral, drawn in 1666 after his return from France and before the Great Fire of London.

*Design for St Edmund King and Martyr, London,
c. 1670. Although initialled by Wren, it was drawn
by his associate Edward Pearce – a typical example
of how the architect delegated work in his office.*

interest. It was probably Wren's mathematical expertise rather than any knowledge of building that led Charles II to offer him the position of Surveyor of Tangiers in 1661, which he declined on grounds of ill health. In the same year Wren was consulted on the repair of St Paul's Cathedral. In 1663 he assisted his uncle, Matthew Wren, in the building of a new chapel for Pembroke College, Cambridge, and produced designs for the Sheldonian Theatre for the University of Oxford. These early tentative ventures into architecture, together with a wish to meet French scientists, were probably the motivation behind Wren's visit to France in 1665 when Oxford University was closed because of the plague. On his return he prepared a design for a new dome for St Paul's Cathedral to replace the badly deteriorating tower. Although approved, the scheme could not be completed.

The Great Fire of London was the defining event that changed the course of Wren's career. Beginning early in the morning of 2 September 1666 in a baker's shop in Pudding Lane, it burned for four days and destroyed 13,200 houses, 87 parish churches and St Paul's. Wren was quick to respond, presenting a plan for rebuilding the City to the king only six days after the fire, and subsequently being appointed to the committee that drafted the new building regulations, although the exact part he played is not known. Their direct result was the London brick terraced house, which was to change completely the appearance of the capital and shape the way it was built for the next two hundred years. Wren's appointment to design fifty new City churches was of more obvious significance. The production of the drawings for these was beyond the capacity of a single individual, so Wren organized an architectural office specifically to do the work, delegating the drawing to draughtsmen but overseeing its operation in every detail. This is one of the first such offices known to have existed in England. Indeed, delegation was the key to Wren's success. He himself had been delegated the work of looking after St Paul's Cathedral by the official surveyor, Sir John Denham, who was also Surveyor-General of the Royal Works. On Denham's death in 1669 Wren was officially appointed to both posts and at a stroke became the most important architect in England. The surveyorship of the King's Works gave him a residence in Whitehall, a salary and a staff of expert craftsmen. He became active at court and was officially in charge of the maintenance of the royal palaces. At St Paul's he set up another office to oversee his greatest project, the rebuilding of the cathedral. Although he retained his professorship at Oxford until 1671 it was clear that his future lay elsewhere. Throughout his career Wren maintained his interest in science and regularly attended the meetings of the Royal Society, but after 1669 he was first and foremost an architect.

ARCHITECTURAL OUTPUT

For the next forty years Wren dominated English architecture. His work was mostly for the Crown, the Church and universities – institutions that all kept written records,

An early design for the Royal Hospital for Seamen, Greenwich, c. 1695. The idea of the central chapel was later abandoned to preserve views of Inigo Jones's Queen's House.

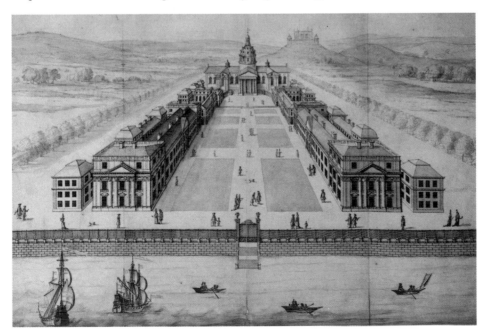

so there is an unparalleled quantity of documentary material relating to his architectural work. Yet we know remarkably little about his character and personal life. Those few accounts we do have stress his brilliance in conversation, and his ability to retain office through six monarchs shows the remarkable respect he commanded.

Wren's architectural output was so prodigious that only the briefest summary can be given here. In the first decade (1670–79) he made a start on thirty-one of the City churches; completed several buildings for Oxford colleges and a new chapel for Emmanuel College, Cambridge; began work on a new library for Trinity College, Cambridge; and built a new Customs House on the Thames, the observatory at Greenwich, Drury Lane Theatre, London Temple Bar, the Monument and a new library for Lincoln Cathedral. The most notable works from the second decade (1680–89) are the vast Winchester Palace (begun for Charles II, but abandoned unfinished at his death in 1685) and the Royal Hospital, Chelsea. He also started work on a further nineteen churches, including St Clement Danes, St Anne's, Soho, and St James's, Piccadilly; completed Abingdon Town Hall, the Court House at Windsor and the Navy Office in Seething Lane; and carried out major works at Whitehall Palace. The principal projects of the third decade (1690–99) were major extensions to Hampton Court and Kensington Palace for William and Mary, and the start of works on the Royal Hospital for Seamen at Greenwich, a scheme so large that it was not completed until many years after his death. Other works in this period, apart from ordinary repairs to the palaces, include many of the steeples for the City churches; designs for William and Mary College in Williamsburg, Virginia; works to Eton College, Christ's Hospital, and Sir John Moore's School in Appleby, Leicestershire; and the fitting out of the House of Commons. By the beginning of the fourth decade (1699–1710) Wren was in his late seventies and there was an inevitable slowing of pace. Nevertheless, he was still actively involved in the ongoing works at Greenwich, designed Marlborough House and Winslow Hall (Berkshire) and a new home for the Royal Society, and oversaw the major remodelling of Westminster Abbey. His primary focus in this period, however, was undoubtedly the push to finish St Paul's Cathedral. After 1711 he was effectively retired, retaining only the surveyorships of St Paul's and Westminster Abbey. Throughout the whole four decades one project dominated beyond all others: his masterwork, the rebuilding of St Paul's Cathedral.

LASTING CONTRIBUTION

By 1720 the skyline of London was dominated by buildings designed by Wren, although critics since have been divided on the quality of his output. John Summerson described Wren's approach to design as 'empirical', drawing a parallel with his scientific work. Certainly there is evidence that Wren approached design as a series of problems to be solved. His architecture is often described as 'English Baroque', which had little in common with Italian Baroque. His interiors are restrained by comparison. They are essentially rectilinear, composed of flat façades, rather than complex curvilinear exercises in three-dimensional modelling. Much of this can be explained by the tension in English architecture of the period, which sought to avoid anything that might be described as 'popish' while still responding to the latest continental trends. The main influences in the early decades are French and Dutch rather than Italian.

Portrait of Wren surrounded by symbols of his many achievements. It was begun by Antonio Verrio shortly before his death in 1707, and completed by Godfrey Kneller and James Thornhill.

The interior of the library at Trinity College, Cambridge, built between 1676 and 1684.

Nevertheless, it would be wrong to see Wren's work as devoid of all architectural innovation, as clever jigsaws composed of architectural quotations. Many of his buildings are extraordinarily innovative and as spectacular today as they were 300 years ago. One recurring theme is surprise: the creation of a particularly unexpected interior through the use of a clever conceit. Prime examples of this can be found in the wonderful domed interiors of St Stephen Walbrook and St Mary Abchurch, whose external appearances give no hint of the different worlds within. Similarly, nothing on the exterior of the library of Trinity College, Cambridge, prepares the viewer for the scale and light of its reading room.

Another aspect of Wren's work is its technical innovation. It is in the realm of building technology that his scientific contribution is most evident. This has often been overlooked because it is mostly hidden and has come to light only as buildings have been taken apart to make repairs. In all his building work Wren acted as the engineer as well as the architect (neither role was properly defined in the 17th century). His technical virtuosity can be seen most clearly in the extraordinary triple structure of the dome of St Paul's, which arose out of discussions with his great friend Robert

Hooke about the correct mathematical shapes for arches and domes. His other innovations are harder to see. In his House of Commons (destr.) the galleries were supported on iron columns. At Hampton Court he went further and hung the first floor from the roof trusses using long iron rods. Similar devices were used to repair the Bodleian Library in Oxford and to strengthen the bookcases in the library at Trinity College, Cambridge. Such innovations were centuries ahead of their time. In taking control of the design of the technical aspects of a building – from foundations to roof trusses – away from craftsmen, Wren established the norm for the following century, when the architect would be expected to handle all aspects of building design, from the plumbing to the decorative detail. Wren himself had started as an amateur architect, but his lasting contribution was to move what had been in England very much an amateur pursuit closer to an established profession.

Drawings for the repair of Duke Humfrey's Library, Bodleian Library, Oxford, c. 1700, showing the new buttresses and iron reinforcements inserted by Wren to prevent collapse.

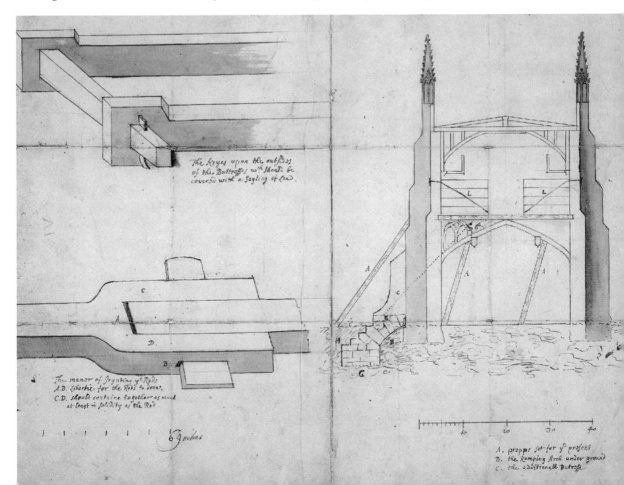

SÉBASTIEN LE PRESTRE DE VAUBAN

Foremost military engineer of the 17th century

1633–1707

ORN AND RAISED IN MORVAN, IN BURGUNDY, Sébastien Le Prestre de Vauban went on to become the greatest military engineer of his day and was still considered the ultimate authority on the topics of siegecraft and fortifications long after his death. The wars waged by Louis XIV throughout his reign, from the late 1660s to the early 1700s, gave Vauban countless opportunities to demonstrate his many talents and allowed the French to take over from the Italians as masters of this type of warfare. Even today, Vauban remains perhaps the most celebrated of all military engineers, with a huge and multifaceted legacy. His built work includes fortifications, towns, buildings and masterpieces of civil engineering, while his writings include memoirs, projects and essays extending far beyond the field of war to embrace economics, taxation, statistics, politics, hydraulic engineering and agriculture.

Attaining the rank of King's Ordinary Engineer in 1655, at the age of twenty-two, Vauban began a career that lasted fifty-two years, culminating in 1703 in the award of the title Marshal of France. In 1678 he became Inspector-General of fortifications and, at the head of a band of almost three hundred engineers, found himself entrusted with maintenance of France's land and sea defences. Ten years later he was made Lieutenant General of the King's Armies. An expert in both siege operations and the building of fortifications, he shared two of the king's passions: war and construction.

Nicknamed the 'taker of cities', Vauban took part in no fewer than fifty successful sieges, allowing France to take cities as large as Lille and Strasbourg. Throughout the second half of the 17th century he instigated a wide-ranging renewal of the attack techniques of siege warfare, digging zigzag trenches at the siege of Maastricht in 1673, raising trench cavaliers made of earth at the siege of Luxembourg in 1684, and employing ricochet firing at the siege of Ath in 1697. In his eyes, no stronghold was impregnable if the attacking forces made use of his techniques, which had the principal goal of 'using more powder and spilling less blood'. An innovator, Vauban eventually developed a rational approach to siegecraft, breaking it down into a logical

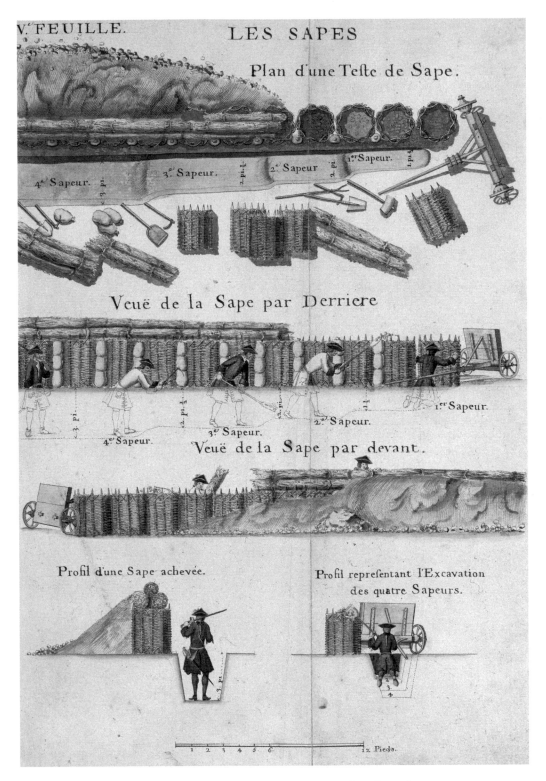

V.ᵉ FEUILLE.

LES SAPES

Plan d'une Teſte de Sape.

4.ᵉ Sapeur. 3.ᵉ Sapeur. 2.ᵉ Sapeur. 1.ᵉʳ Sapeur.

Veuë de la Sape par Derriere

4.ᵉ Sapeur. 3.ᵉ Sapeur. 2.ᵉ Sapeur. 1.ᵉʳ Sapeur.

Veuë de la Sape par devant.

Profil d'une Sape achevée.

Profil repreſentant l'Excavation
des quatre Sapeurs.

1 2 3 4 5 6. 12. Pieds.

Diagrams of sapping trenches, from Vauban's Traité de l'attaque des places fortes *(1704)*.

sequence of twelve phases that required a maximum of forty-eight days to take a besieged site. In doing so, he defined a classic attack strategy that remained in practical use until the mid-19th century. At the insistent request of the king, he laid out the principles of his method in his *Traité de l'attaque des places fortes* ('Treatise on attacking strongholds'), written in 1704. Illustrated with several plates, the work was originally intended to remain secret but was eventually published in 1737 after several illicit versions were found to be circulating. It was subsequently translated into fifteen languages, including Russian and Turkish.

DESTROYER AND BUILDER

Paradoxically, Vauban began his career as an engineer by demolishing the fortifications of Nancy in 1661, the year Louis XIV took over the governing of France. It was not until 1664 that he was given his first opportunity to build new fortifications, at Brisach in Alsace. Throughout his life, through wars and peace treaties, he would alternate between creation and destruction. Alongside countless site-specific interventions to forts, bastions and curtain walls, he fully remodelled almost 150 fortifications. He also built ten new forts and produced hundreds of other designs, some of which were still being worked on half a century after his death. Whether he was improving existing fortifications or creating them from scratch, his first task was always to model the terrain

in order to create the relief that the principles of fortification demanded: a space must be seen if it is to be defended. The shape and layout were determined by the concepts of flanking and defilade. Before building commenced, he had trenches dug and then used the rubble from the trenches to raise bastions. A defensive slope called the 'glacis' would also be built around the entire site. Vauban used the landscape as a basic element in all his projects, reshaping the ground to shelter troops and planting trees to hide the smoke of cannons that could bring down curtain walls and bastions. The skilful control of water allowed him to flood ditches deliberately for defensive purposes. However, Vauban refused throughout his life to publish a theoretical work on fortifications, in the style of his *Traité de l'attaque*, in the belief that good sense and experience were more important than theory, and that all engineers already knew the basic principles of fortification.

ABOVE *A mine destroying a fortification, from Vauban's* Traité de l'attaque des places
(1704). OPPOSITE *Vauban the great military engineer in an early 18th-century portrait.*

Vauban never forgot his country origins and went beyond his role as an engineer to develop a geopolitical strategy to defend the kingdom of France. From 1673 onwards, as military campaigns and peace treaties came and went, Vauban encouraged the king to consider France as a *pré carré* (squared field), giving the kingdom greater unity by preventing territorial enclaves and creating a more linear frontier that would be easier and less expensive to defend. In an area where natural frontiers – rivers or mountains – were not available, such as on the flat terrain that extends from the North Sea to the Meuse, he designed and built two lines of fortifications, like soldiers in battle formation: the first, stretching from Dunkirk to Dinan, included fifteen forts, while the second, from Gravelines to Charleville, had thirteen. The efficiency of this defensive plan, known as the *ceinture de fer* (belt of iron), protected France from foreign invasion until the Revolution. Nor did Vauban ignore the country's largest city, Paris, unsuccessfully proposing the reconstruction of a defensive wall.

TOWN PLANNING, HYDRAULICS AND ARCHITECTURE

After leading the victorious siege of Lille, Vauban designed a citadel for the town in 1667. Pentagonal and with a radiating concentric plan, its layout and construction are the embodiment of his style of fortified structure, surrounded by bastions and curtain walls. Although his first attempt, it was nonetheless a masterstroke, making Vauban the heir and successor of the greatest Italian engineers. He also became the privileged adviser to the king and his ministers for all fortification projects. But always a pragmatist, he began to employ an internal chequered grid pattern from the following year onwards, when he built the citadel of Arras. This eliminated narrowly angled streets,

Neuf-Brisach in Alsace is often considered Vauban's masterpiece. He designed the town from scratch in 1698, employing a regular grid plan within octagonal fortifications.

made construction of buildings easier and improved functionality. All his subsequent designs for new fortified towns took the form of a regular polygon, within which the land was divided into right-angled blocks: these included Longwy (1679), Sarrelouis (1680), Huningue (1679), Mont-Louis (1681) and Mont-Dauphin (1692). Neuf-Brisach, on the plains of Alsace, was Vauban's final new fortified town, designed in 1698 to replace the lost German town of Brisach, situated on the right bank of the Rhine. Within a perfect octagon, Vauban created regular quadrilateral divisions that determined the architectural layout. He also built a canal to bring raw materials to the site. Neuf-Brisach was another Vauban masterpiece, making him a town planner before his time.

While fortifications make up the main body of his work, Vauban's remit also included France's maritime defences: with 3,000 kilometres (almost 2,000 miles) of coastline, the task was immense. His forts on the islands of Île de Ré, Île d'Oléron and Belle-Île-en-Mer were a particular challenge, and he redesigned ports including Toulon, Brest and Dunkirk. Vauban also designed canals and locks, channels and dykes; his many military and civil hydraulic projects included drainage ditches and aqueducts for the Canal du Midi, which links the Mediterranean and the Atlantic, and the aqueduct of Maintenon, which carries water from the river Eure to the grounds of the château of Versailles.

As well as fortifications and ports, Vauban designed a large number of other buildings, chiefly barracks. When Louis XIV decided that armies required permanent accommodation rather than being billeted with civilians, Vauban was inspired by Spanish-style *barracas* and suggested a standard building for troops with a variant for the officers, based on a module of three rows and two storeys. He was also commissioned to build powder magazines, creating a basic design in stone covered by a 'bomb-proof' barrel vault. This standardized approach to military building was then adapted to locally available materials and techniques, leading to results that were both coherent and diverse. Vauban also sunk wells and built water tanks to ensure an independent water supply to these sites. He designed and built arsenals for cannons and guns, storehouses, stables, bakehouses, hospitals, homes, churches and chapels, creating a blend of military, civil and religious architecture.

Alongside Gustave Eiffel and Le Corbusier, Vauban is one of the most widely recognized of French architects. His work has had a deep and lasting effect on the landscape, cities and architecture of France. This was commemorated in Quebec on 7 July 2008, when a diverse and representative selection of twelve of Vauban's major fortified sites was given UNESCO World Heritage protection: Arras, Besançon, Blaye, Briançon, Camaret-sur-Mer, Longwy, Mont-Dauphin, Mont-Louis, Neuf-Brisach, Saint-Martin-de-Ré, Saint-Vaast-la-Hougue and Villefranche-de-Conflent.

Plans for a barracks in Verdun (1698), showing Vauban's preference for a standard but highly adaptable modular design.

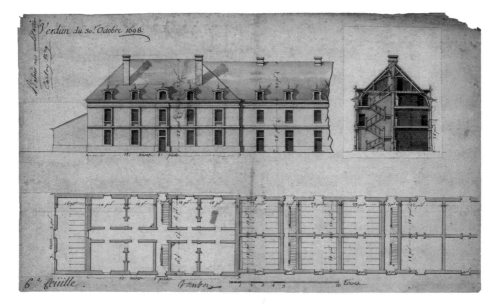

THE AGE OF IRON

The 19th century is sometimes characterized as the age of the battle of the styles, in which the romantic force of Gothic was pitted against the strength of the classical tradition, expressed in the genius of architects such as Karl Friedrich Schinkel in Germany, Claude-Nicolas Ledoux in France and John Soane in England. But the 19th century was equally the age of iron, which provided the raw material for a new transport infrastructure of turnpike roads, canals and railways. The arched cast-iron bridge over the river Severn at Coalbrookdale (by Abraham Darby III and T. F. Pritchard, 1779) was the first large-scale iron structure in the world, but it was essentially a handmade one-off. The bridges designed by the Scottish architect–engineer Thomas Telford, including the road bridge across the Menai Straits in Wales, were far more economical in structural terms. The domed roof of the Halle au Blé in Paris (1811), a collaboration between the engineer J. Brunet and the architect François-Joseph Bélanger, marked a move towards the use of standardized components. Despite the rhetoric of A. W. N. Pugin, John Ruskin and others, the use of iron, including increasingly large quantities of wrought iron, could not be confined to engineering structures – railway and canal bridges, markets, mills and warehouses – but soon invaded the world of architecture. Schinkel, for example, who toured Britain to inspect the new buildings generated by the Industrial Revolution, made free use of iron in his buildings.

In Britain the 1851 Crystal Palace, brainchild of Joseph Paxton, showed what could be achieved when iron was married to another material now also in mass production: glass. The structural ideas behind the Crystal Palace were established by Paxton in the glasshouses he designed for the 6th Duke of Devonshire and by the Irish engineer and iron-founder Richard Turner in his palm houses in Dublin and at Kew Gardens near London. The lessons of the pioneering glasshouses and of the Crystal Palace were applied in the design of the great railway stations of Britain. Richard Turner was co-designer of the roof at Lime Street Station in Liverpool (1849): fabricated in wrought iron, at 47 metres (154 feet) it was the greatest clear, unsupported span yet achieved anywhere. Perhaps the finest of them all, London Paddington

(1852), was the work of Isambard Kingdom Brunel. Like A. W. N. Pugin, he was the son of a French émigré father, and a figure of colossal achievement and even greater aspiration, who created the Great Western Railway and built the first ocean liners. London's most prominent railway monument, St Pancras Station (1868), with a train shed by the engineers W. H. Barlow and R. M. Ordish, was prefaced by a hotel (1876) designed by the great Gothic Revival architect George Gilbert Scott, but inside Scott used iron freely and frankly. Even the University Museum at Oxford (1861), of which Ruskin was the principal promoter, had an interior of iron and glass behind its elaborate Gothic exterior.

If many British architects, in contrast to the engineers, remained nervous about exposing iron construction, very different attitudes prevailed in France. Eugène-Emmanuel Viollet-le-Duc, on one level an active restorer of medieval cathedrals including Notre-Dame in Paris, was even more significantly a theorist of lasting influence, whose writings were to find a particular resonance in the United States and would influence the pioneers of the Modern Movement. Viollet-le-Duc's championship of rational and honest building, which was in tune with the thinking of Ruskin and Pugin, embraced the use of iron and fostered the development of an architecture in which metallic construction was freely displayed, not hidden away or simply used as a substitute for more traditional materials. This agenda found powerful expression in the work of architects such as Henri Labrouste and Victor Baltard, the former responsible for two monumental libraries and the latter for the extraordinary church of St-Augustin, in which exposed iron is combined with lavish Gothic detail, and for Paris's lost central markets, Les Halles (demolished in 1971).

James Bogardus pioneered the metal-framed building, launching the United States as the focus of architectural innovation in the second half of the 19th century. His influence can be seen in the many cast-iron fronted buildings in the SoHo district of Lower Manhattan in New York. His factory, itself a remarkable all-iron structure, manufactured the components, a reflection of the increasing independence of the United States as an industrial nation. The invention of a working passenger elevator by Elisha Otis – the first (steam-driven) was installed in the Haughwout Building at 488 Broadway in 1859 – was fundamental to the future development of high-rise buildings. Equally important was the introduction of steel, a lighter and more flexible material than cast iron, which became the raw material of the first skyscrapers. It made possible some of the greatest engineering achievements of the 20th century. John Fowler's Forth Railway Bridge, opened in 1890, was the first all-steel bridge, suggesting that Britain remained an innovative force.

THOMAS TELFORD

Innovator of cast-iron bridge design

1757–1834

THOMAS TELFORD, FIRST PRESIDENT of the Institution of Civil Engineers, was a master of masonry, pioneer of the aesthetic of cast-iron bridge design, and the first engineer to build an internationally recognized 'longest span' bridge – the Menai suspension bridge. There is scarcely a corner of the British Isles where Telford's work cannot be seen, and perhaps most remarkable of all is that he was able to surmount the disadvantages of a modest social background to become the articulate father of his profession. A veritable child of the Scottish Enlightenment, Thomas Telford was born in one of the most isolated communities in Britain, at Westerkirk, in Dumfries and Galloway. He trained as a mason, but just as important for his later career were the relationships he developed with the leaders of the local community, notably William Pulteney. In 1780 Telford went to Edinburgh, the first sign of a restless ambition that was to sustain him throughout his life. He worked as a mason in the New Town and spent his spare time reading and observing architecture. In 1782 he moved to London where he worked on Somerset House. Around this time he was also undertaking work in his native Eskdale and for William Pulteney at Sudborough Rectory.

In 1784 Telford went to Portsmouth to work on the Dockyard Commissioner's house and chapel, the first significant project for which he was in overall charge. This exposed him to civil engineering construction in the docks. In 1786, under Pulteney's patronage, Telford moved to Shrewsbury to carry out restoration work at the castle, and in 1787 he became County Surveyor. He took on an increasing volume of civil engineering work and, beginning with Montford Bridge (1790–92), he was responsible for the design and reconstruction of over forty bridges

ABOVE *The Menai suspension bridge as painted for Telford by G. Arnold in 1826, the year of its completion.* OPPOSITE *Portrait of Telford by Samuel Lane, engraved by E. Turrell for the* Atlas to the Life of Thomas Telford *(1838).*

in the county. His duties also encompassed public buildings, and he was the architect of a number of churches. Meanwhile, Telford's horizons continued to broaden. From 1790 he was consultant to the British Fisheries Society, which involved surveying the coasts of Scotland to identify sites for harbours and piers. Of particular note is his work at Pulteney Town, Wick, which demonstrated his ability as an architect and planner in addition to his skills as an engineer. At Loch Bay, Skye, he successfully trialled the use of Parker's 'Roman' cement, an important step in the development of modern Portland cements. This also showed Telford's willingness to innovate, most famously displayed in his bridge building.

BUILDING BRIDGES AND CANALS

Telford's nonconventional design for the cast-iron Buildwas Bridge (1795–96) showed a determination to break with the convention established by the structural form of Ironbridge. Driven by a desire to make a more economic and rational use of the material, this ultimately found its expression in a series of cast-iron arches commencing with Bonar Bridge (1810–12). They were an aesthetic triumph and the beginning of

Bonar Bridge, 1810–12, from William Daniell's A Voyage round Great Britain *(1814–25). The poet Robert Southey described his first encounter with the bridge thus: 'At last I came in sight of something like a spider's web in the air – if this be it, thought I, it will never do! But presently I came upon it, and oh, it is the finest thing that ever was made by God or Man!'*

his collaboration with the Shropshire ironmaster William Hazledine. Bonar Bridge was part of Telford's work for the government in the Highlands that had stemmed from his involvement with the Fisheries Society. In 1801–2 he carried out surveys, recommending a range of improvements to harbours and inland communications to stimulate the economy and stem emigration. As a consequence, commissions were set up in 1803 for works in the Highlands and building the Caledonian Canal. Despite the apparent simplicity of linking a series of lochs along the Great Glen to create the canal, the civil engineering challenges were great – none more so than at the eastern end, where a depth of 128 metres (420 feet) of mud was pre-consolidated by the use of fill to enable the lock to be excavated. In all, twenty-four locks had to be built.

The canal was only the most spectacular of Telford's work in the Highlands, which continued until the end of his life. Aside from many small masonry bridges, there were major crossings such as that at Dunkeld (1805–9), numerous piers, road improvements, and work on churches. He built a number of major bridges – at Pathhead, Lothian, and Dean Bridge (1829–32), a tall slender structure in the centre of Edinburgh. Here and elsewhere he employed hollow piers and spandrels to reduce weight and facilitate inspection, a practice widely adopted by others. His Over Bridge at Gloucester (1825–28) was another late masterpiece.

Telford was the last of the great canal engineers. Invited to be 'General Agent' to the Ellesmere Canal Company in 1793, he rapidly mastered the essentials of canal design and construction and proved innovative almost from the first. His advocacy of the use of exposed cast iron for aqueduct troughs, first employed at Longdon on the Shrewsbury Canal (1795–96) but most spectacularly at Pontcysyllte on the Ellesmere Canal (1794–1805), heralded him as a structural artist of premier rank. He was responsible for major improvements on the Trent and Mersey Canal, and completely re-engineered the Birmingham Canal in the 1820s with deep cuttings to prevent its meandering. He used a similar heavily engineered approach for the Birmingham and Liverpool Canal. Telford was consulted about the Gotha Canal across southern Sweden, the first major overseas consultancy project for a British engineer, and as his reputation grew he corresponded with engineers and clients from Canada to India.

ROADS, HARBOURS AND LONG-SPAN BRIDGES

Described as the 'colossus of roads', Telford set standards for road construction that anticipated modern practice. The Holyhead Road provides the finest examples of his work as a road engineer, with toll houses, mileposts and sun-ray toll gates offering further evidence of his architectural work. He was also responsible for the Glasgow to

Telford's Pontcysyllte Aqueduct (1805), a revolutionary structure comprising nineteen cast-iron spans each measuring 13.7 metres (45 feet).

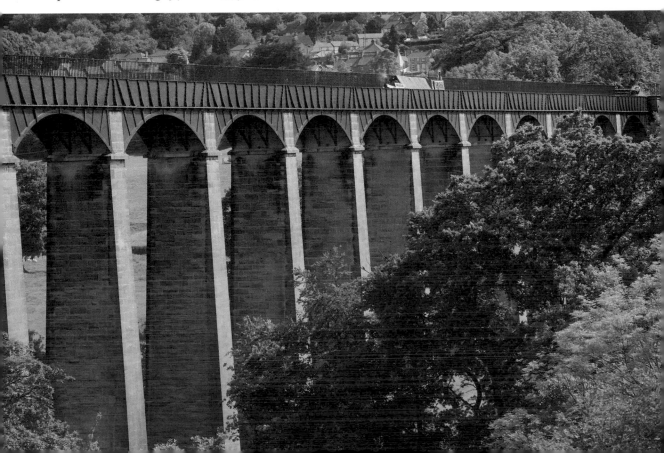

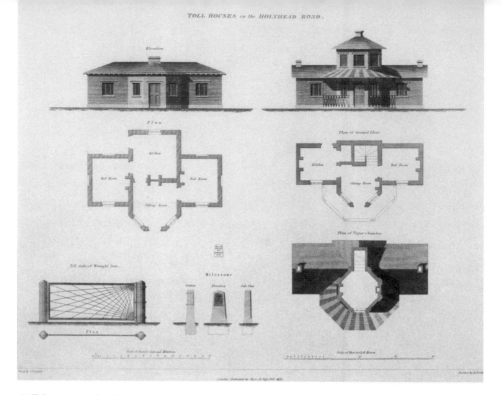

Toll houses on the Holyhead Road: an engraving by E. Turrell from the Atlas to the Life of Thomas Telford *(1838). Throughout his career as a civil engineer Telford took every opportunity to display his architectural ambition.*

Carlisle and Lanarkshire roads, surveys of the Great North Road and roads from Carlisle to Portpatrick and Edinburgh. Telford's dock and harbour works were relatively modest compared to those of his contemporaries William Jessop and John Rennie. Nonetheless they included significant harbour work at Aberdeen and Holyhead, and docks at Dundee (1814–34) and St Katharine Docks (1826–30) in London.

More spectacular were Telford's ambitious schemes for long-span bridges. The first to be developed was for a 183-metre (600-foot) cast-iron arch span to replace the medieval London Bridge (1799–1803), a project that brought him national attention. Even grander was the proposal to traverse Runcorn Gap with a wrought-iron suspension bridge over 300 metres (nearly 1,000 feet) in span. When Telford began work on Runcorn in 1814 the modern concept of a level-deck suspension bridge was unknown in Britain, and only at an experimental stage in North America. He realized that no existing technology could deliver a bridge of the necessary span, and although funding for Runcorn was never available he took forward what he had learned into the design of the suspension bridge over the Menai Straits (1819–26). This bridge had the world's longest span, at over 180 metres (300 feet), and represents one of the first great triumphs of British civil engineering. Since Menai's completion almost all the world's longest spans have been suspension structures.

By the age of sixty Telford was the leading engineer in Britain. He acted as Engineer to the Exchequer Bill Loan Commissioners from 1817 until his death, and as a consequence he was involved as a consultant in most civil engineering projects of the 1820s and early 1830s. This included early railway schemes such as the Liverpool and Manchester Railway. But Telford's legacy was not confined to the built environment he created. Acutely aware of the problems he had experienced in acquiring engineering knowledge, he agreed to become the first president of the Institution of Civil Engineers in 1820. He was able to use his influence to secure its first charter in 1828, establishing the institution as a professional learned society that became a model for others worldwide. His success owed much to his skills in identifying people of ability, making use of their knowledge and delegating to those he trusted, enabling him to achieve an incredible amount. He was buried in Westminster Abbey, the first civil engineer to be so honoured.

Sea lock at Clachnaharry on the Caledonian Canal: engraving by E. Turrell from the Atlas to the Life of Thomas Telford *(1838)*.

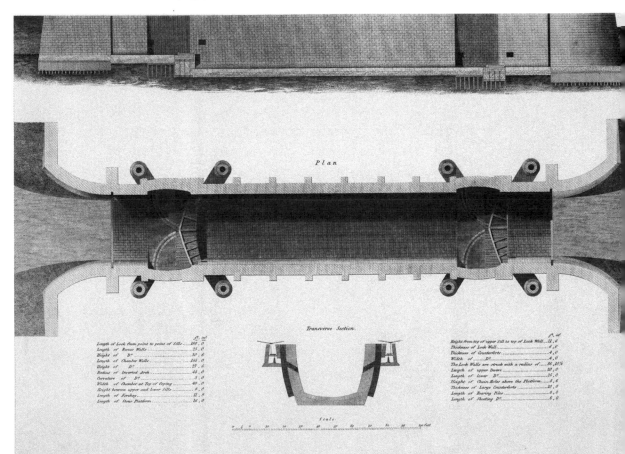

KARL FRIEDRICH SCHINKEL

Genius and engineer

1781–1841

KARL FRIEDRICH SCHINKEL MERITS A PLACE among the most important artists of the first half of the 19th century. His formative influence extended across the whole of northern Germany and beyond, not only within his specialist field of architecture but to all areas of fine art, from painting and graphics via monument designs and theatre sets to interiors and designs for furniture and objects. Nonetheless, Schinkel's main artistic focus clearly lay in the realm of architecture, and he simultaneously utilized his talents as a practising architect, writer on architectural theory and town planner. As a member of the Prussian public works office he also shaped national building policies for many years and thus imposed a style.

Schinkel was born in the small town of Neuruppin, north of Berlin. His father, a high-ranking Protestant clergyman, died in 1787, and in 1794 the family moved to the Prussian capital. At an exhibition at the Akademie der Künste in 1797, the sixteen-year-old Schinkel discovered his passion for architecture after seeing an architectural sketch by the young artistic prodigy Friedrich Gilly. A year later he persuaded Friedrich's father, the architect David Gilly, to accept him as a pupil. By 1800 Schinkel had completed his studies at the new Berlin Bauakademie. His artistic development was strongly influenced by his training, and in particular his contact with Friedrich Gilly. In Gilly's sketchbooks, Schinkel encountered the leading trends in European architecture for the first time, and, following the tragic early death of his young friend in 1800, Schinkel completed some of Gilly's architectural projects.

An inheritance from his mother allowed Schinkel the financial freedom to travel to Italy and France in 1803–5. Italy in particular had a considerable influence on him, and classicism, with its close references to the architecture of the ancient world, became a major theme in his work. This style was not yet dominant in Europe at the dawn of the 19th century, but the thorough study of ancient Roman buildings is likely to have instilled principles in Schinkel that can be detected in his subsequent work and led him to strive for a synthesis of beauty and functionality. The classical ruins also seem to have had a profoundly stimulating effect on his creative imagination.

Schinkel in Naples, by Franz Ludwig Catel, 1824. The portrait dates from the architect's second trip to Italy, when Schinkel was captivated above all by the country's classical ruins.

He later designed an antique-style villa for the Prussian Crown Prince (later King Friedrich Wilhelm IV) in Potsdam, but it was never built. Nonetheless, the Italian style became a guiding influence on many other projects; references to specific buildings as well as general aspects of the 'country architecture' of Italy can be seen reflected in the design and layout of Schinkel's later buildings. Time and again, Schinkel impressed his clients with reasonably priced and technologically functional buildings, within which he managed to reconcile the apparently conflicting demands of low costs and conceptual ideals.

CREATION OF A NATIONAL STYLE

When Schinkel returned to Berlin in 1805 after his first trip to Italy, conditions for architects were extremely unfavourable. As a result of the Napoleonic expansion policy and the Prussian defeats at Jena and Auerstedt, all major building projects had come to a standstill. During this period, which did not end until 1815, with the redrawing of Europe by the Congress of Vienna, Schinkel shifted his attention to painting and the design of popular panoramas, which the people of Berlin could buy tickets to view. In these works, Schinkel obtained some strikingly naturalistic effects through the skilful interplay of illusionistic painting, artful techniques and optical illusions; he also produced works based on his travel sketchbooks (including his *Panorama of Palermo*) and current events such as the 1812 Fire of Moscow.

In his paintings of this period – mostly small-format works that were easy to sell – Schinkel made increasing use of an architectural style that had come to be an alternative to the classicism that was dominant in the second decade of the 19th century, and that also marked his architectural work: the (Neo-)Gothic. In the context of the fervent patriotism surrounding the War of the Sixth Coalition, Gothic was viewed as the German national style. Strongly influenced by the Romantic movement, Schinkel produced several significant designs for memorial buildings, including a mausoleum for Queen Luise, who died in 1810, and for a 'cathedral in commemoration of the War of the Sixth Coalition'. The historicized architecture of these imposingly sized buildings was also a reference to Prussian history.

By 1810 Schinkel was employed in the Prussian public works office. He received his first commissions for public buildings, including the Neue Wache (New Guardhouse) on the avenue Unter den Linden (1816–18), and proved that his predominantly classical-style designs could be executed. These were soon followed by monumental building projects that shaped the new face of Berlin – then known as 'Athens on the Spree' – and included some of Schinkel's masterpieces, such as the Schauspielhaus in the Gendarmenmarkt (1818–21), the Schlossbrücke (1821–24) and what today is the Altes Museum in the Lustgarten (1823–30). The latter building can be seen as an example of Schinkel's architectural self-image: he wanted to use the stunningly impressive architecture to make museum visitors receptive to art and have a pedagogical effect on them at the same time. He reserved a full third of the building's area for the imposing entrance and the central rotunda, inspired by the Pantheon in Rome. A cycle of frescoes on the portico (not completed until after his death and destroyed during the Second World War) was testimony to Schinkel's exuberant imagination as well as his profoundly humanistic education.

Proposed mausoleum for Queen Luise, 1810. Schinkel viewed the Gothic style as fundamentally German.

Rotunda of the Altes Museum, Berlin, 1823–30, in a watercolour by Carl Emanuel Conrad – one of the earliest examples of purpose-built museum architecture.

Alongside such lavish cultural buildings, designed to impress visitors with their cleverly executed architectural programme and stunning sense of space, Schinkel could also work in a more austere and calculated style. One example of this is the Berlin Bauakademie (1831–35), where he later moved into residential lodgings with his family. The building (also destroyed during the Second World War) was characterized by a new and unusual rigour and rationality, and allows Schinkel to be viewed retrospectively as one of the pioneers of architectural Modernism. He found inspiration for the Bauakademie on a trip to England, during which he encountered rational industrial architecture for the first time and transferred its formal language – further enriched with a complex iconographical programme – to Germany. The Bauakademie was also one of the few projects on which he could work as he wished, free from the demands of clients. Perhaps this was the key to the uncompromising clarity of its cube-like structure. Another major area of his work was ecclesiastical architecture. Schinkel's church buildings and designs feature a broad and skilful application of different styles, as can be seen in the Neo-Gothic Friedrichswerder Church (1824–30) in Berlin, which shows the influence of English models.

INFLUENCE AND LEGACY

These and many other plans were published by Schinkel in his substantial *Sammlung architektonischer Entwürfe* ('Collection of architectural designs'); this work not only provided documentation but was also to have an influential effect on less talented architects. From decorative arts (such as altar candlesticks or pews) to the design of a so-called *Normal-Kirche* ('standard church') as a model for small rural parishes, Schinkel imposed a tasteful form of standardization upon the clumsy and unartistic works of less skilful professionals. Consequently, a 'Schinkel school' began to develop, mainly in Northern Europe (and most especially in the Prussian provinces, of course), although Schinkel himself was not a teacher. In his role as a high-ranking city planner he proposed the development of an institutional policy for the preservation of historic monuments in Prussia. He also worked on designs for art galleries and museums.

Karl Friedrich Schinkel combined the qualities of an artistic genius with those of an engineer, meaning that many of his projects could actually be realized. Even his

The Berlin Bauakademie, or School of Architecture (1831–35), in which Schinkel rejected historicist styles in favour of a highly innovative rational design.

Unrealized designs for a Neoclassical villa at Orianda, in the Crimea, for the Tsarina Alexandra, 1838. Schinkel described the project – one of his last – as a 'beautiful dream'.

smaller projects were planned and executed with great precision and a sense for well-balanced proportions. He also found surprising and harmonious solutions to the grouping of buildings, to town planning and to the creation of connections with the landscape. In addition, Schinkel's work aimed to make an impression on the buildings' users. Combined with this was a rather didactic aspect – a wish to improve society and people through art for art's sake. Perhaps Schinkel's most spectacular and successful designs are those that exist only on paper, but that caught the imagination of his predominantly aristocratic and royal clients. He designed a new palace on the Acropolis for the Bavarian-born king of Greece and a classical-style villa complex in the Crimea for the tsarina of Russia, but neither of these projects was ever built. Nevertheless, these unbuilt designs may give a better insight into Schinkel's architectural imagination than his completed buildings. He also remained a role model after his death. His architectural motifs and maxims have cast a long shadow and shaped the many European cities in which his students and successors have worked.

JAMES BOGARDUS

Inventor of cast-iron architecture

1800–1874

THE TERM 'CAST-IRON ARCHITECTURE' IS BEST RESERVED for a typically American type of construction that flourished in the second half of the 19th century in commercial districts of burgeoning cities across the United States. This architectural method relied on the strength of cast iron for vertical supports and employed prefabricated iron modules, structural and ornamental, cast in various architectural styles and bolted together to form multi-storey, self-supporting façades. Cast iron was fire-resistant and made possible large windows to let in natural light, going beyond iron post-and-lintel shop fronts with large display windows set in traditional masonry structures. The first total iron front was built by the American inventor James Bogardus, who had seen iron used extensively in Britain. He was a tireless apostle, and other builders quickly adopted his technique.

James Bogardus was born near the town of Catskill on New York's Hudson River and apprenticed to a watchmaker at the age of fourteen, where he also learned the craft of engraving. He briefly had a small watch-repair shop in Catskill, but his real business was invention, and in about 1830 he moved to the larger arena of New York City. In all, Bogardus was awarded thirteen US patents (as well as a British one) for inventions ranging from clocks and spinning machinery to engraving machines, gas meters, an iron grinding mill and construction techniques for cast-iron architecture. The young inventor went to London in 1836 to protect his gas meter patent rights and, although ultimately unsuccessful, he stayed for four years working on various engraving projects. In Britain Bogardus observed

Portrait of James Bogardus, painted in 1831 or 1832 – just after the young inventor moved to New York City and married Margaret Maclay.

first hand the widespread and increasing use of iron for structural purposes in bridges, aqueducts and railway facilities. In London he could see Thomas Telford's massive iron columns supporting St Katharine Docks (1826–30), John Nash's use of iron columns in the North Lodge of Buckingham Palace (1825) and Carlton House Terrace (1833), and John Fowler's Covent Garden (1828–30), where delicate iron columns supported an iron-framed glass roof.

He also visited Paris, Rome and Venice, where he saw the great buildings of antiquity and the Renaissance, marked by repeating patterns of architectural elements. He later wrote that in Italy he 'first conceived the idea of emulating them in modern times, by the aid of cast iron'. This was the germ of his most famous invention: building multi-storey, weight-bearing cast-iron façades to mimic the stone palazzos of earlier times, employing for this purpose iron castings that were mass produced, interchangeable and styled to suit the Victorian taste for ornamentation. Bogardus returned to New York City in 1840 just as the US was entering its own iron age, having earlier lagged behind Britain in manufacturing and employing iron for architectural purposes. But in the 1840s and 1850s domestic production of iron rose steeply, coinciding with rapid urban and commercial growth. Iron was increasingly used in buildings by artisans and architects, most notably in the form of post-and-lintel shop fronts such as those offered in the 1830s by Jordan Mott or from 1842 by Daniel Badger.

TURNING HIS VISION INTO REALITY

After producing his iron grinding mill on a modest scale for six years, Bogardus decided to construct a factory to manufacture it, taking this as an opportunity to realize his vision of cast-iron architecture. During 1847 he developed practical plans for the structure and built a scale model to promote his idea among architects and investors, many of whom were initially sceptical or hostile. Having gained financial backing, he acquired a plot on Duane Street in Lower Manhattan and in May 1848 laid the foundations for his factory. Not an iron founder himself, Bogardus contracted with local firms to cast simple structural components for his factory: C-shaped beams, tall half-round fluted columns with flanges and a spandrel to fill the enframed space below the large window opening. These components were then bolted together to create structural modules that were in turn bolted together to form a repeating pattern across the façade. Cast-iron ornamental elements could then be bolted on in various combinations to produce different looks.

But before his factory could be built, Bogardus accepted a commission from Dr John Milhau, a chemist and civic leader, to replace the brick front of his three-storey

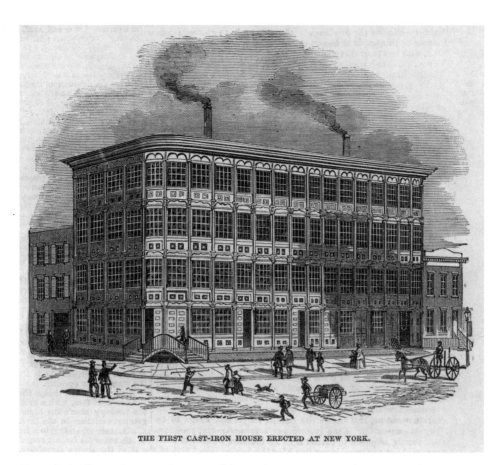

THE FIRST CAST-IRON HOUSE ERECTED AT NEW YORK.

Bogardus's all-iron factory at Duane and Centre Streets in New York City, erected 1849. Bogardus used the image to promote his idea of cast-iron buildings.

pharmacy at 183 Broadway in Lower Manhattan with a cast-iron front. Using the iron castings prepared for his factory, Bogardus was able to erect the new front in just three days. The building was transformed into five storeys with an additional window on each floor. The Milhau Pharmacy (1848; façade since removed) became the first multi-storey, self-supporting total iron front and proved that Bogardus's ideas were sound. Almost at once he received another commission, this time from Edgar Laing, to erect a set of five stores with a wraparound cast-iron front. The four-storey Laing Stores (1849) consisted of twenty-one bays with traditional timber and brick party walls and had relatively little ornamentation. The Laing Stores survived for more than a century but were eventually demolished in 1971 to allow redevelopment of the area. We know a great deal about Bogardus's system of cast-iron architecture because when the structure was taken down the iron front was carefully dismantled and documented.

Bogardus's own factory (1849; destr. 1859) was finally completed shortly thereafter. Four storeys tall, it was constructed of the same elements as the Milhau Pharmacy and the Laing Stores but with more ornamentation, and was notable for its

ABOVE *Bogardus's magnificent iron double frontage for the* Baltimore Sun *newspaper, 1850–51. His first large commission, the Sun Iron Building was destroyed in Baltimore's great fire in 1904.* OPPOSITE *Illustration from Bogardus's 1856 pamphlet demonstrating how successfully – and cheaply – ornate designs could be reproduced in cast iron.*

many large glass windows separated by slender cast-iron columns. Bogardus thought the factory best demonstrated his building system and titled the promotional lithograph of the structure 'The First Cast-Iron House Erected', although the factory had been pre-empted by the Milhau Pharmacy and the Laing Stores. Bogardus claimed the factory was entirely of iron – framing, façade, roof and floors – but some architectural historians contest this, arguing on the basis of limited circumstantial evidence that timbers were used in framing the building. This debate does not negate the fact that by 1849 Bogardus had proved it was possible to construct handsome, modern cast-iron fronts rapidly and economically.

Bogardus readily admitted that he had succeeded by combining well-established methods of iron construction. He received a patent in 1850 for aspects of his cast-iron techniques, but not for the system as a whole, presumably because many of the elements were already known. Indeed, soon many builders were erecting complete cast-iron fronts for forward-looking businesses that wanted attractive quarters for their enterprises at modest cost.

THE POPULARITY OF CAST-IRON BUILDING

Before he withdrew from the field in 1862, Bogardus had built more than thirty cast-iron buildings: among these were the Sun Iron Building in Baltimore (1850–51; destr. 1904), iron framed with two iron façades, and the largest iron building in the US at the time; and (in New York City) the Harper & Brothers Publishing plant (1854–55; destr. 1925), combining cast-iron columns with wrought-iron beams and bow-string girders that were left exposed in the interior, emphasizing fire-resistance; 254 Canal Street (1856–57), a commercial building with two large cast-iron façades; and 75 Murray Street (1857), a small gem for a firm selling china. Bogardus not only built structures but also proselytized for cast-iron architecture, often with the help of his well-educated aide John W. Thomson. In particular, Bogardus is known for publishing in 1856 a sixteen-page pamphlet, *Cast Iron Buildings: Their Construction and Advantages* (reprinted in 1858), in which he explained and defended the new architecture.

Interspersed with Bogardus's commercial buildings were five cast-iron towers that pointed the way to the future. Three were open frames: two fire watchtowers for New York City's Fire Department, the first (1851) 30.5 metres (100 feet) high and the second (1853) 38.1 metres (125 feet)

high (both destr. about 1885), and a Santo Domingo lighthouse nearly 30 metres (75 feet) high (1853; destr.). The other two were extremely tall walled towers for the manufacture of lead shot: McCullough Shot Tower (1855), at 51.8 metres (170 feet) high, and Tatham Shot Tower (1856), at 66.1 metres (217 feet) high (both destr. 1907). These shot towers presaged later skyscraper construction, with curtain walls of brick that enclosed the weight-bearing iron framework to prevent the wind from blowing the molten lead shot as it dropped from the top of the tower.

Many builders rushed into the field of cast-iron architecture that Bogardus had opened up in 1848–49. One such figure was Daniel Badger, whose company, Architectural Iron Works, supplied iron for many famous cast-iron buildings, including the handsome Haughwout Building (1857) in New York City. The extensive catalogue of his firm's wares, *Illustrations of Iron Architecture* (1865), remains the best record of the art and practice of cast-iron architecture in 19th-century America, where it became the choice in urban commercial districts for three or four decades before the modern skyscraper emerged. Bogardus can rightfully be considered the inventor of cast-iron architecture, despite employing many elements and techniques that were already accessible. His invention suited the era and quickly became a staple of the general culture.

In New York Bogardus erected the first iron shot tower ever built (1855). Its iron frame, sheathed in brick to keep molten lead from being blown astray by winds, foreshadows the skyscraper.

JOSEPH PAXTON

Landscape gardener and architect

1803–1865

JOSEPH PAXTON WAS A DESIGNER AND BUILDER OF GARDENS, landscape parks, glasshouses, exhibition buildings, winter gardens, water features and architecture. His training as a gardener was good preparation for his remarkable career, and his keen powers of observation, study, analysis and organization were combined with a broad range of interests, including horticulture, the layout of parks and cemeteries, architecture, heating and ventilation, metropolitan improvements, water supply and sewage disposal. He was the seventh son of nine children, and his father, a farm labourer in Bedfordshire, died when Joseph was only seven years old. Following appointments at an early age as a gardener on two private estates, and then in the garden of the Royal Horticultural Society, his exceptional abilities were recognized by the 6th Duke of Devonshire, who appointed him head gardener at Chatsworth in Derbyshire in 1826. Paxton enjoyed the encouragement and trust of the duke and over time assumed considerable responsibility for the management of his estates, remaining in his service until the duke's death in 1858. The nature of Paxton's special role enabled him to accept numerous commissions from others that included celebrated achievements of national prominence.

CHATSWORTH

From the 1830s through the 1850s Paxton created the most celebrated garden of the day at Chatsworth, which attracted international attention for its design and execution. Remarkable works included the creation of waterworks, reservoirs, the spectacular Emperor fountain and aqueduct, extensive walks through the landscape, and shrubbery and woodland plantations. His projects for public parks and pleasure

Engraved portrait of Joseph Paxton, made around the time of the Great Exhibition of 1851.

Paxton's plan of Birkenhead Park, drawn by John Robertson, 1843. Separated from the public park by a serpentine carriage pleasure drive were villas and terraces, developed to finance a portion of the cost.

grounds such as Prince's Park in Liverpool (1842), Upton Park in Slough (1843), Birkenhead Park (1843), Buxton Park (1852), People's Park in Halifax (1856–57), Baxter Park in Dundee (1859), Public Park in Dunfermline (1864–65) and the spectacular landscape created for the Sydenham Crystal Palace (1856) were enormously influential and his assistants, John Gibson, Edward Kemp and Edward Milner, would all become recognized landscape designers in their own right.

Perhaps Paxton's major achievement at Chatsworth was the creation of a wide range of glass buildings, recognized as the most extensive of their kind anywhere, which housed the duke's unrivalled collection of exotic plants. Over a fifteen-year period Paxton perfected the design of a unique system for a building envelope constructed of wood and glass that later would be used on the Great Exhibition Building in Hyde Park in London. The 'ridge-and-furrow' system evolved through experimentation and was applied to structures of different shapes and sizes. In contrast to others of his day, Paxton was convinced of the superiority of wood over iron in the construction of glasshouses, and his ridge-and-furrow system was especially designed so that water (both externally and internally, in the form of condensation) would quickly run away to prevent decay of the timber. Special steam-powered routing machines were devised to perfect optimum timber sections for glazing bars, ridge rafters and valley gutter rafters before they received a simple painted finish.

The Great Stove or Conservatory at Chatsworth (1836–41; destr. 1920), the most remarkable structure of its kind anywhere in Europe, was conceived on a scale that had never before been attempted. Paxton worked in collaboration with the architect Decimus Burton, who was responsible for preparing drawings of the building in 1836. Considerably larger than the great glasshouses recently erected at Syon House and Woburn Abbey, the Great Stove was 84.4 metres (277 feet) in length and 37.5 metres (123 feet) in width, and the height at the centre of the building was 20.4 metres (67 feet). The interior was divided into three areas by two rows of cast-iron columns forming a central higher barrel-vaulted nave with a clear span of 21.3 metres (70 feet) flanked on either side by two aisles. Paxton adapted his ridge-and-furrow roof system to a curved form and supported it on great laminated timber arches. The glasshouse

The Great Stove at Chatsworth was largely constructed of timber and glass. Great laminated timber arches forming the central barrel vault and perimeter aisles were supported internally on cast-iron columns.

was heated by eight great coal-fired boilers housed beneath the floor, and the smoke travelled through flues in an underground tunnel to a chimney hidden in a wood a distance away.

In 1849 Paxton developed a horizontal ridge-and-furrow roof for a rectangular glasshouse 18.7 metres (61½ feet) long by 14.2 metres (46¾ feet) wide that was specifically designed for the cultivation of the large-leafed *Victoria regia* water lily. The roof was carried on light horizontal wrought-iron beams supported on hollow cast-iron columns that served as rainwater downpipes. Although the dimensions were different, this roof was directly related to the one he would use on the Great Exhibition Building, which covered 71,832 square metres (17¾ acres) in Hyde Park. In June 1850 Paxton patented his design for 'Improvements in the construction of the description of roofs known as ridge and valley roofs'.

THE GREAT EXHIBITION BUILDING

Although he had not entered a design for the competition announced in March 1850 for the Great Exhibition Building, Paxton realized that the alternative scheme prepared by the Building Committee in June of that year could not be achieved within the time available. At a meeting in Derby on 11 June he produced the famous blotting-paper sketch of the building, suggesting how his ridge-and-furrow roofing system could be applied to a multi-storeyed structure of enormous scale. With the help of assistants at Chatsworth and the engineer William Barlow, drawings were prepared to show to the commissioners and later to Prince Albert, and on 6 July the proposal was published in the *Illustrated London News*. A tender for the scheme was produced by Birmingham contractors Fox Henderson and the glass manufacturer Robert Chance, and on 15 July the Building Committee recommended its acceptance, barely more than a month after Paxton had first sketched out his idea.

The Great Exhibition Building (1851), dubbed by *Punch* 'the Crystal Palace', was particularly notable for the application of standard mass-produced building components to a structure of enormous scale, which enabled it to be erected in a remarkably short time. It was 563.3 metres (1,848 feet) in length and 124.4 metres (408 feet) in width. A central nave spanning 21.9 metres (72 feet) and 19.2 m (63 feet) in height was flanked on either side by two aisles 7.3 metres (24 feet) in width. Internally the space was divided by tiers of columns – 3,300 of them – supporting cast-iron trusses. At the centre a barrel-vaulted transept formed by great laminated timber arches rising 32.9 m (108 feet) at the centre and spanning 21.9 metres (72 feet) was introduced so as to preserve large oak trees enclosed beneath the glass roof. Over 83,612 square metres

(900,000 square feet) of glass and 16,990 cubic metres (600,000 cubic feet) of timber were used in the building. Paxton was knighted after the Exhibition.

The future of the Great Exhibition Building, which was intended to be only temporary, was already being discussed almost as soon as it was finished. When it became clear that it would not be allowed to remain in Hyde Park, Paxton raised support for

BELOW *Sketch for the 1851 Great Exhibition Building, which Paxton drew on blotting paper while attending a railway meeting in Derby, 11 June 1850.* OVERLEAF *Drawing of the interior of the building for the Great Exhibition of 1851, Hyde Park, London.*

Aerial view of the Crystal Palace, terraced gardens and waterworks at Sydenham, 1854.

its dismantling and re-erection at Sydenham, south of London, where as a winter garden it would form the centrepiece of extensive pleasure grounds laid out to his design. The new structure at Sydenham opened in 1854 and was even more spectacular in its overall form, boasting three barrel vaults rising above the longitudinal roof. Sited at the top of Sydenham Hill, the multi-storeyed structure dominated the terraced gardens and water features arranged on a series of terraced levels below. It was eventually destroyed by fire in 1936.

Although he never trained as an architect, Paxton was responsible for notable architectural works of different types, such as the rebuilding of Edensor village (1834–42) on the Chatsworth estate, as well as great country houses and castles within landed estates, including Burton Closes in Derbyshire for John Allcard (1846), Bolton Abbey in Yorkshire for the Duke of Devonshire (1844), Mentmore in Buckinghamshire for Baron Mayer de Rothschild (1850–55), Lismore Castle in Co. Waterford for the Duke of Devonshire (1850–58) and Ferrières near Paris for Baron James de Rothschild (1855–59). Paxton worked closely with architectural assistants such as John Robertson and George Stokes, who was to marry Paxton's daughter.

Paxton's works as a gardener represent the finest combination of the 18th-century landscape tradition and leading 19th-century horticultural practice, yet these represent only one area of his extraordinarily varied and wide-ranging activities. His achievement in the realm of public parks was particularly notable, and his experiments in the application of glass to buildings directly influenced two of the most remarkable structures of the 19th century, the Great Exhibition Building and the Sydenham Crystal Palace.

VICTOR BALTARD

Municipal architect of Paris

1805–1874

VICTOR BALTARD WAS BORN IN PARIS, the son of Louis-Pierre Baltard (1764–1846), himself a famous architect who was professor of theory at the École des Beaux-Arts in Paris from 1818 to 1846, architect of the prisons of the Seine and a member of the Conseil des Bâtiments Civils. Victor entered the École des Beaux-Arts in 1824, where he studied under François Debret and Charles Percier as well as his own father. He won several prizes there, allowing him to study from 1834 to 1838 at the Villa Medici, seat of the Académie de France in Rome. Back in Paris, in 1840 he was given the post of Inspector of Festivals and Artistic Works for the city of Paris, a job that placed him in charge of restoration and decorative work on the churches of Paris for twenty years and also gave him the opportunity to design several decorative schemes for city festivals as well as for the opening in 1862 of the Boulevard du Prince Eugène (Boulevard Voltaire).

THE CHURCHES OF PARIS

Baltard's work on a number of Parisian churches, most of them Gothic, encompassed decoration, restoration and also extension projects. In conjunction with the ecclesiastical authorities, he was in charge of determining the overall decorative style and its implementation in different areas of the buildings. Additionally, and perhaps most importantly, he suggested the names of the artists who would carry out the decorative programmes (Hippolyte Flandrin, Jean-Louis Bézard and Théodore Chasseriau). In this way, he became responsible for the decoration of the churches of St-Séverin, St-Louis d'Antin, St-Germain des Prés, Ste-Elisabeth and St-Gervais. He restored the bays of St-Germain l'Auxerrois and designed the altar and organ case at St-Eustache. He

Victor Baltard towards the end of his life, photographed by Pierre-Ambroise Richebourg.

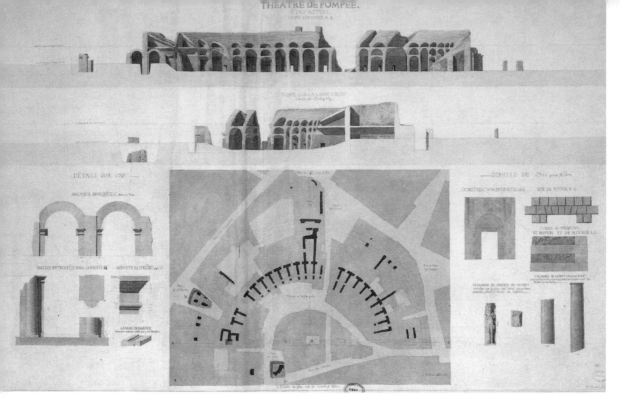

Plan and elevation of the ruined Theatre of Pompey, Rome, drawn by Baltard in 1837–38 while at the Académie de France.

added Chapels of the Catechism to St-Jacques du Haut-Pas, St-Philippe du Roule and St-Etienne du Mont. He rebuilt the chevet of St-Nicolas du Chardonnet and built the entrance porch of St-Jean-St-François.

His largest project involved the church of St-Leu-St-Gilles (1857–62). The newly opened Boulevard de Sébastopol cut through the building and meant that the three chapels situated behind the choir had to be pulled down. This made it necessary to rebuild the apse, which would then become the main façade of the church, looking onto the new boulevard. Baltard also had to rebuild the ambulatory to fit the line of the boulevard and cut off the curve of the apse so that it did not jut out into the street. On the boulevard he built new chapels and a rectory. His reconstruction of the façade was a skilful composition that won much praise. He also designed an extraordinary Chapel of the Virgin, covered by a flat vault supported by four large, open diaphragm arches, in pairs, delimiting a large square central ceiling and nine smaller ones, each supported by two diaphragm arches, all built from cement. Baltard admired the art of the late Middle Ages and the early Renaissance, and his aim was always to respect the original architecture without resorting to copies of the past.

The church of St-Augustin was Baltard's masterpiece, characterized by the sumptuous nature of its eclectic architecture and its unusual layout. The commission came in 1859 directly from Georges-Eugène Haussmann, who took advantage of the opening up of the Boulevard Malesherbes to set aside a narrow wedge-shaped plot of land, intended for a church, on the corner of the Avenue César Caire. Construction took place between 1860 and 1871. The complex structure is dominated by a dome with a cupola 60 metres (197 feet) high; the square nave has chamfered corners and the ribbed dome sits on pendentives. The nave, the choir (Chapel of the Virgin) and two side chapels (each a half-octagon) that form a transept all meet in the centre. Although there are no specific references, this centred plan recalls Byzantine architecture, as does the decoration, although the dome in particular is obviously inspired by the Italian Renaissance, as is the stone cladding. One of the church's most notable characteristics, much criticized at the time, is the metal framework that forms the interior. Because the narrowness of the plot prohibited the use of buttresses to support the vaults of the nave, Baltard chose to cover it with a metal framework resting on iron pillars, with no lateral supports. It was therefore the shape of the site that determined the architectural structure, a strikingly original approach.

Baltard also oversaw the completion of the Hôtel du Timbre on the Rue de la Banque, initially begun by Paul Lelong (1846–51). He entered competitions for the

The nave of St-Augustin, Paris, 1860–71. Baltard's innovative metal structure is clearly visible.

tomb of Napoleon (1841) and the reconstruction of the Hôtel de Ville in 1873, but was unsuccessful, and he designed an unrealized set of plans for the Hôtel de Ville in Amiens (1864–68). As a diocesan architect, Baltard worked on the St-Sulpice seminary (1849–54). A Protestant himself, he converted the former chapel of the Pentemont convent into a Protestant church (1844–52) and won the commission to build the Protestant church of Nérac (Lot-et-Garonne), with its majestic octagonal plan, in 1852–53. He also designed the decoration for the Chapel of the Virgin in the cathedral of Troyes (Aube, 1841–45), although not without fierce debate on the precise form of Gothic style that should be adopted. As chief architect of the city of Paris (from 1860), he was involved in the Hôtel de Ville project, adding the annex buildings that stand opposite it. Baltard also made a speciality of designing tombs: at Père Lachaise cemetery, his most successful were those of Victor Cousin (1866), his painter friends Hippolyte Flandrin (1864) and J.-A.-D. Ingres (1868), and Louis-James-Alfred Lefébure-Weli (1873). Baltard also built his own villa in Sceaux (near Paris) and restored Haussmann's château in Cestas (Gironde).

LES HALLES

After having taken it upon himself, between 1841 and 1843, to come up with new designs for Paris's central market of Les Halles, to stand on the site of the old market, Baltard was named architect of the 'expansion and improvement works on Les Halles Centrales' in 1845, alongside Félix-Emmanuel Callet (Grand Prix winner in 1819 and official architect of the city of Paris). After the precise extent of the site was fixed in 1847, Baltard and Callet were asked to 'give the planned buildings a monumental look'. In 1848 they submitted plans for eight pavilions, each consisting of a huge iron framework, surrounded by monumental stone gates and walls. In 1851 Baltard's sixth set of plans was approved by the city council and the Minister of the Interior, despite fierce competition from other architects. Construction of the first

Baltard and Callet's design for a stone-clad pavilion at Les Halles, Paris, 1851.

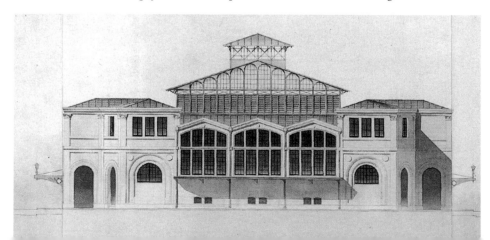

View of Les Halles shortly after construction. In their final, revised design, produced in 1853, Baltard and Callet left the iron framework fully visible.

pavilion began, with stone cladding that mostly hid the metal framework within. This 'stone pavilion' became a public joke, and by 1853 a storm of criticism had been unleashed. Napoleon III was among the dissenters, saying that he preferred a construction style closer to that used for new railway stations – 'Huge umbrellas are what I need; nothing more!' – and bringing a halt to the building work. Baltard and Callet explained that their designs were only following the guidelines of the programme, and in 1853 they even returned to their 1848 plans, in which the metal framework was more obvious. The emperor's critical comments implicitly launched a sort of unofficial competition, and competing projects grew ever more numerous.

The eventual plans consisted of ten pavilions divided into two groups, six to the east and four to the west. Each pavilion stood over cellars that served as storage areas, covered by brick and iron groin vaults supported by a quincunx of iron posts. The outer cladding also used iron (for the supporting columns) and brick (for the partition walls). This base was topped by large arched windows. The iron framework of the aisles and lanterns was supported by more cast-iron columns, and the lanterns (double height in the larger pavilions) had glazed skylights. Large vertical bays situated on the plane of the walls that divided the aisles and the high zinc roofs allowed the circulation of air and light. The streets around the two groups of pavilions were covered by simple double-pitched roofs, pierced by skylights. When building work was finally completed in 1874, the year of Baltard's death, Henri Delaborde wrote: 'Les Halles Centrales seems to be the most successful example of the type of architecture that truly belongs to the times in which we live: architecture that stems from our own needs and modern ideas.'

STEVEN BRINDLE

ISAMBARD KINGDOM BRUNEL

Visionary railway engineer and ship designer

1806–1859

'THE RAILWAY IS NOW IN PROGRESS. I am their engineer to the finest work in England – a handsome salary – £2,000 a year – on excellent terms with my Directors and all going smoothly, but what a fight we have had.' Thus wrote the 29-year-old Brunel in his diary on 31 December 1835. He was the engineer for the Great Western Railway's line from London to Bristol, and in the previous month work had started on the Wharncliffe Viaduct on the west side of London: thousands of navvies, marshalled by his contractors, were about to do his bidding. His entire experience of railways was one look at the Stockton to Darlington line in the north-east, and a single return journey on the Liverpool and Manchester Railway.

EARLY CHALLENGES

Brunel's fortune was to live in the age when Britain, the world's first industrial society, was equipping itself with the first railway network. His father, Marc Isambard Brunel, was born at Hacqueville in Normandy in 1769. In 1799 he came to England to offer the Royal Navy a totally new idea – mechanized production of the wooden rigging blocks for its battleships – and the Block Mill at Portsmouth became the world's earliest mechanized production line. Isambard, born in Portsmouth to Marc and his English wife Sophia, was apprenticed initially to Louis Breguet, a famous Paris watchmaker, and then to Maudslay, Son & Field in London, the best mechanical engineers of the day. By the time he was twenty he was ready to help in his father's greatest project, a tunnel beneath the Thames between Rotherhithe and Wapping.

Cross-section of Brunel's design for the Thames Tunnel, produced shortly after the first flood on 18 May 1827. The tunnel was not completed until January 1842.

The Clifton Suspension Bridge, Avon. The towers were built to Brunel's design c. 1836–43, but work stopped when the bridge company became insolvent. The project was completed in 1864 by the engineers John Hawkshaw and William Barlow, as a memorial to Brunel.

The Thames Tunnel was an idea so daring that most contemporaries would have declared it impossible: others had tried digging trial holes and found the treacherous ground giving way above them. Marc devised a means of protecting the tunnellers by housing them in a great iron framework, the tunnelling shield. They scooped out the earth ahead of them, the shield was pushed forward on screw-jacks, the bricklayers working immediately behind carried the tunnel forward a short distance, and the process started again. It was dangerous work in the stinking, fetid mud. In 1826 Isambard was appointed Resident Engineer, at a salary of £200 per annum. The work became ever more dangerous and traumatic: the tunnel flooded and was sealed and pumped out, but on 11 January 1828 it flooded again. Isambard, in the tunnel at the time, was very nearly killed. The Thames Tunnel Company had to suspend work, and it looked as if both the Brunels' careers were over, almost before Isambard's had begun.

Isambard went to Bristol to convalesce, where he won the competition for a daring new Clifton Suspension Bridge over the Avon gorge with a design for the longest-span suspension bridge in the world at 214 metres (702 feet). It was not completed until after his death, in 1864. He also secured some humbler but useful work improving the docks, as Bristol's merchants and bankers were worried that their city was being left behind by Liverpool in the race for the Atlantic slave trade. The Liverpool and Manchester Railway was more of a threat, for it was swiftly followed by further plans for railways south to Birmingham, and on to London. So the Bristolians

Brunel (upper right) and colleagues, including Robert Stephenson (upper left), at the abortive launch of the SS Great Eastern *at Millwall Dock, London, November 1857.*

eventually set up their own railway company, and on 7 March 1833 they appointed Isambard to survey the route for their line. It was the turning point of his career.

DESIGNER OF RAILWAYS

For nine weeks Brunel worked twenty-hour days on horseback until he had found his ideal route. In June he was appointed as engineer to design the line, playing a vital role in steering the legislation for the Great Western Railway Company (GWR) through Parliament on 31 August 1835, after the tremendous fight referred to in his diary. He had grasped that the whole point of a trunk route was that it should be as level and straight as possible: it didn't matter if it missed out the smaller towns (which it did) – they could be picked up by slower branch lines, later. For its first 83.5 kilometres (52 miles), from London to Didcot, Brunel's line rises at an average gradient of 1 in 1,320 (4 feet per mile).

Brunel's originality of mind went much further, leading him to question the 'standard' gauge – with rails spaced 143.5 centimetres (4 feet 8½ inches) apart – that George and Robert Stephenson, father and son, the doyens of the northern railway establishment, had chosen, based on the colliery tramways on which George had started work as a boy. Instead, Brunel persuaded the GWR to allow him to build their railway with a broad gauge, with rails 2.1 metres (7 feet) apart. Brunel reasoned that a broader gauge would allow for larger and heavier locomotives, with a lower centre of gravity, which would be more stable at high speeds and offer more flexibility and room for growth in the future. Brunel expected to control all aspects of the railway's design himself. His broad gauge was a brilliant conception, but the GWR's first locomotives, built to his specifications, were unreliable and underpowered. The business was probably saved by a brilliant young locomotive superintendent, Daniel Gooch, who was to become Brunel's key ally in the expansion of the broad-gauge empire.

Ceding control of the locomotives to Gooch, Brunel nevertheless controlled all other aspects of the voluminous work from his London office at Duke Street in Westminster. He was a difficult man to work for, expecting very high standards of work and unrestricted working hours from his assistant engineers and contractors alike. He spared himself least of all, regularly working through the night. About fifty of Brunel's sketchbooks survive, and they demonstrate the extent to which he was responsible for the original design of bridges, tunnels, stations and other structures. Brunel wanted his line to be beautiful as well as serviceable: as the sketchbooks show, he designed Egyptian-style viaducts, castellated tunnel portals and Gothic bridges. He gave Temple Meads Station (1839–40) in Bristol a gigantic timber roof with false hammer beams, modelled Bath Station on an Elizabethan country house, and gave the Box Tunnel a classical archway on a heroic scale. Perhaps the finest station of all was London Paddington (1852).

Digging the Box Tunnel, the longest then conceived, was the most difficult and traumatic part of the whole process. It took over four years and cost more than a hundred lives. When it was completed in June 1841, the line could open from London to Bristol. Indeed, the GWR could already run their trains further, for they had set up a

The west façade of the Box Tunnel (1836–41), designed in a classical style by Brunel. This lithograph is from John Cooke Bourne's History of the Great Western Railway *(1846).*

host of subsidiary companies – the Bristol and Exeter Railway, the South Wales Railway, the Oxford and Rugby Railway, and so on – all with Brunel as their chief engineer, and all laid to the broad gauge. By the time of his death, Brunel had supervised the construction of over 1,930 kilometres (1,200 miles) of railway in England and Wales.

Brunel had too restless and brilliant a mind to be satisfied with easy solutions to problems, but this was not always good news for his shareholders. The most notorious case was the South Devon Railway, where the difficult terrain and steep gradients convinced him that here was a suitable place to try out a new technology, atmospheric traction, whereby the train would be pulled along by a vacuum created in a pipe running between the rails. Unfortunately, the materials technology of the time was simply not up to maintaining the vacuum consistently: after a year of experiment, he was forced to call it off and convert the line to locomotive running, and the South Devon shareholders lost over £240,000 as a result. This has led to Brunel being charged with extravagance, but there are many more instances where his genius as a designer created brilliantly economical solutions. A case in point was the Cornwall Railway, for

The Royal Albert Bridge, built to carry the Cornwall Railway over the Tamar at Saltash, under construction in the summer of 1858. The second truss has been floated into position and is gradually being raised on hydraulic jacks.

which he had to design 86.9 kilometres (54 miles) of track over difficult terrain, for a total budget of only £600,000. Brunel responded with a series of designs for timber viaducts, masterpieces of economical design: all have since been replaced in stone, but that was the point – the timber viaducts were there to get the railway running and earning revenue, so that they could be replaced later in more permanent form.

Brunel designed hundreds of bridges, in brick, stone, timber, cast iron and wrought iron. His late wrought-iron bridges are the most celebrated, culminating in the Royal Albert Bridge at Saltash over the Tamar estuary between Devon and Cornwall. Erected between 1854 and 1859, this created an entirely new form, the 'closed suspension bridge', in which all the forces are kept within the structure rather than being transferred to external anchorage points.

STEAMSHIP DESIGN

If Brunel had designed only railways, he would certainly be acknowledged as one of the great engineers of all time. Yet there was another aspect to his career, as one of the most influential ship designers of all time. This began in 1835, as he was planning the GWR. In an apparently casual dinner conversation, he said: 'Why not make it [the railway] longer, and have a steamboat go from Bristol to New York, and call it the Great Western.' Conventional wisdom had it that, because the small steamboats of the age could carry enough coal only for short crossings, it followed that no steamship could carry enough coal to cross the Atlantic. Brunel had the insight that the reverse was true: the larger the ship, the more favourable the power-to-weight ratio would be. A big enough ship could indeed cross the Atlantic, without being at the mercy of the winds. His charisma and the support of a group of GWR shareholders created the Great Western Steamship Company, and the SS *Great Western* (1835–38) was built to Brunel's specifications. It was the first purpose-built long-distance steamship in history, and on its maiden voyage in April 1838 crossed the Atlantic in fourteen days.

The SS *Great Western* had a wooden hull. Brunel next envisaged an iron-hulled vessel twice the size, and the SS *Great Britain* (1838–45) has a fair claim to be the most revolutionary ship design in history. Brunel originally planned to use paddle wheels, but in 1840 he saw the *Archimedes*, the world's first and only propeller-driven boat, invented by Francis Pettit Smith, and he persuaded his directors to suspend construction while he investigated further. Brunel's propeller design for the *Great Britain* was so good that even modern propellers are only 5–10 per cent more efficient. The *Great Britain* crossed the Atlantic in seven days on its maiden voyage in 1845: Brunel had once again revolutionized transport.

His third great ship, the SS *Great Eastern*, has often been seen as Brunel's greatest folly: it was certainly an astounding engineering vision. In 1853 Brunel set out to solve the problem of how a steamship could reach the Far East, given the lack of coal supplies at the far end, by carrying enough coal for the journey there and back. After a few pages of calculations and sketches he was envisaging a ship of 183 metres (600 feet) in length and 27,000 tons displacement – six times the size of the *Great Britain*, which had itself been the largest ship in the world when launched. Construction of the *Great Eastern* was immensely traumatic and protracted, bankrupting the Eastern Steam Navigation Company and its first builder, John Scott Russell, leaving Brunel to run the work himself. The first attempt to launch the completed hull, in January 1857, was an expensive fiasco, as it jammed fast on the launching ways. The ship eventually set sail on its maiden voyage on 7 September 1859, and the next day an explosion on board, caused by a closed steam valve, killed five men. The *Great Eastern* was by far the largest mechanical object yet built, and no one had ever tried to control so big a machine before. Brunel had invested so much in the *Great Eastern* – morally, intellectually and financially – that the disaster probably hastened his death only a week later, aged fifty-three, of kidney failure. The *Great Eastern* never made a profit: it was a marvel of design, but too big and before its time. George Bernard Shaw once observed that, as reasonable people adapt themselves to their circumstances, all progress must depend on the unreasonable man. Brunel was not a reasonable man, but he was a designer of genius, perhaps the supreme genius of the heroic age of engineering.

A page from one of Brunel's sketchbooks of 1853 showing the first sketch of his third ship, the SS Great Eastern.

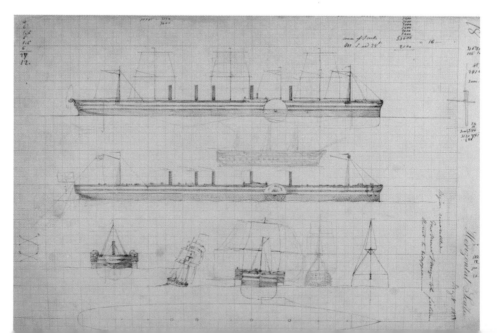

A. W. N. PUGIN

Realist and revolutionary

1812–1852

OR ALL ITS MANY BEAUTIES AND IDIOSYNCRASIES, the story of English architecture has few theorists and fewer revolutionaries. The one name that stands out – Augustus Welby Northmore Pugin – is that of a man who was so unusual a person, so radical an architect and so controversial a polemicist that he has suffered one of the oddest fates in architectural history. During the Victorian period, before and after his death, he was either derided or adored; then he was forgotten completely for half a century. From the 1940s onwards his reputation was paradoxically revived by Modernist historians, who saw him as one of the fathers of the dogmatic, unornamented style of the mid-20th century, although originally he had been best known as a wildly ornate decorative designer, in particular for the Palace of Westminster. Pugin's contribution to the way Western architecture has developed over the last 150 years is still highly contentious. But what is beyond doubt is that he had an almost freakish capacity for work, constantly generating the images and ideas that by the end of the 19th century would make English domestic architecture the envy of the world.

Pugin was born in Bloomsbury to parents who lived at the centre of what passed then for

Pugin's portrait at the Palace of Westminster, painted by his friend J. R. Herbert in 1845. The restless architect spared only twenty minutes to sit for the artist.

bohemian life in London. His father, the French émigré Auguste Charles Pugin, drew buildings and ornaments for John Nash, in effect as a subcontracted designer – a common practice before large architectural offices were established. Perhaps more significantly, however, he also worked with the topographical writer and publisher John Britton on illustrations for Britton's many books on medieval architecture. Britton's contribution to this growing genre was his insistence that measured drawings of old buildings should be absolutely accurate, and A. C. Pugin produced fine examples of these, good enough to show, sometimes through partial reconstruction, what Gothic churches and cathedrals had actually been like. Until then most antiquarian illustrations had been inaccurate or romanticized; the significance of this new scientific type of survey cannot be underestimated at a time when architects were hungry for reliable information.

FORMULATION AND PUBLICATION OF PUGIN'S THEORIES

The younger Pugin helped measure and draw up these structures, and this contributed to what became his encyclopaedic knowledge of medieval architecture. It also developed in him a strong sense not only of the structural and practical sophistication of Gothic architecture when compared to much modern building, but also an understanding of the significance of each of the elements of construction, however small. The 1820s and 1830s were an era of architectural disasters, and many new buildings were failing both technically and aesthetically. Furthermore, architects were faced with design problems – for technical installations such as efficient modern kitchens and plumbing, or for whole new building types such as railway stations – to which the conventional, symmetrical, Neoclassical approach to architecture offered no solution. So Pugin seems to have developed very early on the idea that the whole modern way of designing was fundamentally wrong, and that the only route out of an architectural dead end was to start again, from the point in the late 15th century when the Renaissance had begun to subvert English design.

Pugin was a prodigy as a designer and assisted the already established architect Charles Barry with the drawings that won the competition for the new Houses of Parliament in 1835. He always remained behind the scenes at the Palace of

Westminster, however; it was the publication (by himself) of his book *Contrasts* in 1836 that launched his career. He was by this time a Roman Catholic convert, living in an eccentrically medievalizing house of his own design outside Salisbury, and his book was an attack on modern life and modern architecture. The first part, rarely read, consists of his own version of history in which the course of English architecture was perverted by the Reformation. The second part, however – a series of satirical illustrations – has been pored over by architects ever since. Here the 24-year-old

OPPOSITE *Pugin's designs for wallpaper at the Palace of Westminster demonstrate his remarkable ability to reinvent medieval imagery. This example dates from 1851.* BELOW *St Giles, Cheadle, 1841–46: the closest Pugin came to achieving the high standards of design and execution he strove for all his life.*

savaged the work of leading contemporary designers such as Nash, Cockerell and Smirke, along with many lesser names mischievously mixed up with them, by contrasting their feeble efforts with the splendours of England's Gothic past. His message was that a good, moral society produces good, moral buildings – an entirely new idea – and that fakery and façadism offered no solutions to the problems of modern construction.

In a later book, *The True Principles of Pointed or Christian Architecture* of 1841, Pugin explained to architects through simple language and illustrations what this good, moral building was and how to achieve it. 'There should be no features about a building', he wrote, 'that are not necessary for convenience, construction, or propriety … the smallest detail should *have a meaning or serve a purpose*.' Essentially, materials and building techniques ought to express their uses and physical properties: a roof, for example, should primarily function as a roof, throwing off the rain and expressing its internal construction; even a detail as small as a hinge should look like a hinge, rather than being a piece of mechanically pressed metal hidden inside a door. Although his inspiration was Gothic and medieval, Pugin's doctrines fit within a family of contemporary ideas, mainly French, suggesting that the basic elements of life should be addressed rationally, coherently and expressively – an approach usually called 'realism'.

ECCLESIASTICAL AND DOMESTIC DESIGN

Pugin was taken up by only a small number of clients, but they were influential men who gave him the opportunity to design an astonishing number of buildings during a short architectural career of scarcely fifteen years. First among these was John Talbot, 16th Earl of Shrewsbury, a committed supporter of England's newly enfranchised Roman Catholics, who needed not only churches but convents, schools, monasteries and clergy houses; Shrewsbury made it a condition of his support for each new building project that Pugin be taken on as architect. For Shrewsbury Pugin designed his masterpiece, St Giles (1841–46) in the Staffordshire village of Cheadle – a re-creation of a perfect late 15th-century church. The building was decorated from top to bottom with sculpture, murals, tiles, stained glass, liturgical vestments and ornaments in brass and silver – for Pugin, helped by his continuing work at the Houses of Parliament, had begun to revive medieval skills in the applied arts as well. In fact he designed so much

The contrast between Pugin's 'Mediaeval Court' and the iron and glass 'Crystal Palace' in which it was housed emphasizes the extraordinary richness and vitality of Victorian design.

during his life that enthusiastic admirers, including George Gilbert Scott, William Butterfield and the whole first generation of English Neo-Gothic architects, were given a treasury of Gothic design on which to draw.

Pugin's ecclesiastical architecture eventually included four major Roman Catholic cathedrals – St Chad (1839–41) in Birmingham, St Barnabas (1841–44) in Nottingham, St Mary (1842–44) in Newcastle upon Tyne, and St George (1841–48) in Southwark, London – as well as more churches than he had years in his life. But his domestic architecture was perhaps his most original and influential work. He designed institutional buildings such as convents that closely mirrored (and indeed determined) the way residents lived their daily lives, usually in the form of long, winding corridor routes linking different types of room: a far cry from the symmetrical architecture of the Georgians. His houses, such as The Grange (1843–44), his own cliff-top home at Ramsgate in Kent, were similarly revolutionary. Every detail was worked out afresh, and plans and elevations were expressive both of what went on inside and how they were constructed. Pugin rejected compromise; he had nothing in common with fashionable 'picturesque' architects who designed romantic homes, possibly in a version of the Gothic style, that melted into the landscape. His religious fervour was an expression of his passion for seeing buildings designed logically and built well, even when he scarcely had the means to do it properly himself. A frenetic worker and constant traveller, Pugin produced his last significant public project at the Great Exhibition in 1851, when he displayed work for the applied arts at his 'Mediaeval Court'. He died the following year, aged only forty but utterly exhausted, having recently designed the clock tower of the Palace of Westminster. Every time his work and life are rediscovered they yield much that is entirely new.

Pugin is buried in his church of St Augustine, located next door to The Grange, the revolutionary house he designed for himself in Ramsgate in 1843–44.

EUGÈNE-EMMANUEL VIOLLET-LE-DUC

Gothic as constructive will

1814–1879

THE PROMINENT ARCHITECTURAL HISTORIAN John Summerson once claimed that Viollet-le-Duc was one of only two supremely eminent theorists in the history of architecture. This declaration, made in the heyday of modern functionalism, may no longer sound as convincing as it did in the 1940s, yet Viollet-le-Duc remains unmatched for the polemical force with which he developed the constructive argument for architecture. He was the most important influence for the development of continental Art Nouveau from France to Russia, and, following Henry Van Brunt's English translation of his two-volume *Entretiens sur l'architecture* (1858–72), he was among the most widely read architectural authors in the US during the late 19th century. Frank Lloyd Wright admitted in his autobiography that he once thought Viollet-le-Duc's *Dictionnaire raisonné de l'architecture française du XIe au XVIe siècle* (1853–68) 'was the only really sensible book on architecture in the world'.

Viollet-le-Duc's key role in the advent of architectural Modernism may be surprising, given that the majority of his writing is devoted to Gothic architecture and his architectural practice was largely dominated by restoration work. Few of France's major medieval monuments were spared his often over-zealous hand: the church of La Madeleine at Vézelay (from 1840), the basilica at St-Denis (from 1846), the cathedrals of Amiens (1849–74) and Reims (1860–74), the château of Pierrefonds (1857–79) and the fortified town of Carcassonne (from 1846) were all substantially transformed by Viollet-le-Duc. His most famous restoration is Notre-Dame de Paris (1845–64), where not a stone was left untouched. Even the fifty-six demonic gargoyles circling the upper gallery – among the most famous medieval icons in Paris – are his modern creations.

Portrait of Viollet-le-Duc, engraved by Léopold Massard, c. 1867.

The Middle Ages were for Viollet-le-Duc an inexhaustible reservoir of both architectural knowledge and fantasy. His structural rationalism cannot be separated from such historical investment in the past. Born in Paris into a prominent artistic and literary family and trained in classical letters and art by his uncle, the influential art critic Étienne Delécluze, Viollet-le-Duc came of age in the midst of the Romantic revolution that swept France in the 1830s. Refusing to attend the École des Beaux-Arts for fear of being swallowed by its academic doctrine, he was drawn instead towards the Romantic fascination with history, especially the Middle Ages, making a series of pilgrimages to southern France, Normandy, Chartres and Mont Saint-Michel, and spending restless hours completing meticulous drawings of France's architectural heritage. Viollet-le-Duc's drawing talent was nothing short of prodigious. His first achievement, at age twenty, was winning a medal at the Parisian salon of 1834 for a watercolour hung in the painting section. Thanks to money earned from a painting commissioned by King Louis-Philippe in 1835, he was able to spend the following two years travelling in Italy. He brought back hundreds of drawings, notably a series of ambitious pictorial essays in which he tried to bring history back to life.

A REVELATION IN RESTORATION

The turning point of Viollet-le-Duc's career came when he was entrusted to restore the church of La Madeleine at Vézelay in 1840. The job was not only an exercise in archaeological judgment, but also an extremely difficult problem of structural stability. A complete vault in the narthex of the dilapidated church collapsed in the first

BELOW *Cross-section of the narthex of La Madeleine, Vézelay, as restored by Viollet-le-Duc c. 1840.* OPPOSITE *One of Viollet-le-Duc's gargoyles on the upper gallery of Notre-Dame, Paris, sculpted by Victor Joseph Pyanet, c. 1849.*

years of the restoration. The accident would have been fatal to the whole monument had Viollet-le-Duc not previously rebuilt the most deteriorated arcades of the main nave, where stones simply crumbled into dust in the hands of the mason. The work, successfully completed, was revelatory for Viollet-le-Duc. First, it brought to light his practical abilities that would form such a useful complement to his drawing talent. But, more fundamentally, it showed him how structural issues could be mobilized profitably within the process of historical recovery he had initiated in the 1830s. The logic of structure moved the question away from a static, external taxonomy of form towards an internal understanding of the dynamics of style formation. Thinking the medieval church through its constructive logic was a deeper way to seize history: not merely a pictorial visualization, but putting oneself in the position of the very builder who had constructed the building in the first place. Viollet-le-Duc's entire career unfolded from this process of identification with the constructive gestures of medieval masons.

In the wake of his first success at Vézelay, Viollet-le-Duc won with his partner Jean-Baptiste Lassus the prestigious commission to restore Notre-Dame, Paris, in 1844. The project sealed his professional reputation and crystallized his association with Gothic in the public eye. The Middle Ages had been at first only a private refuge, but now it would provide the footing for an entire architectural revolution. Viollet-le-Duc, together with a group of zealous defenders of *l'art chrétien*, developed a militant anti-academicism seeking to revive the old French ways of building, an architectural polemic organized around the twin notions of rationalism and nationalism. Gothic was not only structurally more rational than the classicism taught at the École des Beaux-Arts, but it also had deeper roots within the French soil.

WIDENING INFLUENCE

With the 1848 Revolution and the advent of the Second Empire, and thanks to his powerful ally Prosper Mérimée, Viollet-le-Duc was able to consolidate his position in the administration of historical monuments and diocesan services. His dominion over these offices would be so absolute that he soon found himself at the head of a whole battalion of diocesan architects working all over France from which the rationalist precepts in his famous *Dictionnaire raisonné de l'architecture* could spread widely. Viollet-le-Duc claimed that he had 'formed a small army of artists … marching united and directing newcomers following the same principles'. In 1863 he sought

E. Viollet-le-Duc del.

Cl. Sauvageot, sc.

MAÇONNERIE

A. MOREL, Éditeur.

Imp. Lemercier. Paris.

to expand his control further by reaching out to the spiritual centre of the architectural discipline, fomenting with Mérimée an extremely ambitious reform of the École des Beaux-Arts.

It was around this period that Viollet-le-Duc, increasingly irritated at being pigeonholed as a Gothic Revivalist, finally turned his attention to modern iron industrial construction. His famous series of visionary projects in iron – published and illustrated in the eleventh, twelfth and thirteenth parts of his *Entretiens sur l'architecture* – were designed in the short period between 1864 and 1868. All these projects were big assembly rooms with large-span roofs inspired by crystalline or cellular structures. Iron was paradigmatically used for large spaces, but Viollet-le-Duc was not concerned with the usual stock of shed-like buildings such as greenhouses, train stations, market halls or exposition buildings. His attention was directed instead to the great assembly spaces of the modern secular age: concert halls, civic halls, town halls, etc. He deplored the fact that, in a time 'when meetings are becoming so large that no hall is capacious enough to hold them', architects had not succeeded in building a single space 'in which a crowd may be at ease, breathe comfortably, and come in and go out freely'. The 19th century, he added, was thus compelled to have recourse to medieval cathedrals to find room for the multitude – an effective way to show that his iron proposals began where Gothic left off.

These speculative projects, which all remained unbuilt, display a rather contorted structural logic, with iron members often used as prosthesis, bracketing masonry vaults. Viollet-le-Duc was not an advocate of straightforward modern engineering structures.

OPPOSITE *Plate from Viollet-le-Duc's* Entretiens sur l'architecture *showing an iron framework used in the roof of a large assembly room, c. 1868.* BELOW *Design for a covered market constructed using iron struts, from the* Entretiens sur l'architecture, c. 1868.

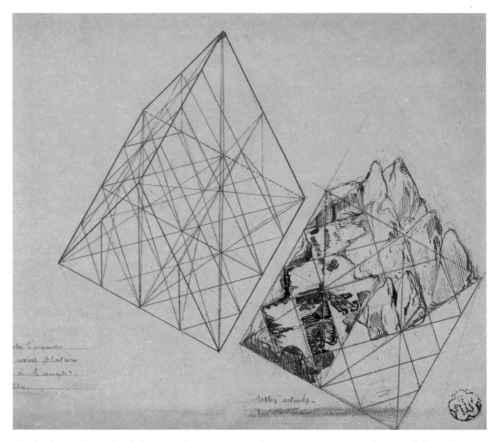

Viollet-le-Duc's study of the crystalline structure of a mountain peak at Blaitière de la Vallée Blanche, Mont Blanc, c. 1874.

He sought something more complex, tied to both his understanding of the historical evolution of architectural forms and his fascination with nature's productive principles. Following the disastrous Franco-Prussian War of 1870–71, a grieving Viollet-le-Duc spent much of his summers trekking in the Mont Blanc, admiring the structure and formative logic of the great mountain chain and reflecting on the nature of time. In this last decade of his life he cut back on his architectural activities, concentrating instead on other projects such as writing children books: short novellas meant to help regenerate the nation by reaching out directly to 'the children of all classes', teaching French youth how to think and muster the energy 'to get up in the morning and set to work'. By then Viollet-le-Duc was the head of a very active group of disciples, his influence spreading not only through his legacy in patrimonial and diocesan works but through the network of professional journals and architectural publications under his control. By the time of his death in Lausanne in 1879, Viollet-le-Duc, although still considered a renegade by the establishment, had almost acquired the status of a living legend. His rationalist teaching would reverberate well beyond his own lifetime.

John Fowler

Renowned developer of urban railways

1817–1898

JOHN FOWLER IS BEST KNOWN AS THE ENGINEER for the London Metropolitan Railway and the Forth Railway Bridge, the achievement of either of which would justify calling its creator a great engineer. In his lifetime he was associated with over a thousand projects, chiefly but not exclusively related to railways, and these frequently involved long spans and new concepts or materials. He was also an expert manager and delegator, able to persuade clients, shareholders and associates of the soundness of his judgment.

John Fowler was born in Sheffield, the son of a land surveyor. He received his early training with the Leather family, whose engineering practice was largely concerned with navigation and water supply. However, with them, and then with the locomotive pioneer and iron master John Urpeth Rastrick, he gained experience of railway surveying. He helped Rastrick design the masonry viaducts on the London–Brighton line in the late 1830s and then returned north to take charge of the construction of the Stockton to Hartlepool railway for George Leather, becoming engineer to the company on its opening in March 1841. He was thus one of the few Victorian engineers to have actually been responsible for running a railway. By that time he had already given evidence to Parliament, at the age of twenty, on improvements to Farringdon Street in London. Such precocity was characteristic of his career: in November 1865 he would become the youngest ever president of the Institution of Civil Engineers.

John Fowler in later life, photographed by Elliott & Fry. Fowler was an early and lifelong advocate of record photography on his projects.

Fowler rose during the 1840s through his involvement with railways in Yorkshire and Lincolnshire, many of which became part of the Manchester, Sheffield and Lincolnshire Railway. From the start he showed an ability to find able assistants and to delegate. His younger brother Henry acted as resident engineer on the East

Lincolnshire Railway, and his future brother-in-law, John Whitton, did the same else-where. Another early collaborator was William Wilson, a former employee of the iron fabricators Fox Henderson, who brought expertise of iron structures. The most famous of his assistants was Benjamin Baker, who joined him in 1860.

Parliamentary work inevitably required much of Fowler's time, and in 1844 he moved to London. In March 1851 he took over from Isambard Kingdom Brunel for the completion of the Oxford, Wolverhampton and Worcester Railway. The company had fallen out with the Great Western Railway, and the ambitious Fowler plotted a London extension, but he could not raise the necessary funds.

THE WORLD'S FIRST URBAN RAILWAY

In 1853 Fowler began the struggle, involving eighteen parliamentary bills, to build what became the London Metropolitan Railway, the world's first urban railway. Initially it was a relatively modest proposal to run from King's Cross to Edgware Road, but, as Fowler persuaded sceptical shareholders and railway companies to buy

BELOW *The Metropolitan District Railway under construction near Blackfriars, London, c. 1870; photograph by Henry Flather.* OPPOSITE *The Metropolitan Railway at King's Cross Station, shortly after the line was opened in 1863.*

The central girder of the Forth Railway Bridge under construction, September 1889. The photographer was P. Phillips, son of one of the contractors.

in, the route was extended to Paddington and Farringdon, linking most of the main railway companies north of the river Thames to the City. Inaugurated in January 1863, the line was a great success, despite the discomfort to passengers of underground steam haulage. Extensions followed through the 1860s and early 1870s: north to St John's Wood, west to Hammersmith and – with an independent company, the Metropolitan District Railway – through the West End and north bank of the Thames back to the City. Further progress was stalled by the capital costs associated with the expense of land purchase and also by physical disruption, until the development of the Greathead shield in the late 1880s facilitated tunnelling through London clay. Fowler was again involved as consultant to the first underground lines.

Fowler worked on other lines in the London area such as the London, Tilbury and Southend, as well as the terminus station at Victoria and the lines that made use of it. At various times he was consultant to most of the main lines operating in Britain, succeeding Brunel as consultant to the Great Western Railway. For that company he was involved in track quadrupling and gauge conversion, including the reconstruction of Maidenhead Railway Bridge (1891).

In his early career Fowler had displayed a mastery of masonry, as at Wicker Viaduct in Sheffield (1848), but he also proved an innovative user of other materials.

He was one of the first engineers to adopt William Fairbairn's patent tubular wrought-iron girders, most famously at Torksey Viaduct (1850) over the river Trent. There, the Railway Inspectorate refused the company permission to open the line because of concerns over the deflection of the girders. Fowler, with the support of the Institution of Civil Engineers, argued against this interference. He claimed that the Inspectorate did not understand the concept of continuity in girders. Eventually a compromise enabled both sides to save face.

Fowler did not abandon cast iron at this time. He saw its merits and employed it for economic reasons for the two largest cast-iron railway arches ever built, 61 metres (200 feet) in span, on the Severn Valley Railway in the 1850s. Fowler's Victoria Bridge (1860; now Grosvenor Bridge) was the first railway bridge across the Thames in central London. He used wrought iron because its relative lightness compared with cast iron permitted the reuse of staging and faster erection.

THE FIRTH OF FORTH RAILWAY BRIDGE

Fowler's name is more generally associated with long-span bridges. He considered a crossing of the Thames at Rotherhithe in connection with the Outer Circle Railway, a suspension crossing of the Severn, and also a crossing of the Humber, but his ambition

The famous human model used by Benjamin Baker to illustrate the cantilever principle underpinning the Forth Railway Bridge to the Royal Institution, 1887. The central figure is Kaichi Watanabe, a Japanese engineering student with Fowler and Baker.

saw practical realization with the Forth Railway Bridge, which at the time of its completion in 1890 contained the longest spans in the world: 520 metres (over 1,700 feet). Very much a collaboration with Benjamin Baker, who developed the cantilever design and almost literally proved the value of steel for its construction, this bridge was one of the greatest triumphs of Victorian engineering and remains a symbol of Scotland to this day.

The Forth Railway Bridge is seen as the structure that marked the transition from wrought iron to steel in bridges, and its success restored faith in the civil engineering profession after the collapse of the Firth of Tay Rail Bridge in 1879. Less well known is Fowler's involvement in the use of concrete, and the construction of a pioneer mass concrete arch, 23 metres (75 feet) in span, over the District line near Cromwell Road. The first such structure used lime cement and failed, but a replacement in February 1868 using Portland cement was more successful. Wider adoption was precluded by the quality control necessary for such an innovation. Fowler regularly used concrete in foundation work, and more unusually in 1880–81 for the lining of Harrow School Baths.

Fowler's railway work included a number of large stations, from Victoria in London (1860) to St Enoch's in Glasgow (1876; destr. 1977), Manchester Central (1880), Liverpool Central (1874; destr. 1973) and Sheffield Victoria (1851). The larger-span roofs had crescent trusses, the largest – 64 metres (210 feet) – at Manchester. Fowler's personal involvement was strongest at London Victoria.

Like most leading British engineers, Fowler was responsible for work overseas. He was a long-time consultant to the New South Wales government after his brother-in-law John Whitton emigrated there. His work in Egypt, where he was consultant to the Egyptian government from 1871, involved a proposed railway in Sudan. He received his knighthood as a result of this work, after his surveys were used by the British government in their campaigns there. He was consulted about an English Channel bridge proposal, the Chignecto Ship Railway in Nova Scotia and urban railways in North America.

Fowler was also responsible for a number of dock and land drainage schemes, most famously Millwall Dock (1867–68) in London. This, like Victoria Station, was a commercial venture associated with the contractor John Kelk, among others. Fowler was one the most financially successful Victorian engineers, and few could compare with the range and extent of his work in the second half of the 19th century.

Fowler's presidential address to the Institution of Civil Engineers was the first to address seriously the issue of engineering education and paved the way for its first

Installation of the lock gates at Millwall Dock, London, 1867.

report on the subject. Like Telford before him, he had a great facility for mentoring and delegating, and it was his success as a manager as much as his engineering knowledge that enabled him to achieve so much. He died at Bournemouth, honoured with a baronetcy for his work on the Forth.

CONCRETE AND STEEL

The availability of cast and wrought iron and plate glass in large quantities transformed the world of 19th-century construction, with the mass production of steel inaugurating a new age of high-rise building that still continues to change the face of cities everywhere. Iron and glass made it possible to enclose entire urban quarters: Giuseppe Mengoni's Galleria Vittorio Emanuele II in Milan (1863–77), the biggest element in a comprehensive renovation of the central area around the Duomo, was the largest of innumerable glazed arcades that can now be found in cities on every continent. As a building type it was pioneered in Paris, from where the prefabricated elements of the Galleria's roof were imported. The resilience of the iron construction tradition was reflected in the remarkable tower (controversial in its time but now the iconic symbol of the French capital) that was designed for wrought iron by Gustave Eiffel for the 1889 Universal Exposition in Paris. The form of the tower – for over forty years the world's tallest building – was inspired by Eiffel's railway bridge designs. A multifaceted genius who pioneered the science of aerodynamics, he was also responsible (with his engineers Maurice Koechlin and Émile Nouguier) for the structural framework of New York's Statue of Liberty.

In the United States, the revolutionary idea of the metal-framed building went back to mid-19th century New York, but came to fruition in the Midwestern metropolis of Chicago after the city was devastated by a catastrophic fire in 1871. Chicago was the birthplace of the modern skyscraper, home of William Le Baron Jenney's Leiter and Home Insurance buildings as well as the more radical work of Daniel H. Burnham and John Wellborn Root, architects of the first tall building to rely entirely on a steel frame (1881). It was left to Louis Sullivan to address the aesthetics of the tall building: he developed a theory of architectural decoration, subordinated to the primary expression of structure, which is at odds with his reputation as a pioneer of functionalism (although its essential rationalism contrasted with the more ornamental tendencies associated with the early skyscrapers of New York). Perhaps the best known of all American architects, Frank Lloyd Wright, emerged from Sullivan's office and made his name with a series of 'Prairie houses' (1900–20). He engaged with concrete to spectacular effect at Fallingwater (1938) and in the structurally innovative and spatially awesome Johnson Wax Building (1939), his great 'cathedral of work', with its extraordinarily thin concrete columns. Equally daring towards the end of his long career was the great ramped interior of New York's Solomon R. Guggenheim Museum (1943–59).

If the United States was the leader in the development of metal-framed construction, the possibilities of reinforced concrete were first explored thoroughly in Europe. Building on early experiments in Britain, François Hennebique developed the use of the material internationally from his Paris base. A particular benefit of concrete construction was its potential for spanning large internal spaces. A series of engineers, including the Frenchman Eugène Freyssinet and the Swiss Robert Maillart, used concrete to spectacular effect in the design of bridges and other functional structures, while architects were left to exploit its aesthetic possibilities. Despite its apparent suitability for the sculptural visions of Antoni Gaudí, the Catalan architect made only occasional use of concrete (it would, however, be employed extensively in the ongoing construction of the Sagrada Familia in Barcelona after his death in 1926). Through the first half of the 20th century the more down-to-earth approach of Auguste Perret, whose family background was in the construction industry, established concrete as an acceptable material not only for factories and bridges but for public buildings as well. Fundamentally a rationalist in the mould of Viollet-le-Duc, Perret developed a modern classical language in a series of Parisian projects, treating concrete as a practical material that could also be made visually attractive through the use of fine detail and colour. His work balances a close regard for utilitarian efficiency with a concern for artistic effect and urban decorum, offering the potential for a modern alternative to the more dogmatic functionalism of the International Style associated with Walter Gropius and others. The young Le Corbusier's apprenticeship with Perret certainly galvanized his belief in concrete as the basis for a new architecture. Le Corbusier's early projects contain memories of classicism, seen particularly in the Villa Savoye (1929–31). His late work moved on from the functionalist agenda to idiosyncratic buildings such as the chapel at Ronchamp (1950–55) and the monastery of La Tourette (1960), in which concrete is used to create expressive forms of profound majesty and resonance that continue to influence architects in the 21st century.

GIUSEPPE MENGONI

Architect of Milan's Galleria Vittorio Emanuele II

1829–1877

GIUSEPPE MENGONI'S NAME IS INDISSOLUBLY LINKED with the Galleria Vittorio Emanuele II, which he designed and built in Milan between 1863 and 1877. It was one of the most structurally complex and challenging works in the city, the culmination of a series of decisions taken just after the unification of Italy in 1861 that were intended to breathe new life into the city's infrastructure, institutions and monumental buildings. After more than a century his Galleria retains its fascination, owing to its ideal location between two key points in the centre of Milan (Piazza del Duomo and Piazza della Scala), as well as the reputation of its shops and cafés and the grandeur of its spaces.

A COMBINATION OF SCIENCE AND ART

Giuseppe Mengoni was born in Fontanelice, then part of the Papal States, to a wealthy middle-class family. Following the revolutionary upheavals of 1848, he concentrated on his studies at the University of Bologna's Faculty of Mathematical Physics and the local Academy of Fine Arts, a combination that equipped the future architect to take on complex and wide-ranging projects. In 1861 he took part in a competition to redesign the Piazza del Duomo in Milan, which also included what would become the Galleria Vittorio Emanuele. The success he achieved on this occasion led to an outstanding professional career that brought him commissions to design and build theatres, apartment blocks, banks and covered markets with exposed iron frameworks; he also submitted a town planning proposal for the city of Rome. Mengoni's awareness of modern building techniques and materials, combined with his respect for tradition and traditional forms characterized a career that ended abruptly in December 1877, when he died after falling from the scaffolding of the Galleria Vittorio Emanuele. Although therefore few in number, his works show that he was a versatile, professional and highly skilled architect, perfectly attuned to the

The Galleria Vittorio Emanuele II, Milan, shortly after completion of the main gallery, c. 1867.

dynamics of the 19th century and capable of meeting the many demands of a rapidly changing society.

THE GALLERIA VITTORIO EMANUELE II

Building the Galleria Vittorio Emanuele II was an extremely complicated achievement that required the balancing of political allegiances and administrative concerns, economic interests and town-planning strategies, symbolic meanings and functional requirements, technical problems and artistic issues. It was part of a long debate about how to renovate the Piazza del Duomo in a way that would both enhance the cathedral and modernize the structure of the city centre. In 1859, the year Austrian forces were expelled from Italy, Milan's city council held an initial competition for ideas that was open to all citizens. The competition was held again in 1861, but only for artists

BELOW *Plan by Mengoni showing renovations to the Piazza del Duomo, Milan, and his design for the new Galleria Vittorio Emanuele II, 1865.* **OPPOSITE** *Portrait of Giuseppe Mengoni, 1877.*

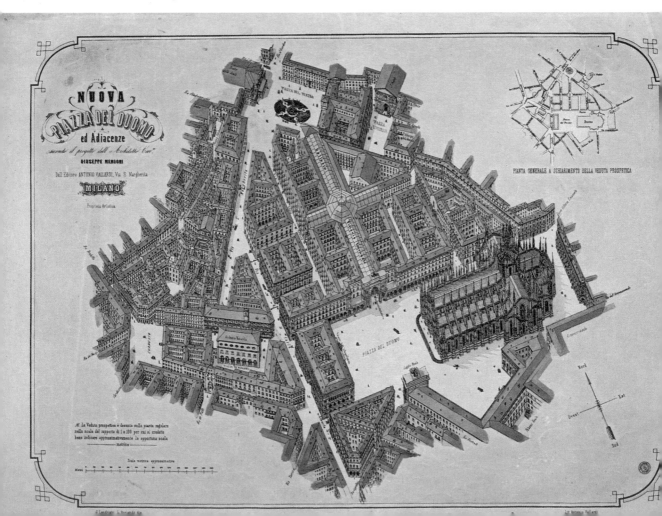

and architects, and as Mengoni was considered one of the best candidates he was invited to take part in the final competition in 1863. His winning design consisted of a vast rectangular piazza surrounded by arcades and linked on its northern side to the Piazza della Scala by a covered passageway, to be filled with elegant shops and cafés. This is the origin of the Galleria's distinctive layout, characterized by the intersection of two streets that meet at right angles in the centre of an octagonal 'piazza'. It was entirely covered over by a translucent iron and glass ceiling – a symbol of modernity and progress.

As both architect and director of works, Mengoni demonstrated his exceptional talents: he had to manage an operation that required complicated negotiations for the expropriation and sale of properties, raising of capital and a great deal of demolition and construction work, while maintaining a delicate balance both between public and private funding and between the speed of the building schedule and the use of technical innovations. The construction company, the City of Milan Improvements Company (formed in London especially for the occasion), took just two years to build the entire Galleria, with the exception of the entrance archway from the Piazza del Duomo (which was finished in 1878). By 1867, the general public could walk through the entire site in its delightful urban setting.

Mengoni altered the original design by enlarging the dimensions of the entire complex and raising the height of the buildings from three to five storeys. His intention was to increase the size of the rentable spaces and their revenues, and thus promote the interests of both the construction company and the city council. This decision also affected the overall atmosphere of the Galleria, which, because of its vast scale and grandiloquent volumetric spaces, succeeded in modernizing and promoting covered passageways as a building type; its broad walkways were 14.5 metres (47½ feet) wide and its tall façades 25–30 metres (82–98½ feet) high. Such 'real streets and real buildings', declared Julien Guadet, professor of Architecture at the École des Beaux-Arts in Paris, in 1880, can only result from a courageous attitude on the part of the architect and from a 'grandiose vision' on the part of the city. The decision to enlarge the design also affected the technical solutions required. The need to create height, using flexible spaces that were as free as possible from load-bearing walls in order to 'respond to the various demands of commercial activity', and the necessity of constructing the heavy iron and glass ceiling above the buildings –

353,000 kilograms (776,600 pounds) of metal – meant that new combinations of materials had to be used. Small cast-iron columns and iron double T-beams were thus combined with traditional masonry work, introducing construction systems virtually unknown at the time in Milan. The metal framework, hidden within the masonry walls and behind the façades, can be seen in all its modernity in the roof, which abandoned the more conventional trusses with angled supports and was instead held up by elegant depressed-arch ribs without horizontal tie beams, providing support for a large cupola that echoed the shape of the octagon below it. The dome reached a height of more than 49 metres (160 feet) at its summit and was approximately 38 metres (125 feet) wide.

In the absence of suitable Italian manufacturing companies, the sections were pre-fabricated in France by the Parisian company of Henri Joret and then installed over a period of about six months: an impressively short time given the prevailing culture and local legislative practices. It is astonishing that Mengoni was able to organize all the most demanding stages of such an unusual building site where approximately

Longitudinal section of the iron and glass roof of the Galleria Vittorio Emanuele II, manufactured in Paris by the firm of Henri Joret.

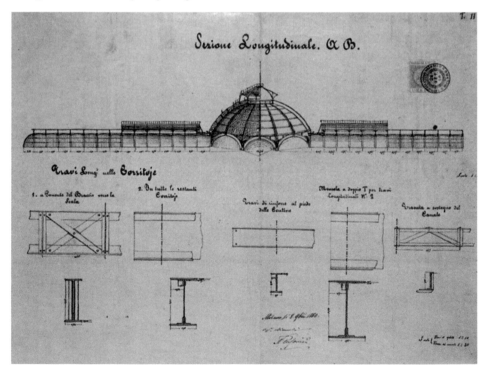

The buildings of the Galleria during construction, 1866. With the exception of the entrance arch, the entire fabric took only two years to build.

1,000 men worked every day, each with different skills and practices. Equally remarkable is how he was able to bring together contributions from public and private funding, not to mention the participation, services and experience of both Italian and foreign companies. However, affairs took a less fortunate turn in 1867, when the work was slowed down by economic and administrative difficulties. It took another ten years to complete the triumphal arch over the entrance from the Piazza del Duomo, but in the meantime the Galleria was enthusiastically patronized and enjoyed by the citizens of Milan, who were delighted by the shops, decorations, light and the new atmosphere and spaciousness created by the 'iron and glass sky'. In 1892 the engineers of Milan's Politecnico observed that it could be credited with having introduced 'iron formally into the city, placing it in competition with classical masonry structures, as it is no longer restricted to a subordinate role, but rather elevated to a new dignity in construction'. Mengoni's Galleria influenced the design of new shopping arcades and helped to make Italy a leader in this type of building, transforming it into a true triumph of space and light and an eternally delightful part of city architecture.

GERALD R. LARSON

WILLIAM LE BARON JENNEY

Developed Chicago's distinctive skyscrapers

1832–1907

WILLIAM LE BARON JENNEY WAS ONE OF A GROUP of architects responsible for the development of the skyscraper in Chicago during the 1880s. Born in Fairhaven, Massachusetts, he received his professional education in civil engineering at the École Centrale des Arts et Manufactures in Paris, completing his studies in 1856. He served in the Union Army as an engineer during the Civil War and resigned his commission as a major in 1866. His first inclination was landscape design, and he approached Frederick Law Olmsted for a job. By 1867 he was working in Chicago as the junior partner of architect Sanford E. Loring, but Loring soon left his practice with Jenney to focus on terracotta manufacturing, while Jenney found employment as the landscape engineer for the West Chicago Park Commission. In 1869 Jenney was contracted by Olmsted to help in the construction of Riverside, a new Chicago suburb, where he designed his first two major architectural commissions, the Riverside water tower and the Riverside Hotel.

Jenney benefited greatly from the 1871 Chicago fire, winning commissions for two major commercial architectural projects, but unfortunately for all of Chicago's architects the 1873 Depression slowed Chicago's reconstruction for six years. In 1874 Jenney's career slid back to where it had been before the fire, as he worked on small houses and churches. As the economy began to rebound in 1879, he was approached by Levi Leiter, Marshall Field's partner, to design a five-storey loft building for the corner of Wells and Monroe. Jenney wanted to maximize the daylight in the interior by keeping the width of the masonry piers the same size in

ABOVE *Portrait of William Le Baron Jenney.* OPPOSITE *Jenney's Home Insurance Building, Chicago, 1884–85.*

Construction of the Fair Store, designed by Jenney c. 1890. The iron framing system is similar to that employed by Jenney in the Second Leiter Building.

the two street elevations of the Leiter Building. He placed cast-iron pilasters that supported the floor beams on the inside face of the piers in the façade that would normally have supported the floor beams. Although iron columns had been used in the exteriors of Chicago's buildings prior to the 1871 fire, this was the first use of iron columns in the exterior of a Chicago building after the fire.

CHICAGO'S FIRST SKYSCRAPERS

After Jenney had completed the Leiter Building (1879; destr.), while younger architects in Chicago were being commissioned to design office buildings that had at least ten storeys – buildings that would soon be called 'skyscrapers' – his practice slowed and he began to assume the role of elder statesman. Daniel H. Burnham and John Wellborn Root designed the Montauk Block, Chicago's first skyscraper, in 1881, as well as the majority of these early skyscrapers. By April 1884, when Jenney was awarded the design for the Home Insurance Building, his only major commission during the ten-year period that followed the completion of the Leiter Building, there were already seven ten-storey and taller skyscrapers built or under construction in Chicago. The Home Insurance Building commission can be viewed as an anomaly in Jenney's career during this time, attributed not to his pre-eminence among Chicago's architectural community but rather to a personal favour from the company's local agent, who was a Civil War acquaintance. Historians in the early 20th century erroneously referred to the Home Insurance Building as both the 'first skyscraper' and the 'first iron skeleton-framed skyscraper', and Jenney was similarly recognized as the 'father of the skyscraper and the iron skeleton frame'. More contemporary research has not sustained these legends. James Bogardus is now considered the inventor of the iron skeleton frame in the United States, with his iron skeleton-framed buildings in New York during the 1850s. Historians also now credit George Post with having designed the first skyscraper, the Equitable Life Insurance Building in New York, in 1867. Burnham and Root are correspondingly credited with having designed Chicago's first skyscraper.

Commentary of the period and examination of the structure of the Home Insurance Building make it apparent that Jenney did not conceive or detail its structure as an independent iron skeleton frame. The two masonry-bearing party walls in the rear of the building, as well as the interior iron cage, were typical for the period. The unique detail in which Jenney departed from standard Chicago construction practices of the early 1880s was his insertion of a cast-iron section within the exterior masonry piers in only the two street façades. These supported the floor beams in a manner similar to the iron sections he had used in the Leiter Building. Jenney's objective, once again, was to diminish the size of the masonry piers in order to maximize the daylight in the interior space. Unlike with a true skeleton frame, however, there were no iron spandrel beams at each floor that would have connected the columns into a rigid framework. The building's exterior relied on the conventional bonding of the masonry in the pier and spandrel to rigidify the structure of the two street façades.

Panorama of Chicago in 1913, with Jenney's Second Leiter Building in the foreground, 1889–91.

DEVELOPMENT OF THE IRON SKELETON FRAME

The first iron skeleton-framed exterior wall in a Chicago skyscraper appeared in the lightcourt of the Phoenix Building, designed by John Wellborn Root in 1885. Root used the now conventional iron column and spandrel frame for the first time to support the lightcourt's masonry enclosure at each floor with the incorporation of iron shelf angles attached to the spandrel beams. Root also used this same detail in all four walls in the lightcourt of the Rookery (1885–88). By 1889, Root was ready to divorce the skyscraper from any reliance on bearing walls for the first time with the design of the Rand McNally Building, which was not only the first all steel-framed skyscraper but also the first to sport an all terracotta-clad exterior.

Manhattan Building, Chicago, 1889–91 – the world's first sixteen-storey building, and technically the most pioneering of Jenney's projects.

While Jenney had not invented the iron skeleton-framed skyscraper nor was he the first Chicago architect to design a building solely supported by an iron frame, he was in the forefront of the Chicago architects who continued to develop the skyscraper after Root had designed the Rand McNally Building. Jenney's first all iron-framed building was also his masterpiece. Soon after construction had started on the Rand McNally Building, Levi Leiter once again commissioned Jenney to design another project, now referred to as the Second Leiter Building: a department store for the corner of State and Van Buren. Jenney designed its eight-storey elevation as a straightforward expression of the underlying skeleton frame.

The Second Leiter Building (1889–91) marked the beginning of the true high point of Jenney's practice, reflected in his taking on William Mundie as his junior partner in 1890. The firm was commissioned to design a number of skyscrapers during the period immediately preceding the 1893 World's Fair. The most technically pioneering of these buildings was the Manhattan Building, completed in 1891. It shares with Burnham and Root's Monadnock Building (1889–92) not only the title of the world's first sixteen-storey building, but also the reputation of being the first skyscraper designed with wind bracing. The sites for both buildings were located on Dearborn Street, which had recently been widened south of Jackson Street, and the width of these lots had correspondingly been reduced to 20.7 metres (68 feet). Both architects were so concerned about the potential deflection caused by the wind in a tall building with such a narrow width that they had simultaneously responded by stiffening the buildings' interior structures against wind loads. In the Manhattan Building, Jenney incorporated diagonal bracing (as did Burnham and Root) in addition to, for the first time in a skyscraper, rigid portal frames.

The 1893 World's Fair, for which Jenney was honoured with the commission to design the Horticultural Building, marked the zenith of his career, and afterwards he seemed content to allow Mundie to assume more and more control of the firm. He retired in 1905 to southern California, where he died in Los Angeles on 15 June 1907.

The Horticultural Building designed by Jenney for the 1893 World's Fair, Chicago.

et son Gendre et Collaborateur M. Salles
Mr G. Eiffel au sommet de la Tour
ND. Phot

GUSTAVE EIFFEL

Engineering mastermind of tall metal structures

1832–1923

GUSTAVE EIFFEL WAS NOT ONLY THE MASTER BUILDER of the mighty Paris landmark that bears his name: he was also an able businessman and entrepreneur who left testimonies of his work in France, Portugal, Spain, Hungary, Romania, the United States, South America and South-east Asia. Ambitious, energetic and decisive, he possessed all the skills of a fully trained engineer combined with originality, a realistic approach to deadlines, an understanding of public relations, and the capacity to attract and retain the best collaborators.

Eiffel was born in Dijon, where his mother ran a family coal and firewood business. His father was a self-educated man whose adventurous spirit and thirst for knowledge Gustave inherited. At the end of three years' study at the École Centrale des Arts et Manufactures, already one of the major engineering schools in France, Eiffel wrote his final dissertation on the construction of a chemical plant, expecting to take over from his uncle as the manager of a paint factory near Dijon. But family relations had soured, so in 1855 – the year of the first Universal Exhibition, in France – Eiffel began a career in engineering. He went to work for Charles Nepveu, a versatile engineer and contractor whose avowed business was the 'construction of steam engines, tools, forgework, boiler building, metalwork, production of stationery and rolling stock for railways and civil engineering'. Soon afterwards Nepveu helped Eiffel get a job with a railroad company, giving him the opportunity to study a small metal bridge with a span of only 22 metres (72 feet). This was to be his first step in a grand career as a builder of bridges for railways, which were then developing rapidly in France. When Eiffel was twenty-six, Nepveu gave him the job of supervising the construction of a 500-metre (1,640-foot) metal railway bridge over the river Garonne in Bordeaux. The bridge was one of the longest built in France at the time and quite an important assignment. The pier foundations were driven by compressed air caissons, which were to become one of Eiffel's specialities.

Gustave Eiffel (left) and his son-in-law Adolphe Salles stand on the spiral staircase at the summit of the Eiffel Tower, Paris, 1889.

RAILWAY VIADUCTS AND BRIDGES

After a few jobs in the South of France for the Compagnie des Chemins de Fer du Midi, which included the Toulouse railway station and several bridges, Eiffel decided in 1864, at the age of thirty-two, to start his own company. He had only limited financial resources but good technical knowledge and a few contacts in the railway business. Within two years as an engineering consultant he was able to buy material and a workshop to become a builder. His first, modest commission was the framework for two synagogues in Paris, and then his company was awarded the contract for building two viaducts, designed by Wilhem Nordling, over the river Sioule in central France. Eiffel's own contribution was to launch a prefabricated deck from the riverbank – a method that later became common. In the early 1870s his business began to prosper and he built several more bridges, the most remarkable being those of the Latour to Millau and Chinon to Les Sables d'Olonne railway lines. He also built structural frameworks and gas storage tanks, and in Bolivia and Peru he constructed jetties, bridges, storage tanks and even a prefabricated church on the Chilean border that still stands today.

In 1875 Eiffel was awarded two major European commissions. The first was the central station in Pest (now Budapest) and the second was a large viaduct (Maria Pia) over the river Douro in Porto, designed by Theophile Seyrig. Together they developed the concept of a very large arch bridge spanning 160 metres (525 feet), which allowed them to cut costs by avoiding any scaffolding across the river and thus to win the international competition, contributing to Eiffel's growing fame. During this time he was responsible for several other bridges in Portugal and Spain, and the structural design of the pavilion of the City of Paris for the Universal Exhibition of 1878. In Paris he built additions to the department store Le Bon Marché in 1879 and two years later the imposing head office of the Banque Crédit Lyonnais.

The success of the Maria Pia viaduct in Portugal brought Eiffel a contract to build a similar bridge on the Marvejols–Neussargues line in central France, crossing the Truyère gorge and thereby saving the costly earthworks necessary to go down and up the valley. Although the Garabit Viaduct differs in some details from the Douro bridge, it is very closely related and still stands as a masterpiece in Eiffel's career. Spanning the valley across 160 metres (525 feet,) and 122 metres (400 feet) above the river, it gives a visual impression of incomparable lightness, the elegance of the shape of the bow echoed in the most minute details of the bridge. Completed in 1884, it opened the way for the construction of the tall 300-metre (985-foot) tower in Paris that would be designed and built using the same principles, calculations and construction, and by the same team of technicians.

The Garabit Viaduct over the Truyère gorge, completed in 1884. With its clear span of 160 metres (525 feet), it was a major achievement for Eiffel's company.

THE STATUE OF LIBERTY AND THE EIFFEL TOWER

In 1884 Eiffel and his team of engineers, notably Maurice Koechlin and Émile Nouguier further demonstrated their talent by designing and building the armature of the Statue of Liberty in New York. The structural framework consists of a pylon that carries, with the support of a light skeleton, the thin copper sheets that give shape to the colossus. The rotating steel dome of the observatory in Nice, built in 1886, is also a good example of resourcefulness. In order to facilitate its mobility, Eiffel made it float on a circular tank filled with salt water to prevent freezing. Aside from these inventions, the company made a considerable profit in the development of portable bridges, which were sold as kits for export throughout the world until 1940.

The Universal Exhibition of 1889 gave Eiffel the chance to go beyond his work as a civil engineer. Before anything had been officially decided, some suggested that a distinctive monument should commemorate the centenary of the French Revolution. The idea of a very high tower had already been put forward elsewhere, including a 305-metre (1,000-foot) example proposed for the Philadelphia 1876 Exhibition, and in May 1884 Koechlin and Nouguier began to consider a tower for Paris, producing a rough sketch and some calculations for a metal pylon made of four main girders,

8 Octobre 1887   10 Novembre 1887   14 Juin 1888   10 Juillet 1888   14 Octobre 1888

widely spaced at the base and joining at the top. It was substantially modified by the architect Stephen Sauvestre, who joined the first level and the four main piles with monumental arches, placed glazed halls on the floors and added some ornamental effects to the façades. Eiffel became quite interested in the idea and took out a patent together with his two engineers in September 1884. Months were spent promoting the project among official circles; eventually the competition for the masterplan and major buildings of the exhibition, launched in 1885, included a very high tower – an explicit reference to Eiffel's project. He won the commission. Eiffel provided almost half the financing for the construction, receiving an allocation from the City of Paris in exchange for the right to operate the tower until 1910 and the rest of the funds through a pool of three banks.

Work on the tower had barely started when an articled entitled 'Protest against Eiffel Tower' appeared in the 14 February 1887 issue of *Le Temps*, the leading French newspaper of the time. Signed by well-known personalities from the artistic establishment, it was a vigorous and indignant protest against 'this offence to French good taste … building this monstrous Eiffel Tower in the heart of our capital'. Descriptions such as 'baroque, mercantile imaginations of a machine builder, a gigantic black factory chimney, like an ink splotch' reflect the general tone of the article. Eiffel replied in an interview that summed up his artistic doctrine, arguing in favour of the 'aesthetics of the tower': 'Can one think that because we are engineers, beauty does not preoccupy us or that we do not try to build beautiful, as well as solid and long lasting structures? Aren't the genuine functions of strength always in keeping with unwritten conditions of harmony?' He continued: 'Yes, I affirm that the curves of the

14 Novembre 1888   26 Décembre 1888   20 Janvier 1889   12 Février 1889   12 Mars 1889

Ten photographs taken between 8 October 1887 and 12 March 1889 recording the progress of the Eiffel Tower's construction.

four corners of the monument, as mathematical calculations determined them … will give a great impression of force and beauty, because they will visibly reflect the strength of the overall conception.' This text still stands as Eiffel's paradoxical aesthetic testimony, based on rational and abstract considerations in keeping with the laws of science and ethics, and in contradiction of his own personal tastes, which were those of the conventional 19th-century bourgeois.

Construction of the tower was a masterpiece of precision, efficiency and speed. The riverside foundations of the monument, which were made using pneumatic caissons, were finished by June 1887. The 1,200 pieces of the Tower required 700 engineering drawings and 3,000 workshop drawings, which kept forty people employed for two years. Each prefabricated part was built to within a tenth of a millimetre at Eiffel's Levallois-Perret factory, just five miles away. There were between 150 and 300 workers on the site, with a team of veterans from the great viaducts at key posts. There were twelve temporary scaffolds 30 metres (98 feet) high, and another set of four scaffolds 45 metres (148 feet) high held the first-floor girders. Climbing cranes were used to hoist the elements. In all, the entire iron tower was built in a mere twenty-two months, and 1889 was a year of triumph for Eiffel. Not only a technical but also a popular success, the tower was considered a symbol of industry and a masterpiece of engineering, the culmination of several decades of daring experiments in construction, and it ensured Eiffel's worldwide fame.

STARTING ANEW AS A SCIENTIST

Unfortunately, Eiffel also became involved in the biggest financial scandal of his time, the Panama Canal affair. The entrepreneur of the canal, Ferdinand de Lesseps, had gained a concession from Colombia to build a canal through the Isthmus of Panama. Confident from his Suez success, he had opted for a level canal, and work started in 1882. However, extreme difficulties – including thousands of lives lost in the jungles of Central America – made it obvious that this was impossible. Eiffel was brought in to build ten huge locks, including their sliding steel doors, with a budget fifteen times that of the Tower. He agreed to deliver within thirty months, and work started in record time: the gates were built while excavations were progressing on the site. But the medical skills of the time could not cope with malaria and yellow fever, and the rest of the canal works were too slow to keep the trust of the investors. Unable to get further private funding, the Panama Canal Company went bankrupt on 4 February 1889, and Lesseps and other trustees were put on trial. Although he was eventually cleared, Eiffel was drawn into the litigation and decided to resign from his position as chairman in order to protect his own company.

Eiffel then began a second career as a theoretical scientist, becoming a pioneer in three new fields: meteorology, radiotelegraphy and aerodynamics. His research in

Construction of the colossal Gatún Locks on the Panama Canal, c. 1912 – some twenty-five years after Eiffel had initially advised on their design.

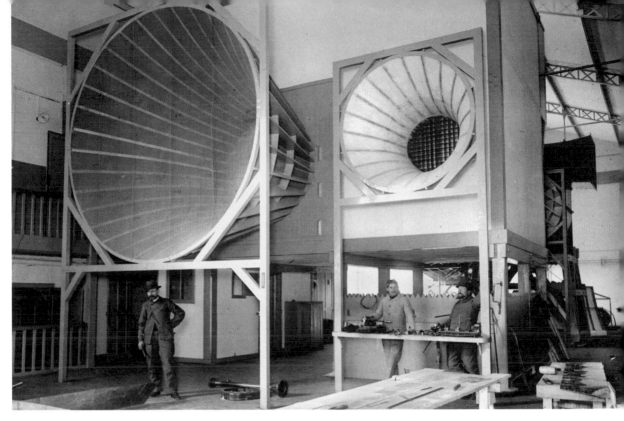

The wind tunnel built by Eiffel in 1912 at 67 Rue Boileau, Paris, to test the aerodynamic performance of structures as well as aeroplane models. The laboratory is still in use today.

meteorology started in 1889 at the top of his Tower, where he fitted an observation station. Later he created other stations on his properties in Sèvres near Paris, Beaulieu on the French Riviera, Ploumanach in Brittany and Vevey in Switzerland. He published the results of these observations in luxurious editions at his own expense. He also encouraged numerous scientific experiments that demonstrated the utility of the Tower, such as a giant pendulum, a mercury barometer, physiological experiments and the first long-distance radio transmission. In October 1898 Eugène Ducretet received signals transmitted from the Tower at the Pantheon, and four years later Captain Ferié established good radio communications with eastern France. From then on, the Tower was considered a site of strategic interest and thus saved from destruction. Perhaps Eiffel's most passionate interest was in aerodynamics: he built a wind tunnel in Paris on the Champ de Mars that was used between 1909 and 1911, followed by a bigger one at Rue Boileau that is still in use. Until the time of his death, at the age of ninety-one, he was usually to be found in his laboratory, directing work and supervising the publication of results obtained by his team of researchers.

FRANÇOIS HENNEBIQUE

Symbol of reinforced concrete

1842–1921

FRANÇOIS HENNEBIQUE WAS AN EMBLEMATIC FIGURE in the early history of reinforced concrete. But what role did he play as a builder? The history whose course he helped to shape is an intriguing marriage of concrete and metal, the story of a coming together of technology and production that created a profound shift in the landscape of architecture in the early 20th century. The nature of this emerging technology was therefore defined at the crossroads of very different working cultures and this shaped the early identity of reinforced concrete as a raw material: multifaceted, heterogeneous, hybrid, even impure. But this composite material's character was also forged by the meeting of the world of industry and the world of craftsmanship. This is a point where two different and conflicting scales come into play – a crossroads where Hennebique operated and where, in a more general sense, the technology of reinforced concrete was shaped.

Diagram of Hennebique's 1897 building system for reinforced concrete – an expansion of his earlier patent of 1892. It is based around the use of iron stirrups, but here the concrete beams are reinforced by additional rods.

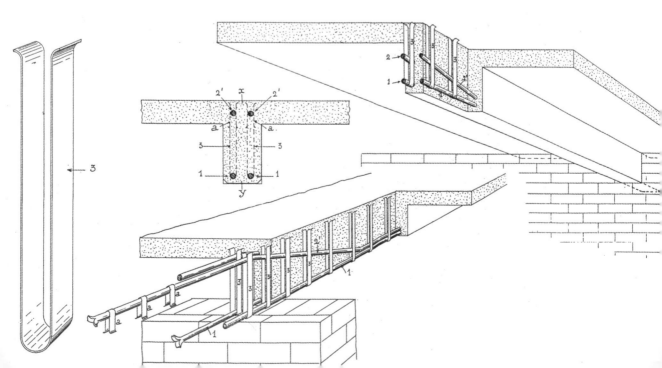

At the heart of the process that Hennebique developed in the early 1890s lay a simple iron stirrup. When the metal is correctly positioned within a mass of concrete, the stirrup connects the two together and resists the effects of shearing stresses. However, this connection also created a relationship between an abstract technique and a functional working method. It is basically a builder's skill, a stonemason's trick, but Hennebique foresaw its many possible applications and exploited its economic potential on an industrial scale. Once the process had been set in motion, he laid down the foundations of a huge commercial and technological empire, which allowed him to exploit and control his own patents all over the world.

NEW MULTINATIONAL BUSINESS STRATEGY

Hennebique's ascent was a swift one: in 1894, with his patents in place, he moved his base from Brussels to Paris. By 1900 he was dealing with a volume of work in France that equalled that of all of his competitors combined. By 1905, while the earliest regulations regarding the use of the new material were being put in place around the world, his network included several hundred construction businesses. The cohesion and efficiency of this production network was backed up by a solid multinational organization that guaranteed all projects – which were overseen by the central office in Paris – and gave advice and technical assistance. This powerful and fast-reacting company soon cornered almost 20 per cent of the world market in reinforced concrete design and construction. The system of commercial exploitation that Hennebique pioneered therefore reflects the unusual bonds and relationships on which the invention itself was based. In a sense, he created a closer connection between the world of metal construction, with which he was very familiar, and the world of masonry. The simplicity and efficiency of his system of combining concrete and metal, the ease with which the predetermined elements required for the building could be calculated and sized – in fact, everything that Hennebique could use to promote his process – functioned in a similar way to the catalogue-based systems of distribution that metalworkers had used for decades to sell their products. The basic prototypes, pre-sized elements, formulae, tables and graphs distributed by Hennebique acted as a sort of substitute for these catalogues. The frontiers of traditional building were being demolished.

But the efficiency of the organization that he set up to distribute his system and conquer the market was nonetheless dependent on a subtly detailed geography whose rather dense fabric was made up of the very landscape of construction that Hennebique was competing against. It was built around branches and agencies, systems of allegiance, networks of influence or convenience, which Hennebique utilized tirelessly to build up his own business. The close relationships that he soon developed with cement producers and ironworks are good examples of this kind of connection: his early clients were often his early suppliers, who brought him into contact with his first licensees (or became licensees themselves). In fact, this convergence of interests informed the system of interactions that he so efficiently exploited. The same kind of networking could be seen at work in his communication strategy, in which images in both hand-drawn and photographic form played a key role. These images were circulated just as concrete was gaining ground, showing off the projects that the earliest contractors had already commissioned.

These early projects were often very daring (for example, the mills in Don and Brébières, in northern France, in 1893, or the flour mill in Nantes in 1894) and became solid anchoring points for the burgeoning business. Around these points, Hennebique spun and manipulated the strands of his web. Beyond the technical experimentation (and risk-taking) that surrounded his process, he saw his early projects as clear demonstrations of the possibilities of combining systematized technology with economic organization, forming a meeting place where innovation could thrive. The Hennebique system proved itself, and concrete grew in status.

BELOW *Lille International Exhibition, 1902: this display of cement bags demonstrates both the impressive load-bearing capacity of a Hennebique floor and the convergence of interests between cement companies and the architect's own firm.* OPPOSITE *The Grands Moulins flour mill in Nantes, 1895. The construction of this 'strong monolithic block' was one of the first major commissions for Hennebique's growing business.*

INNOVATION AND STANDARDIZATION

Another important factor that allowed Hennebique's company to expand to an extent almost unprecedented in the field of building was the unusual system of in-house training for the engineers who made up the firm, who thus acquired the specialist knowledge needed to work with reinforced concrete at the same time as the material itself was being invented. The majority were recruited straight from the École Centrale de Paris (paradoxically, an institution strongly marked by the metal-based approach taught there). The engineers would start out in Paris, at the central office on the Rue Danton, and would then be sent out to regional and overseas branches, as Hennebique's plan of attack demanded. Their mission was to ensure the flow of technical resources between the central office and the branches. In this way, the reputation of reinforced concrete began to grow.

GRANDS MOULINS DE NANTES
ARCHITECTES: MM. Lenoir et Elève à Nantes.
M. Raoulx au Mans.
ENTREPRENEURS Conc.ᵗˢ: MM. E. 4 P. Sée Ing.ʳˢ à Lille.

Fragment de la coupe montrant la salle des machines et les Silos.

The autonomy, cohesion and efficiency of this network of technical assistance were plain to see: in 1905, there were sixty engineers working in the central office in Paris. That number doubled in five years, while in the rest of the world there were just over five hundred. A formidable team of experts soon grew up and out from the central hub of the research office. At the same time, Hennebique fuelled competition between engineers who were well-versed in the theory and practice of reinforced concrete. Much in demand before the First World War, these engineers basically moved from one firm to another and encouraged a cultural cross-fertilization that led to a rapid rise in the popularity of the building material.

The invention of reinforced concrete therefore occurred within a context of developing technical knowledge, which helped shape the way in which the material

The Agence Hennebique in Cairo, c. 1899. The goal of the international offices was to ensure a smooth flow of technical information between the firm's headquarters and outer branches.

itself was formualted. Its invention is therefore inseparable from the process of standardization that accompanied the earliest developments in reinforced concrete. This was primarily a matter of social recognition. At first, builders who were developing techniques for building with reinforced concrete, like Hennebique, operated within a redefined area of industry: they had to break free, knock down barriers, create unusual connections and enable new and productive combinations. By shaping the contours of this new technical field, Hennebique stood out from his competitors: he made the relationship between process, material and product central to his strategy, which involved giving reinforced concrete an image, a public face. From that moment on, in around 1905, as architects and engineers came together to work on projects, reinforced concrete became a shared cultural object – a kind of operator that connects many different social agents.

It is difficult to explain the process by which hybridization occurs: with no beginning or end, no point of origin or attachment (or so many that they cannot be counted), it simply happens. It is the mark left by the interplay of forces that shape history when someone like Hennebique takes control. Perhaps it might be said that this great builder laid the foundations on which the future landscape of materials could be built?

ANTONI GAUDÍ

Architect–craftsman with a unique creative style

1852–1926

GAUDÍ IS WIDELY RECOGNIZED FOR HIS DISTINCTIVE and unusual creations, in which he employed traditional procedures and designed structural forms using his own methods. Indeed, one of the reasons Gaudí's work is considered so important is that his complex forms are far removed from what is standard. While 20th-century architecture moved towards flatness and linearity, Gaudí incorporated more complex geometry. Instead of Gothic vaults and arcades, in his later projects he used catenary arcs, hyperbolic paraboloids and hyperboloids of revolution, which continued to provide him with regulated surfaces that could be incorporated relatively easily with the aid of such simple tools as a measuring stick and line.

This spirit of resistance to cost-effective forms mass-produced by the construction industry set Gaudí apart from the general trend, turning him into an example of perseverance and such uniqueness that, from his earliest years, he simultaneously provoked both enthusiasm and rejection. Gaudí's work is far from neutral, so it is easy to see why it has attracted constant controversy and interpretation. Given his solitary nature and his conception of the architect–craftsman, and because few of his writings and drawings have survived that might have shed light on his own opinions and uncompleted projects, only recently has such interpretation become more definitive. This is based on the examination of his work from many different angles – biographical, symbolic, constructive and formal – all of which provide us with a more complete appreciation and a better appraisal of his work in relation to his time.

He also left two of his masterpieces unfinished. The first is the chapel for the Colonia Güell, a settlement for company workers near Barcelona, of which only the crypt was almost complete in 1915, although photographic documentation of the project's funicular models (including hand-drafted retouching) has survived. The second is the Sagrada Familia ('Holy Family') Temple, its final version represented in plaster models that were destroyed and then reconstructed from their remains and from original photographs. During construction, right up until Gaudí's death and afterwards, the project underwent an evolution in building techniques even greater than that of the medieval cathedrals. Thus, in addition to the polemical interpretation of Gaudí's legacy, controversy exists also over the continuation of his work.

EARLY ECLECTICISM

Antoni Gaudí was born in 1852 in Riudoms, near Reus, where he went to a grammar school before going on to study at Barcelona School of Architecture, graduating in 1878. In his first decade as a professional, works such as Casa Vicens (1883–85) and the entrance and stables of the Güell estate (1887) in Barcelona, and El Capricho (1883–85) in Comillas near Santander, are all notable for their decorative eclecticism of Moorish origin including neo-Mozarabic walls (with colourful ceramic tiles), as well as for Gaudí's skill in creating different forms in elements such as towers, windows and doors, which demonstrate his great mastery and imagination in designing wrought iron and other details. In 1883, at the age of thirty-one, he was also given the task of building the Sagrada Familia, which he would continue to work on for the rest of his life: by the time of his death in 1926 Gaudí had created four different designs for the temple.

From 1886 to 1891 Gaudí designed and built the home of his great patron, the industrialist Eusebio Güell. In what apparently began as a plan to enlarge Güell's house – by creating a room where the owner could enjoy the music of Wagner – this new space became the central hall around which the rest of the living areas were located. Above a semi-basement of stables and a mezzanine for the owner's offices, the central area was situated at an elevated height, topped by a parabolic dome that allowed light to enter through its sides. On the main floor, separated by slender columns and arcades, the galleries that give onto the street and the courtyard cleverly filter the light and the views, creating an attractive transition between the interior and exterior.

Between 1888 and 1894 Gaudí built the Teresian convent in Barcelona. From 1887 until 1893 he designed and built the Episcopal Palace of Astorga, a work that overlapped (between 1891 and 1894) with the construction of an apartment building, Casa de los Botines, also in León. At the beginning of the 20th century Gaudí designed and built Torre Bellesguard (1900–02) and three successive apartment buildings in

Gaudí showing the Sagrada Familia works to a group of visitors, Barcelona, 1915.

Models of the Sagrada Família, photographed in the church's basement sometime after Gaudí's death but before their destruction in 1936.

Barcelona's new development area. These were Casa Calvet (1898–1904), Casa Batlló (1904–6) and Casa Milà (1906–10), which became popularly known as 'La Pedrera' ('The Quarry'). The first of the three is more conventional in its arrangement of court-yards and rooms and its neo-Baroque decor. In contrast, in his project to reform Casa Batlló, Gaudí achieved a surprisingly organic effect through the bow windows on the main floor and the doorways at street level, making them look as if they were fleshy stone forced by thin bony pillars. The succession of spaces for stairways and inner courtyards is also arranged fluidly and vertically. The polychromatic surfaces of the courtyards and the ceramic and painted features on the façades represent a rather mis-chievous alternative when viewed alongside the balconies and decor of the rest of the buildings in the area, which look quite monotonous in comparison. The same could be said about the originality of the attic roof, built on parabolic arches and covered with a ceramic exterior surface, with a tower separating it from the adjoining building.

La Pedrera is also outstanding in its overall originality. Gaudí used a façade of warping stone to create a symphony of waves dotted with openings and balconies. While he uses (with certain limitations) a structure of stone, brick and iron pillars and iron beams that enable him to create an interior free of right angles, the façade's appearance contradicts the idea of a non-bearing wall. With more spatial options

available than in Casa Batlló, in Casa Milà the organization of the circular and oval courtyards (which provide ventilation and light for the interior rooms and space for the lifts) are the key to the overall composition. The attic stands on parabolic arches of ceramic brick, and crowns – at a slanting angle – the building as a whole. The roof terraces and the fanciful forms of the turrets and chimneys represent one of those architectural spectacles where the boundaries between 'construction architecture' and 'sculptural architecture' become blurred.

ANALYSIS OF FORM AND STRUCTURE

Between 1904 and 1914 Gaudí definitively consolidated an idea for a construction in which form and structure would be closely dependent on one another. His experiences with the arches, vaulting and walls at Parc Güell (begun in 1900), created by using forms deriving from graphic static analysis, led him to design a building based on the form of catenary arches. His method involved building a funicular model that, once inverted, would have the desired shape of the building. A series of hanging and tensioned wires, with weights equivalent to the different parts of the building, configured the position of the axes of the linear structural elements, pillars and arches that would be subjected to axial compression. While it is true that at that time the use of the funicular polygon was already well known, it is also true that no one had ever constructed a building as a three-dimensional arrangement of polygons. In addition to lines, chains and bags of pellets to graduate the axial weights, pieces of silk paper were also used to simulate the infill of walls and vaults. Using this upside-down approach, Gaudí prefigured the spaces of the Colonia Güell chapel and its basement or crypt, and subsequently, by drawing on photographs, he obtained views of the building's exterior and interior. These techniques with models were re-examined in the late 1980s by Frei Otto, Rainer Graffe and others, though they have been reappraised more recently for use in digital morphogenetic architecture.

The completed part of the crypt and portico (where the access stairway is located) shows what Gaudí was attempting to do with the main naves. One of his aims, in construction terms, was to move beyond ogival structures in which the horizontal strength of the vaulting was counteracted by exterior buttresses or flying buttresses, which Gaudí disdainfully referred to as 'crutches'. His goal was to eliminate these crutches through the use of funicular arches and leaning columns.

Casa Batlló, Barcelona, 1904–6. In the course of remodelling the existing structure Gaudí added an extra floor, covering the roof with ceramic tiles like scales of a great dragon – a reference to St George, to whom the house is dedicated.

Gaudí's method represents a unique approach in the analysis of building structures. Instead of using other calculating systems that linked buckling with tension, Gaudí sought – more empirically – a structural balance that was compatible with mechanical capacity, first in structures with parabolic arches, and later in three-dimensional funicular polygons, all the way up to the Sagrada Familia. His methods are based on experience, but also on a healthy dose of intuition that enabled him to ascertain the ideal structures, dimensions and geometric shapes. Gaudí conceived his works in solid stone and used traditional building resources and materials. It was only at the end of his life, around 1925, that he considered the use of reinforced concrete. His forms do not separate so clearly the resistant structure from the rest of the building process (as became the dominant trend in the 20th century), and this prevented him from incorporating larger openings and transparencies. However, Gaudí locates

Working model of the Colonia Güell chapel, c. 1908–15. The structure, consisting of wires, weighted bags and silk paper, was hung upside down to simulate the catenary shapes of arcs and vaults.

Perspective view of the Colonia Güell chapel, sketched in pencil onto a photograph of the inverted model.

masses at the points of greatest tension, and sites openings far from the axes – unlike more academic examples of Catalan Modernist architecture, which were less uninhibited and sincere. On the other hand, Gaudí preferred traditional techniques, with which he achieved excellent results.

The experience of designing the chapel for the Colonia Güell helped Gaudí greatly in his transformation of the Sagrada Familia, a building much larger in size. The final version saw the arches replaced by a structure of leaning, tree-like columns that supported the roof vaulting, which was connected by means of paraboloid

The crypt of the Colonia Güell chapel. Rough-cut inclined columns support a web of masonry ribs and vaults.

geometry. Light entered the ceiling by means of a series of hyperboloid holes. In his final years, in addition to redesigning the vaulting, Gaudí threw himself into completing the construction of one of the tower façades so that he could visualize the temple's external appearance. His work was carried out in accordance with the funds contributed by donors, and it was this period that gave rise to the mythical idea of the sculptor–architect who lived in his workshop on the site, recalling the master builders of cathedrals in the Middle Ages.

GAUDÍ'S LEGACY

Positive criticism of Gaudí's work has often emphasized the constructive purity of subordinate spaces, such as basements, attics and auxiliary areas, where one can better appreciate the construction without decoration or added symbols. Nevertheless, attention should also be paid to the spaces with surfaced arches and to the decoration in the main rooms, given that it is in these spaces that Gaudí's achievements – as a builder capable of creating such unusual ambiences – can be fully appreciated. The carved plaster finishes, coffering, tiled surfaces, painting gradients and bright reflections, in addition to all the individual features and furnishings, contribute to the attraction of these spaces, designed to fully satisfy the senses of their users. Structure and building techniques are deployed to create sensations that are still discernible within his structures and in photographs from that time. Gaudí was a great builder not only because of the audacity of his structures, but also because of the originality of their forms – unique, different, highly personal creations that made it difficult for anyone to continue his legacy. While Francesc Berenguer was a loyal collaborator and friend (the Bodegas Güell in Garraf are attributed to both him and Gaudí), Josep Maria Jujol was his 'right-hand man', especially with respect to decoration, and Joan Rubió and Cèsar Martinell continued with his constructive system to a certain extent.

Gaudí's stature as a creative builder is only increased by the way he often employed elements of surprise and playfulness, especially in his freer works. He embodies the paradox that, while rationalists accept the logic of his constructive solutions, he can also be situated among the anti-rationalists. Thus the surrealists appreciate his most fantastical aspects, the symbolists his reflection of ideological and religious signs, and the organicists the way he portrays lessons drawn from nature. With Gaudí, one does not exclude the other, and this is one of the keys to the often passionate interest that his constructions still arouse today.

The Sagrada Familia in 1926, the year of Gaudí's death. Work on the apse wall and façade of the Nativity is largely completed; below is the undulating roof of Gaudí's school, designed as a temporary structure for the education of construction workers' sons, 1909.

LOUIS H. SULLIVAN

Ornamentalist, skyscraper designer and
advocate of an 'American' style

1856–1924

LOUIS SULLIVAN WAS THE PREMIER ARCHITECTURAL ornamentalist in the
United States, the first architect appropriately to express the skyscraper, and
the first to make a concerted effort to create an 'American' style. His training
combined traditional apprenticeship with modern pedagogy. Born of immigrant Irish
and French-Swiss parents in Boston, Massachusetts, Sullivan entered the
Massachusetts Institute of Technology's 'Building and Architecture' programme – the only such course in the US at the time – at the young age
of sixteen, but he was dissatisfied with its curriculum and left after a
year. He worked briefly for Frank Furness in Philadelphia, but there
was a national economic downturn and his family had recently
moved to Chicago, so young Sullivan followed. He secured
employment with William Le Baron Jenney, with whom he
remained until he decided to go to 'the source' (of MIT's curriculum and of Western architectural education) at the École des
Beaux-Arts in Paris, thereafter spending several weeks in Rome
before returning to Chicago. For the next seven years he did free-
lance drafting for an undetermined number of architects, including
Dankmar Adler (1844–1900), who in 1882 elevated him to junior
partner and in 1883 to principal in the renamed Adler & Sullivan. After
the firm was dissolved in 1895, Sullivan worked independently until his
death in 1924.

ORNAMENT AND FAÇADE

Dankmar Adler was a nationally recognized acoustical and structural engineer who
hired Sullivan to compensate for his own limitations as a decorator and designer.
They complemented each other perfectly: after working out building programmes
together, Adler took charge of structural and technical matters while Sullivan dealt

with ornament, interior layout and façade composition – best exemplified, perhaps, by the Auditorium Building in Chicago (1886–90), their largest and most celebrated collaboration. The heaviest and most capacious building in North America, at seventeen floors it was also the tallest in Chicago. A 400-room hotel and 136 offices and shops provided financial underpinning for a 4,200-seat theatre that, with support facilities, constituted a third of the volume of the entire edifice. Adler's theatre acoustics were considered among the finest anywhere, and his ingenious distribution of the tower's weight to prevent uneven foundation settling was deemed a structural masterpiece. Sullivan created an understated but monumental façade befitting the

OPPOSITE *Sullivan in 1885, during his time with Adler & Sullivan.* **BELOW** *The theatre of Adler & Sullivan's Auditorium Building, Chicago, 1886–90.*

auditorium's cultural and economic importance for the city. But it was his ornament, particularly in public areas such as lobbies, stairwells and the main dining room, that especially impressed critics and the public. In the theatre, the most lavishly decorated space of all, chevron mouldings divided acoustical ceiling arches into hexagons enclosing foliated patterns that flowered into electric lights and grilled bosses (resembling beehives) hiding air intakes, examples of how well the partners integrated their separate spheres of expertise.

To label Sullivan's ornament an American version of Art Nouveau, as many have, is to understate its singularity. Based mostly on vegetal forms whose energy suggested the possibility of bursting free of the simple geometries that sometimes accented and contained them, Sullivan's ornament was richer, more sensual and complex, with greater trompe l'oeil effect than its European counterparts – and all the more so when in terracotta, plaster, glass or metallic form it assumed its rightful architectural place. The so-called 'Sullivan School' of ornamentalists who imitated or were influenced by him flourished coast to coast from the 1890s to about 1910, lingering through the dominance of classical and later revivals and the early stages of Modernism until its demise during the Great Depression.

ADDRESSING THE 'SKYSCRAPER PROBLEM'

Ornament also featured prominently in one of his solutions for the 'skyscraper problem', as it was called in the 1890s: how best to express the new office (and occasionally residential) buildings of ten or more storeys that were usually, but not always, supported by steel framing, which all Sullivan's were. From 1890 to 1904 he designed twenty-four (seven of which were constructed), mostly of two types: what he called a 'system of vertical construction', and what some observers label a 'system of skeletal construction'. In the former, exemplified by his first skyscraper, the Wainwright Building (1890) in St Louis, Missouri, Sullivan recessed windows and spandrel-faced beams behind façade columns to create a powerful vertical rhythm from third floor to

ABOVE *The Schlesinger & Mayer (now Carson Pirie Scott) department store, Chicago, 1898–1904. The steel skeleton is presented with a minimum of decoration.* OPPOSITE *Adler & Sullivan's Wainwright Building, St Louis, Missouri, 1890, with its strong vertical accents.*

attic when seen from an acute angle (as urban buildings generally are), thereby implementing the assertion in his most famous essay, 'The Tall Office Building Artistically Considered' of 1896, that since a skyscraper's 'chief characteristic' is loftiness, it 'must be tall, every inch of it tall … rising in sheer exultation … from bottom to top … without a single dissenting line.' In this system, attics, inset masonry elements and entries are highly decorated, with bases and columns often left plain. An exception is his most striking skyscraper, the Guaranty Building (1894–96) in Buffalo, New York, where every bit of its façades is ornamented.

But Sullivan also recognized that the steel frame, a three-dimensional grid of directionally neutral interlocking vertical and horizontal members, was every bit as characteristic of skyscrapers as tallness. His 'system of skeletal construction' is most clearly revealed in a proposal for the Chemical National Bank Building (*c.* 1894) in St Louis. Here, beams and columns are flush with each other, hence no spandrels, windows are minimally inset, and there is no façade ornament except at attic and base, thus highlighting structure more than verticality. Its creamy, monochrome walls were unusually taut for the era, anticipating the lightweight, skin-like façades of later years. Only one of his half-dozen skeletal projects was erected: the Schlesinger & Mayer department store (1898–1904) in Chicago, featuring a highly articulated grid. Refusing either to quote from the past or to negate height, Sullivan's solutions proved to be influential. Indeed, his oft-imitated vertical system reappeared in exaggerated form as late as 1965 on Eero Saarinen's Columbia Broadcasting System headquarters in New York City, and the skeletal system, usually glassier with less masonry, remains ubiquitous.

CREATING A NATIONAL 'DEMOCRATIC' STYLE

Early in his career Sullivan decided that skyscrapers had become the prototypical buildings of a rapidly urbanizing and industrializing United States, epitomizing the creativity, boldness and effective problem-solving – defining features of democracy, he believed – that might serve as a basis upon which to build a long-anticipated national style. In an 1885 speech, 'Characteristics and Tendencies of American Architecture', Sullivan argued that, of all his countrymen, entrepreneurs were best able to 'develop elementary ideas organically ... into subtle, manifold and consistent ramifications', that is, successful business organizations. He therefore urged architects to emulate entrepreneurial daring by referring in commercial design to those aspects of American life he believed would define a national (which is to say, 'democratic') style.

But as time passed and Sullivan's opinion of entrepreneurs and his own colleagues deteriorated, he began publicly to speak out, sometimes intemperately. In the 1896 essay quoted above, he blasted the typical skyscraper as a 'sterile pile, [a] crude, harsh, brutal agglomeration, [a] stark, staring exclamation of eternal strife', the physical outcome of 'lower and fiercer passions', meaning entrepreneurial ruthlessness and greed. Five years later he castigated his profession, particularly the American Institute of Architects, for its timidity, for being 'unoriginal' and designing 'nothing but imitations' while labelling its president, the prominent Bostonian Robert S. Peabody, a 'plain public nuisance' for his 'stupid paltry' annual address. The result of such attacks, of which there were many, was retribution: an abrupt drop in commissions after 1900, and a financial reversal that forced him, out of necessity and against his inclination, to accept small jobs in remote places scattered across the Midwest. The most significant for his thinking, and lasting for his reputation, was a series of nine banks (one remodelled) from 1906 to 1919. The experience of living and working for weeks at a time in hinterland communities changed his views about what democracy meant. While designing big-city, big-budget skyscrapers, Sullivan had taken it to mean uncompromising individualism realized through self-discovery and left to develop independently of others, best exemplified by entrepreneurs although potentially available to everyone. But as he began to design small-budget, small-town banks, he came to envision democracy as a cooperative collectivity in which individualism was enhanced by membership and contribution. 'Individualism without collectivity means sure destruction,' he wrote in 1908 as he completed the bank in Owatonna, Minnesota, 'while collectivism without individuality is an abstraction'.

Sullivan's 1912 essay about his second bank, People's Savings Bank (1909–11) in Cedar Rapids, Iowa, exemplifies his revised thinking. Knowing that 'most of the clients

Banking Room, People's Savings Bank, Cedar Rapids, Iowa, 1909–11. Sullivan sought to reassure customers through a more 'democratic', open arrangement of this principal space.

are of the working class', he focused on the banking room, 'the high point of interest' that 'may be called "democratic" in plan'. He meant, first of all, that the view upon entry was unobstructed: everything was in plain sight, including the vault's massive door, always open during business hours as a reassuring symbol of the availability of valuables and the security of their storage space within the cube-like brick 'strongbox' that was itself the building. Executive areas were not secluded behind closed doors but open to view, and not as luxurious as the banking or waiting rooms for men and women customers. Ornate metal wickets and grilles made dealing with the clerks an aesthetic adventure, while overhead murals depicting agricultural life and the relation of banking to labour paid tribute to the customers themselves. All this, he wrote, 'may be called the modern "human" element of the plan, as it tends to promote a feeling of ease, confidence and friendship between officers, employees and customers' – that is, within the community at large.

The richly decorated entrance of the Merchants' National Bank, Grinnell, Iowa, 1913–14.

But it was not only gorgeously embellished spaces that Sullivan deemed emblems of democracy; it was also how his banks were made. Eight of the nine were clad in 'tapestry brick', a new product made possible by cutting and grinding clay in such a way as to produce a coarse texture that, after firing, 'showed a veritable gamut of colours', he wrote in a 1910 essay while working in Cedar Rapids. These bricks 'are at their best when laid up with a raked-out joint leaving the individual brick to play its part as a unity … and the mass free to express its colour and texture in a broad way'. If 'person' were substituted for 'brick' and 'society' for 'mass', Sullivan's democratic as well as his architectural vision becomes clear: the ensemble is composed of innumerable individuals working together for the good of all but never losing their distinctive identities. 'It used to be said that it took two to make a building,' he continued, 'the owner and the architect.' But in fact it also took 'the intelligent brick manufacturer' and craftspeople 'working in their various ways and contributing technical support … Such is the development of modern society,' he concluded: 'each [contributor] reacting upon each and all.' Experiencing his banks and understanding how they were made, Sullivan thought, might increase awareness of what democratic life ought to be. Decoration was also crucial. Sullivan's banks are known for their ornate façades, especially Merchants' National (1913–14) in Grinnell, Iowa. Its most stunning feature is above the entry, an oculus centred in an over-scaled decorative burst that was meant to be eye-catching – to make people stop, stare, and reflect – because Sullivan intended it to represent democracy in action. Its complex network of squares, diamonds and circles is a more intense version of tapestry bricks in ensemble: that is, a celebration of community wherein each geometry depends upon but bursts the bounds of the next, proclaiming its independence while simultaneously working in concert with others to achieve architectural harmony and, metaphorically, the collective cooperation that Sullivan understood – perhaps hoped is more accurate – democracy should be.

Sullivan's banks were praised by critics and the public, remain cherished in their communities, and are now understood to be among his finest buildings. But they did not revive his career while he lived. During the thirteen years from 1909 until his last built work in 1922 – a music store façade – he received only nineteen commissions, twelve of which were erected, including eight of the banks. Whether this was because his highly ornamented style had gone out of fashion or because his 'anti-establishment' views frightened away potential clients, the fact is that his income declined to virtually nothing. By the late 1910s he was relying on handouts from friends and colleagues, including Frank Lloyd Wright, his devoted employee from 1888 to 1893. *The Autobiography of an Idea* and *A System of Architectural Ornament According with a Philosophy of Man's Powers* (both 1924) were among his final published works. On 13 April 1924, the day before he died, Sullivan gave Wright a sheaf of drawings, some of which Wright later published in *Genius and the Mobocracy* (1949), a tribute to his 'beloved master', which he closed thus: 'whenever the practice of architecture today rises to the dignity of an ideal … the origin of that practice … stems from one [man], Louis H. Sullivan.' An overstatement, perhaps, but it is a sentiment Sullivan himself would surely have appreciated.

ROBERT MCCARTER

FRANK LLOYD WRIGHT

Architect of the space within

1867–1959

F RANK LLOYD WRIGHT WAS AMERICA'S MOST SIGNIFICANT ARCHITECT, and his work served as the primary inspiration for the emergence of modern architecture around the world. Over his seventy-two-year career Wright designed more than six hundred built and six hundred unbuilt projects of unparalleled diversity. Yet he always described his life's work as being one singular effort, emphasizing its underlying fundamental principles. His first principle was the primacy of the interior space of inhabitation, which he called 'the space within', in determining the spatial composition. The second principle was that space is given its essential character through the way it is constructed, by working with what Wright called 'the nature of materials'. The third principle was that architecture makes a place *in* nature, when interior and exterior space are woven together to make an integral whole, and Wright believed the design of a building should start with the ground from which it is to grow.

Wright was raised in Madison, Wisconsin, and his upbringing emphasized the study of natural forms, the Unitarian faith and American Transcendental philosophy, in particular the writings of Ralph Waldo Emerson. His education as an architect took place from 1888 to 1893 in Chicago, when he apprenticed in the office of Louis Sullivan. Rejecting Beaux-Arts classicism, Sullivan believed that an appropriate American architecture would only develop on a regional basis, with variations dependent on local climate, landscape, building methods and materials, and Wright was to realize this prophecy.

THE SPACE WITHIN

Wright's first achievement in establishing a truly American architecture came with his perfection of a particularly American building type – the single-family suburban house. By 1910, when his designs were first extensively published in Europe by Wasmuth, Wright had completed almost 150 built works, the vast majority of them houses. The Prairie House, as it later came to be called, was first defined in his two prototype designs of 1901, which were published in the popular women's magazine

Living room of the Frederick Robie House, Chicago, 1908. Wright designed everything visible in this period photograph, including the furnishings, lighting and stained-glass windows.

Ladies' Home Journal. Of the Prairie houses, the Frederick Robie House in Chicago, Illinois (1908), was Wright's greatest urban residential design, engaging its compressed site to create a dynamic sequence of interlocking spaces culminating in the famous living room and dining room, joined by their common ceiling that passes through the open centre of the fireplace. The Darwin Martin House in Buffalo, New York (1904), five structures comprising a series of interpenetrating cruciform spaces woven into the landscape, was Wright's greatest suburban residential design. Its plan was a masterpiece of formal composition, and the inhabitation of its exquisitely articulated interior spaces was a profoundly meaningful experience.

In Wright's Prairie House, the solid fireplace mass anchored the centre while the space opened out in all directions at eye level, the out-riding walls and overhanging eaves acting to layer the house into the earth, giving the suburban site a geometric order so that the house and the landscape were inextricably bound to one another. These houses combined the formal order of symmetrical planning with the dynamism of interpenetrating spaces to produce the open, multifunctioning interiors, integrated with surrounding nature, that have since become the most popular characteristic of modern domestic architecture. The Prairie houses crystallized a modern interpretation of the dwelling place, allowing the inhabitant simultaneously to experience comfort and inspiration, shelter and outlook, freedom and order.

In addition to the reinvention of the American house, Wright's Prairie period (1900–20) also saw him evolve new forms for public architecture. At the turn of the century an appropriate form for American public architecture had yet to emerge; the steel-framed skyscraper perfected by Sullivan had proved incapable of attaining the monumental character necessary to house the public realm. Wright realized his vision of an appropriate monumentality for public buildings with his design and construction of the Larkin Building in Buffalo, New York (1904; destr. 1950), housing the offices of a manufacturing firm, and Unity Temple in Oak Park, Illinois (1908), a Unitarian sanctuary. The plans of these two buildings are simple rectangles, with mezzanines surrounding and overlooking a central multi-storey space, lit by high clerestory windows and continuous skylights, and allowing no views out at eye level. On the exterior these buildings are closed and solid, with a severity of form unlike anything else of their time, seeming to relate more to the stark rectilinearity of ancient monuments.

Exterior of the Larkin Building, Buffalo, 1904. Describing it as a 'simple cliff of brick', Wright placed services and stairs in the corner towers, and the main workroom at the centre.

For Wright, the public building invariably took the form of an introverted compound, seen from the outside as a grouping of powerful independent masses bound together by mutual purpose. Entry occurred between these masses, leading to a low, dark, horizontal, rotating movement sequence, which compressed and then released the occupant into the tall, light, hidden, vertical central space. The singularity of the central space, ordered through Wright's 'perfect' geometries of the square and cube, and the way it fuses form, structure, material and light, is profoundly monumental. Wright intended that his public buildings be experienced as sacred spaces, whatever their function, their introspective interiors flooded from above with transcendent light to create a morally edifying effect for their inhabitants.

After a personal and professional crisis in 1909, Wright constructed his home and studio, called Taliesin (1911), outside Spring Green, Wisconsin. Like a number of his larger houses of the period, Taliesin is organized around an exterior garden courtyard, framing but not entirely enclosing the brow of the hill upon which it is built. During the next ten years Wright designed a series of public courtyard buildings, the plans of which, in contrast to his asymmetrical courtyard houses, were rigorously symmetrical, illustrating Wright's use of symmetry to distinguish between the public and private realms. The Midway Gardens in Chicago (1913; destr. 1929), an indoor and outdoor garden for music and dining, is perhaps Wright's most completely resolved total work of art, for here he designed not only the architecture but also the bandshell, interiors, furniture, dishes, sculpture, decorations and landscaping. The Imperial Hotel in Tokyo, Japan (1914–22; destr. 1968) was a monumental and yet subtly scaled building designed to float on a field of structural piers sunk into the unstable soil – an innovative seismic precaution almost immediately tested when the building survived the devastating 1923 Tokyo earthquake.

IN THE NATURE OF MATERIALS

Wright engaged new materials with almost every design, yet reinforced concrete proved to be the most consistently challenging for him. Despite his early success in the all-concrete Unity Temple, Wright remained critical of concrete's inherent lack of order, its ability to be formed into any shape the designer desired – unlike all other construction materials, concrete did not exhibit a 'nature' that would determine its appropriate use. In 1906, while Unity Temple was in construction, Wright developed the concrete block system that he would realize only seventeen years later in his Concrete Block houses, such as the Samuel Freeman House in Los Angeles (1923), built with reinforced-concrete blocks cast in custom-designed forms. In the Concrete Block houses, Wright

found a means of expression suitable to reinforced concrete, the modular order of the concrete blocks giving character to this previously formless material.

DWELLING IN NATURE

In 1932 Wright published *An Autobiography*, which brought new clients, and opened the Taliesin Fellowship, an apprenticeship school and office housed in the new drafting room, which provided both an architectural and farming workforce. The Edgar Kaufmann House in Mill Run, Pennsylvania (1938), called Fallingwater, together with his own winter home and studio, Taliesin West in Scottsdale, Arizona (1940), exemplified Wright's belief that architecture is born of its place and can thus never be the product of an 'International Style', as modern architecture was first called in 1932. Fallingwater, built above a mountain stream, is Wright's greatest 'natural' house, a place where people can truly be at home in nature. Taliesin West, built in the desert north-east of Phoenix, celebrated both the ephemerality of life, with its canvas roofs that were replaced seasonally, and the permanence of place, with its concrete walls into which were cast massive stones, marked by the carvings of the original Native American inhabitants of this landscape.

The Johnson Wax Building in Racine, Wisconsin (1939), is Wright's great 'cathedral of work'. Its innovative thin-shell concrete columns stand in small brass shoes that delicately touch the floor of the central workroom, clad in streamlined brick and top-lit by glass tubing laid up like masonry in clerestories and skylights. Like the drafting room at

OPPOSITE *Fallingwater, Mill Run, Pennsylvania, 1938. Anchored to the rock by solid masonry walls, the reinforced-concrete floors and ceilings cantilever out over the waterfall.*
BELOW *The 'great workroom' of the Johnson Wax Building, Racine, Wisconsin, 1939.*

Taliesin, employees work in a room that feels as if it were in the forest, among the column-trees, in the light filtering down through the skylight-leaves. Though dedicated to work and not worship, the central room of the Johnson Wax Building illustrates the way Wright celebrated everyday rituals and functions by housing them in sacred spaces.

Broadacre City (1934) was Wright's visionary proposal that sought to establish an ordered pattern of cultivation and inhabitation for the unprecedented scale of the Jeffersonian grid, while providing each household a place in nature. The plan wove public, commercial and religious structures into an underlying fabric of single-family houses, so as to give the suburb an appropriate and precise spatial and social order. The Herbert Jacobs House in Madison, Wisconsin (1937), was the first of Wright's so-called 'Usonian' houses, small, affordable and energy-efficient homes for the rapidly growing American middle class. Wright designed hundreds of Usonian houses for the widest variety of climates and construction types, and each house is a masterpiece of spatial generosity within a remarkably small total floor area, allowing the daily lives of each family to be suffused with sunlight and nurtured by nature.

The last ten years of Wright's life were incredibly productive, with hundreds of designs emerging from Taliesin. Among the best works of this period was the Solomon R. Guggenheim Museum (1943–59), built facing Central Park in New York City. A glorious expression of the plastic formal possibilities of reinforced concrete, the museum also provides a remarkably dynamic spatial experience, suspending the art and its spectators in a continuously spiralling volume that opens towards the sky. The Beth Shalom Synagogue in Elkins Park, Pennsylvania (1954), with its seating within a folded concrete base anchored to the earth, and its roof a translucent tent scaled to the heavens, is a powerful summary of the human condition as both permanent dweller and perpetual wanderer. Perhaps Wright's most brilliant site design, though unfinished at his death, is the Marin County Civic Center in San Rafael, California (1957–59), a series of horizontal planes bridging between the low hills.

It can be argued that Wright's greatest accomplishments were his designs, from throughout his career, for hundreds of modest, inexpensive yet place-engaging and experience-enriching dwellings. In a surprisingly humble definition, he believed architecture to be the background or framework for the daily life that takes place within it, and the intellectual and formal order of his designs was always directed towards the physical comfort and spiritual engagement of the inhabitant. Wright's systematic conception, linking place, material and interior spatial order to human occupation and experience, was unmatched in the 20th century.

Solomon R. Guggenheim Museum, New York City, 1943–59. Artworks are displayed on the outer walls of the upwardly spiralling concrete ramp.

AUGUSTE PERRET

An aesthetic language and doctrine for concrete construction

1874–1954

AUGUSTE PERRET, A PROMINENT FRENCH ARCHITECT AND BUILDER in the first half of the 20th century, was an important advocate for reinforced-concrete construction. He contributed to the architectural discipline a distinct aesthetic language for concrete as well as a comprehensive doctrine for architectural design. Recognized in the first decades of the century as a progressive innovator by a younger generation of architects led by Le Corbusier in particular, Perret was greatly admired as a *constructeur*, whose expertise as a builder, theorist and architect offered a decisive model for a committed and disciplined professional practice. Working with his brothers Gustave and Claude in the family firm – Perret Frères, a construction business inherited from their father – Auguste was an entrepreneur with full control within the office of the conceptual and construction process from the earliest design work to the finished details.

Perret designed churches, theatres, artists' studios, museums, industrial warehouses and large-scale urban development projects, especially in Paris, Amiens, Le Havre and Casablanca. Giving full architectural expression to the reinforced-concrete frame, Perret elevated reinforced concrete in the eyes of the French public, bringing it from a coarse material primarily used in industrial buildings to a highly refined medium for structural design handled with the care of fine wood or stone. In particular, he contributed to future generations' understanding of the technological potential and constructional techniques of this new material. By the middle decades of the century Perret had established a reputation both through his doctrine and practice as a leading advocate for concrete construction. He exercised an influential role in shaping French modern architecture through his participation in debates regarding such issues as volume, structure and material in the journals *L'Architecture d'Aujourd'hui*, *L'Architecture Vivant* and *Techniques et Architecture*.

Auguste Perret (with beard and bow-tie) in the studio at 51–55 Rue Raynouard, Paris, c. 1937. Perret designed the building with an apartment for his own use.

MODERNIZING CLASSICISM

Rooted in a long tradition of French structural rationalist theory (especially Eugène-Emmanuel Viollet-le-Duc, Auguste Choisy and Julien Guadet), Perret balanced his critical position between these 19th-century theorists and the demands of a new architecture appropriate to the 20th century. He thereby aligned himself with a modernizing classicism as a determinative system. His work was rooted in a belief in the continuing potential of classicism to inform a new architectural order, as well as a deep appreciation for historical continuity within the formal French architectural tradition.

Often grouped by historians with Peter Behrens, Frank Lloyd Wright and Otto Wagner, Perret is considered part of this heroic generation of builders. Perret's first reinforced-concrete frame building was an apartment building constructed at 25 bis Rue Franklin in Paris (1904). With a structural system first patented by François Hennebique in 1892, the skeletal frame of this multi-storeyed building was clearly revealed on the façade, emphasized by ceramic tile patterns designed by the ceramicist Alexandre Bigot. In a parking garage on the Rue de Ponthieu (1906), Perret

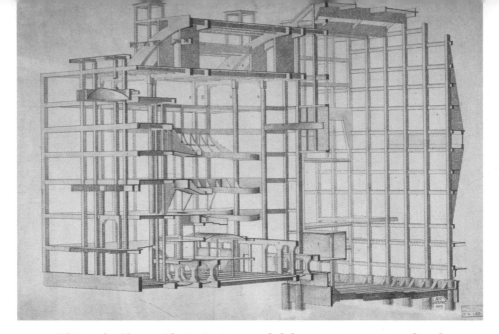

ABOVE *Théâtre des Champs-Elysées, Paris: an exploded axonometric view revealing the structural framework of reinforced concrete, 1911–13.* OPPOSITE *Interior view of Notre Dame du Raincy during construction, 1922–24, showing the vaulted ceiling, supporting columns and perforated wall screens, all made of concrete.*

demonstrated his ability to achieve the maximum monumental value even in a modest structure through the careful use of spatial composition, proportion and the regulating discipline of the structural frame, which is fully expressed here on the front façade. In the Théâtre des Champs-Elysées (1911–13), derived from an earlier design by Henri van de Velde, Perret most fully embraced the ideal of a Modernist classicism. The building's structure itself is a carefully worked-through system, again employing a concrete structural frame, while the façade was decorated with bas-reliefs by the sculptor Antoine Bourdelle and the interior dome with murals by the painter Maurice Denis.

The church of Notre Dame du Raincy (1922–24) manifests the inherent tension in Perret's work between his allegiance to a long architectural lineage, as exhibited by his extension of the Greco-Gothic tradition, and his deployment of certain modern radical gestures such as the full exploration of the potential of reinforced concrete. Built in Raincy, a working-class town north-east of Paris, this church is composed entirely of unclad reinforced concrete, demonstrating the monumental potential of concrete while also expressing its tensile strength in slender columns. Widely publicized at the time of its construction, this building became a major model for the rethinking of traditional church design in the 20th century, influencing especially the Czech architect Antonin Raymond, who worked in the United States and Japan. The curtain walls of the church are composed of prefabricated concrete grilles filled with coloured glass designed by Maurice Denis and executed by the glass artist Marguerite

Musée des Travaux Publics, Paris, 1936–48: construction view of the staircase in the Grand Hall.

Huré. The nave is composed of tapered columns carrying low-arching vaults that achieve an interior of unusual lightness and grace. Through its homogeneity and control of language, the church rapidly established Perret as a leading exponent of this new architectural system.

In another apartment building, at 51–55 Rue Raynouard, Paris (1930–32), Perret exhibited his attachment to the humanistic form of the traditional French window, celebrating the understated urban domesticity of Paris's 16th arrondissement in his own penthouse apartment. Like that at 25 bis Rue Franklin, the Rue Raynouard apartment building was also a speculative project on a particularly difficult site, in this case triangular and steeply sloping. Here, according to his principles of economy, Perret made full advantage of all the deviations permitted by the building laws.

Perret's Musée des Travaux Publics (1936–48), built at Place d'Iéna on a large triangular site near the Palais de Chaillot, demonstrates most vividly his interest in a new French architectural order appropriate to the material of concrete. Here his craft precision in handling concrete is fully evident in the elegant detailing, the colouring of the different stone aggregates in the concrete and the textures achieved by bush-hammering. The Mobilier National (1946) was built in the form of a *hôtel particulier* as a warehouse and restoration studio for furniture owned by the French state.

Perret's later works were an extension of his early urban exploration. For example, he was responsible for the postwar reconstruction of Le Havre (1949–56), working with a team of devoted followers to carry out his doctrine on a large scale. Perret himself was responsible for the town square and the centrally planned church of St-Joseph (1952), which serves as a beacon on the Normandy coastline. The urban plan is based on a strict elementarist model, and within this standardized structural system the city could be expanded as necessary.

CULTURAL CONTRIBUTION

Like his colleague, the poet and social critic Paul Valéry, Perret understood the creative process to be a function of a particular kind of distilled intellectual insight. For him, the compositional methods underlying his designs were not unlike writing poetry, in that they entailed a disciplined process of repetition and syntactical refinement, controlled by the constraints of cultural habit and context. Many of these cultural and social intentions, as well as the design methods underlying them, are synthesized in Perret's laconic aphorisms. He published a collection of these maxims in 1952 as *Contribution à une théorie de l'architecture*.

Perret's cultural contribution parallels trends in Parisian literary and intellectual circles prior to the Second World War, which sought to achieve a modern reinterpretation of the French classicist tradition. For example, in Valéry's Socratic dialogue on architecture, *Eupalinos, or the Architect* (1921), there is an allegiance to a classicist ideal that seeks a means of articulating an encounter between the more stable aspirations of French culture and the transitory processes of change and modern innovation. Perret, considered to be the model for Eupalinos, has had his work described as complex, even enigmatic, seeking a balance between the principles of constructional economy and a Modernist pursuit of the technical and aesthetic potential of new materials. He is therefore an architect and builder whose clarity of form may be said to hide the complexity and subtlety of his intent.

LUDWIG MIES VAN DER ROHE

The last great inventor of form

1886–1969

A FTER LE CORBUSIER DIED IN 1965, Reyner Banham wrote an obituary in *The Architectural Review* entitled 'The Last Formgiver', but, despite Mies van der Rohe's disavowal ('Form is not the object of our work'), the last great form-inventor actually died in 1969. Mies was born in Aachen, the son of a master stonemason. He never went to an architectural school, was apprenticed to Peter Behrens and then after the First World War established a small personal practice in Berlin. He emigrated from his native Germany to the United States in 1938, both for work and to build up the new architectural school at the Illinois Institute of Technology. He abandoned his earlier experiments in concrete frame to adopt the steel and glass buildings by which he is best known. While still in Europe he had experimented with projects for tall buildings, flexibility in housing (the Wiessenhof, Stuttgart, 1927), and the open plan for domestic homes (Tugendhat House, Brno, 1928–30). The results of these experiments were filed away and later reused in the US – as he noted in a letter to Erich Mendelsohn. So when the chance came to construct tall buildings in Chicago, Mies already had some clear ideas: the buildings were not invented from scratch.

INVENTION AND INNOVATION

The first steel-framed apartment buildings in the world, 860–880 Lake Shore Drive Apartments (1948–51), twenty-six storeys high, were also notable for their invention in terms of structures and services. Mies's engineer Frank Kornacker designed the steel structures with little knowledge of how much they would sway. Ove Arup told a story of a party on the topmost floor during tempestuous winds, when the water sloshed out of the bathroom sink. Such dangerous engineering would not now be allowed, of course. Likewise, the air-handling systems extracting from bathrooms and kitchens proved noisy and unbalanced when the inadequate lifts activated. Mies had wanted air conditioning, which the developer Herbert Greenwald could not afford. Simply supporting environmental standards was also experimental in this novel development, but would be made to work in the apartment buildings Mies built later for Greenwald. Most questioned were the stanchions attached to the mullions that clearly supported no structure. In an interview published in *Architectural Forum* in November 1952, Mies explained: 'First I am going to tell you the real reason for those mullions, and then I am going to tell you a good reason by itself. It was very important to preserve and extend the rhythm which the mullions set up on the rest of the building. We looked at it on the model without the steel section [I-beams] attached to the corner columns and it did not look right. That is the real reason. Now the other reason is that the steel section was needed to stiffen the plate which covers the corner column so this plate would not ripple, and also we needed it for the strength when the sections were hoisted into place. No, of course, that's a very good reason – but the other one is the real reason.'

860–880 Lake Shore Drive Apartments, Chicago, under construction. The building was completed in 1951.

At the same time that Mies was designing the Lake Shore Drive Apartments he worked on the Farnsworth House in Plano, Illinois (1945–50), a single-storey clear-span weekend retreat lifted above the then known floodplain of the Fox River. This pavilion, totally glazed, with an asymmetrically placed central core of bathrooms and a linear kitchen, has become the standard by which all minimal housing is judged. Immediately after, Mies received the commission for the Seagram Building (1954–58), a glazed and bronze-framed building that stepped back from Park Avenue to provide the first new public open space New York had seen in years. Mies's final major project marked a return to Berlin, a single-storey clear-span exhibition space for the Neue Nationalgalerie (1962–68). The forms that Mies employed – the tower, the big hall and the pavilion – make it easy to attack him as a formalist. On the contrary, he could be remarkably pragmatic in adapting to the availability of building materials, the shapes of the sites and the demands of clients, all of which in others might have led to compromise, the enemy of formalism. The little he wrote, virtually cursory remarks,

Plan of the Farnsworth House, Plano, Illinois, 1951 – a country retreat harmoniously integrated with its surroundings, and now one of the best-known houses of the 20th century.

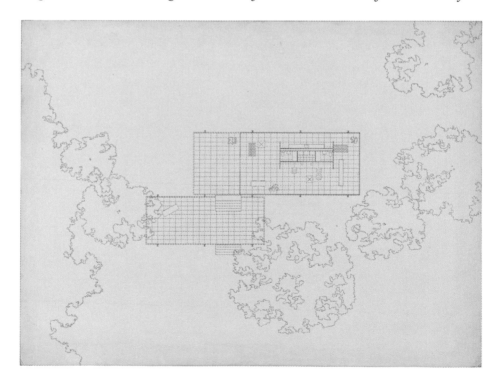

Neue Nationalgalerie, Berlin, 1962–68. Mies's clear-span glass pavilion, positioned on the museum's roof space, is sheltered by a square steel roof borne on eight exterior columns.

gives few clues, but anecdotes suggest a gentle, non-authoritarian figure, one prepared to explore all possibilities and then to think about them over protracted periods. So in the end only the fact of the building itself can confirm the difference between the good reason and the real reason.

VISION OF THE FUTURE

Mies's output barely sustained his reputation to his death in 1969, and soon he was branded as the enemy of pluralism, the father of all those 'glass and steel' buildings that defined the emerging late 20th-century urban landscape and whose critics blame him for the anonymity of cities. Two exhibitions opened in New York in 2001, 'Mies in Berlin' and 'Mies in America'; these, together with the counter-argument mounted some years before by Manfredo Tafuri, suggest that Mies's work is actually the architecture of silence and order. It slides the Modernist armoury of expression – function, materials and structure – under an orderly surface that absorbs the uses to which such buildings might be put as a contrast to the *anomie* of urban life, the chaos of Berlin as Mies had experienced it in the 1920s and 1930s. The work is as close to value-free as it is possible to come. This is precisely why Mies is one of the greatest builders in the history of architecture, and not just the 20th century: rather like those who explored and experimented within the archaeological revival of antiquity in the 15th and 16th centuries, reinventing what we now call classical architecture, Mies slowly and gradually developed a vocabulary of orderly architecture and thereby laid the ground for the works of the European architects broadly categorized as rationalists. This private but determined architect still offers a vision of the future, almost timeless and hieratic, that reaches beyond the times in which his types were constructed.

LE CORBUSIER

In concrete or stone, wood or metal?

1887–1965

THERE IS A PHOTOGRAPH OF THE YOUNG Charles-Édouard Jeanneret and two of his friends in smocks working a sgraffito pattern of pine cones into the façade of his first work of architecture, the Villa Fallet (1907–8). This is almost the last time that Le Corbusier, as he renamed himself in the 1920s, was caught contributing directly to the building process. He did not very often visit building sites and was frequently disappointed at the quality of workmanship in his buildings. And yet Le Corbusier can be thought of as a great builder of the 20th century. Over seventy buildings were constructed to his designs, and he wrote more than fifty books, several of them translated into many languages, all of which provided architects with new ways of thinking about building. Part of his impact came from reinforcing the message of international Modernism: the separation of structure from enclosure, the use of roof terraces and large expanses of plate glass and the opening up of space in the interior. But part of it came from a counter-current against Modernism that Le Corbusier initiated as early as 1929, when he rediscovered the use of natural materials such as stone, wood and tiles, and a reinforced concrete rendered more tactile by leaving the impression of the wooden shuttering on the surface. His architecture became increasingly sculptural and colourful, especially after the Second World War. In all his work, however, Le Corbusier evolved his forms, inside and out, in a kind of dialogue with the structural process.

PRINCIPLES OF MODERNISM

The diagram the young Jeanneret drew in 1915, in an abortive attempt to patent a radically new approach to construction – the so-called Dom-Ino house – was a complete expression of the fundamental principle of Modernism. Separating the structure from enclosure meant that any part of the walls could be made of glass, and the

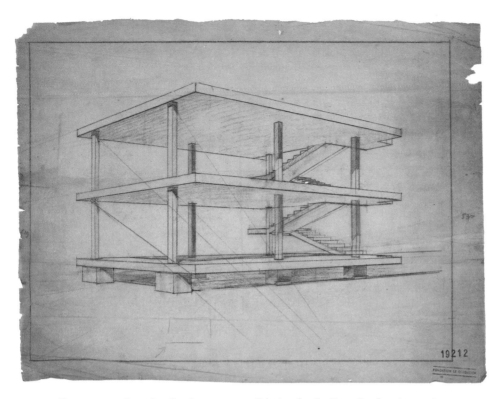

ABOVE *Preparatory drawing for the patent application for the Dom-Ino housing project, 1915.*
OPPOSITE *Octave Matthey, Charles-Édouard Jeanneret (Le Corbusier) and Louis Houriet at work on the gable of the Villa Fallet, 1907.*

internal walls could take any form on each floor. So radical was this idea that even Jeanneret failed to grasp its full significance for a while, designing houses with the Dom-Ino system in which none of the concrete struts were exposed and in which conventional windows were used. The exposed concrete posts – dubbed 'pilotis' by Le Corbusier in the 1920s – became a hallmark of his work and that of most International Modern architects.

This fundamental principle took as its starting point 'structural rationalism', the idea that the form of a building should be determined by its structure. It was famously summed up in Le Corbusier's 'Five Points of a New Architecture' (1926): 'pilotis' (thin reinforced-concrete columns), raising the building off the ground; the free plan, benefiting from the pilotis that take the strain of the building and allow each floor to be arranged differently; the free façade, because the structure also allowed the façade to be composed freely; the *fenêtre en longueur* – windows that stretch the width of a building, supported from the floor slabs; and the roof garden, exploiting the flat roof to recover the area taken up by the building.

Le Corbusier demonstrated his five points in his lectures by drawing a diagram. The traditional type of house, made of load-bearing walls, required that each floor plan

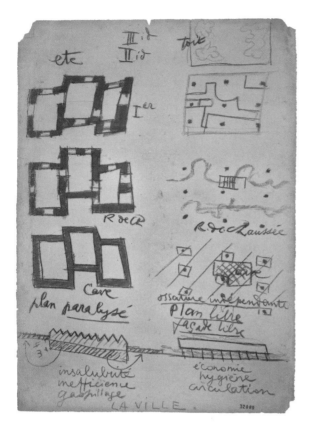

Drawing made during a lecture entitled 'The Plan of the Modern House', given in Buenos Aires, October 1929.

follow the one below. Furthermore, every opening in an external wall weakened the structure. In contrast, the reinforced-concrete building allowed light and air to flow through underneath, contributing, he claimed, to economy, hygiene and open circulation. Although these five points were based on a logic derived from structure, they quickly became a set of stylistic tropes, which Le Corbusier and his many imitators used again and again in the 1920s and 1930s. Unlike his former master Auguste Perret, who was a convinced believer in structural rationalism, Le Corbusier had no real interest in expressing the structure on the exterior of his buildings. The miracle wrought by reinforced-concrete construction allowed Le Corbusier to do certain things, but his measure of value was formal and aesthetic, rather than the moral judgment of the structural rationalist, who asks whether a building 'honestly' expresses its structure.

It was part of the tradition of Western architecture that structural systems should be made visible in a satisfying form, even if it meant twisting structural logic to do so. Thus the Greek system of trabeated construction (columns supporting entablatures) developed during the Roman Empire (and later in the Renaissance) into a visual language of pilasters and attached half-columns in which the original structural logic no longer applied. A similar formalism creeps into modern architecture in the application of the five points. Le Corbusier's Villa Savoye at Poissy, near Versailles (1929–31), is a clear example where the form dominates over any real logic of construction: the south-east entrance façade looks as if it supports the wall above, whereas in fact the floor above is cantilevered out from the line of pilotis.

Le Corbusier later went on to apply the same principle to the separation of the other functions of enclosure: providing protection from the sun, ventilation, privacy

ABOVE *Southeast façade of Le Corbusier and Pierre Jeanneret's Villa Savoye, Poissy (near Versailles), 1928–31.* BELOW *Kindergarten on the roof of the Unité d'Habitation, Marseilles, 1945–52, showing the use of concrete* brises-soleil.

or opening windows onto a fine view. Protection from the sun could be achieved with thin vertical concrete baffles, organized in subtly proportioned cadences, which he called *ondulatoires*. Alternatively, for the façades of buildings he developed the more massive *brise-soleil*, a frame of concrete baffles angled to prevent the strongest sun from penetrating the interior while allowing the morning and evening light to flood in. On 5 September 1951 he patented a system, which he dubbed the 'fourth wall', for dividing up a façade into panels of glass, plywood or aluminium and ventilating strips, incorporating cupboards and other fitments on the inside, all based on his proportional system known as the Modulor.

REINFORCED CONCRETE

The material most commonly associated with Le Corbusier is reinforced concrete, and he tried in vain to find ways of exploiting its full industrialized potential. In the housing estate at Pessac near Bordeaux (1925–26), he persuaded his patron to purchase very expensive Ingersoll-Rand equipment capable of spraying concrete onto a mesh of steel wires for reinforcement. This 'gunnite' material proved impossible to control and was quickly abandoned for the handmade methods used in all his 1920s Purist villas: breeze-block walls finished by hand in cement render. Only in this way could the perfect precision of the Machine Age be represented with the techniques of the time. Curiously, 'gunnite' later reappeared in the chapel of Notre Dame du Haut, Ronchamp (1950–55), where it was used to create the moulded, curving forms of the walls.

Reinforced concrete began as a symbol of progress in the machine era – a stimulus to revolutionary change – and developed into a proof of enduring humanity in the face of modernization. Concrete passed from the machine to the hand, from pure form to the tactile, from the perfect to the flawed, from geometric to biomorphic form. These changes can be identified in two ways: as a kind of alchemical transformation over time, passing through other materials (wood, stone, brick), and as a deep, conceptual ambiguity from the outset within the practice and theory of concrete.

Le Corbusier quickly lost interest in the idea that structural stresses had to appear to be reduced to a minimum, supported by improbably thin steel or concrete frames. For the dormitory building he and his cousin Pierre Jeanneret constructed for the Swiss students at the Cité Universitaire, Paris (1930–31), he abandoned a project based on thin steel struts and created massive concrete piers modelled, as he said, on a dog bone he had picked up and kept. He wanted to express the drama of the structure in a sculptural form. On these organically profiled piers, for the first time, the delicate surface left by the unplaned wooden shuttering used to mould them can be seen. Also visible in this building is the use of ragstone walls – *pierre meulière* – which were used everywhere in Paris for construction when out of sight of the public. In the penthouse apartment he designed for himself in the Rue Nungesser et Coli (1931–34), the *pierre meulière* of the party wall was left exposed, complete with the red brick chimney flue, which created a fine decorative effect. This use of the humble *pierre meulière* allowed Le Corbusier to exploit the colour and texture of stone without joining the camp of the academic architects, who employed dressed and carved stone in their classical façades.

Another of the five points to go was the flat roof. Ever since visiting Barcelona in 1928, he had been fascinated with the Catalan vaults made of thin tiles cemented edge

Notre Dame du Haut, Ronchamp, 1950–55.

House for André and Suzanne Jaoul, Neuilly, Paris, 1951–55: the living room.

to edge. In his penthouse studio he used concrete vaults imitating factory buildings, and in the little weekend house at La Celle St Cloud in 1935 he again employed concrete vaults, covering them with earth and grass. In the wonderful Sarabhai House (1951) in Ahmedabad, in India, he again used concrete vaults covered with vegetation. In Paris, however, he returned to the source of his interest in vaults and built two houses in Neuilly for André Jaoul and his son (1951–55), using genuine Catalan brick vaults tensioned with steel cables. The warmth of colour of the Catalan brick tiles and the enclosing form of the vaults create a much greater sense of intimacy than in Le Corbusier's houses of the 1920s. The two parallel vaults, one larger than the other, are used as a discipline to organize the plan into different functions. The rough concrete of the over-sized beams contrasts with the red vaults and white walls. The addition of a double-height space for the salon, flooded with light, adds to the surprise.

THE PLEASURE OF NEW MATERIALS

From 1929 Le Corbusier had begun to rediscover the pleasure of using new materials, richer textures and more complex forms, abandoning the 'Five Points of a New Architecture' that he had coined only three years previously. The summer house he and Pierre Jeanneret designed in 1935 for the Commander of the Salvation Army in France, Albin Peyron, at Les Mathes, north of Bordeaux, is a poem in modest arrangement of space for a simple, open-air existence in the summer months. The bedrooms are located on the far (east) side, while the master bedroom and shared living room, on the first floor, has a window onto the view to the sea, as does the dining room below. In fine weather the family would have lived outdoors on the covered balcony and terrace. The woodwork on this house benefited from the detailing of the Japanese architect Junzo Sakakura, then working as an assistant in Le Corbusier's practice.

Le Corbusier and Pierre Jeanneret, House for Albin Peyron, Les Mathes, near Royan, 1935.

Le Corbusier's final tribute to wood was the cabin he designed in 1949 for himself and his wife, for their vacations on the rocks at Roquebrune-Cap-Martin. Working with his favourite carpenter, the Corsican Charles Barberis, Le Corbusier designed an extremely compact plan, based on the Modulor dimension of 3.66 metres (12 feet). Everything had its place, and the surfaces were articulated with plywood panels and coloured insulating board. Although all the details have a handmade feel to them, the whole cabin was made in Corsica and brought to Roquebrune by rail, the train stopping just above the house for the panels to be unloaded. It was here, and in a tiny builder's hut nearby, that Le Corbusier worked on many of his projects during the last fifteen years of his life, and where he died swimming from the beach in 1965.

Le Corbusier's cabin at Roquebrune-Cap-Martin, 1949, designed for his personal use.

KONSTANTIN MELNIKOV

Leap into the unknown

1890–1974

KONSTANTIN MELNIKOV WAS BORN IN MOSCOW. From 1905 to 1910 he took a general course at the Moscow School of Painting, Sculpture and Architecture, after which he studied painting until 1914, when he transferred directly to year four of the architecture course. He graduated as an architect in 1917, a momentous year in the history of Russia. In 1920 he was appointed professor at Vkhutemas (the Higher Art and Technical Studios), founded that same year from a merger of his old school and the Stroganov School of Applied Art. Over the next four years Melnikov took part in several architectural competitions for projects in Moscow: model workers' houses (1922–23), the Palace of Labour (1923), the Arkos joint-stock company building and the Moscow bureau of *Leningrad Pravda* newspaper (1924). His first design to be built was the Makhorka tobacco pavilion, for an agricultural exhibition in 1923. This wooden structure attracted the attention of both the press and fellow architects with the freshness of its composition.

'BRILLIANT DECADE'

He further developed the wooden theme in his designs for the New Sukharev market in Moscow (1924–26; destr.) and the Soviet Pavilion for the 1925 Paris Exhibition. Melnikov's Paris pavilion, a clear milestone in his work, brought him international recognition and success. Le Corbusier declared it to be 'the only pavilion at the exhibition worth seeing'. Recognition brought a commission to design a 1,000-space taxi garage in Paris, for which he produced two different designs. Although it was never built, working on the designs aroused Melnikov's interest in the garages that were starting to be built in Moscow. He set about studying the functional details and came up with a drive-in drive-out parking system that avoided the use of reverse gear. Melnikov designed and built two garages in Moscow: Bakhmetevskaya Street bus garage and Novo-Ryazanskaya Street truck garage (1926–29).

Melnikov in his home on Krivoarbatsky Lane, Moscow, completed 1927.

The year 1927 was one of Melnikov's most productive. He designed a series of workers' clubs, six of which were built over the next few years: the Frunze club (1927–29), Rusakov club (1927–29), Kauchuk rubber factory club (1927–29), Svoboda factory club (1927–29) and Burevestnik factory club (1929–31), all in Moscow, and the porcelain factory club at Dulyovo (1927–28). The most famous of these is the

Melnikov's Soviet Pavilion for the Exposition Internationale des Arts Décoratifs et Industriels Modernes, Paris, 1925.

Rusakov club, with a system that allows the three seating areas to be transformed into one large auditorium if required. Another, which was never built, was a design for the Zuev club (1927–29). It consisted of five intersecting cylinders and was the precursor for the design of his own house (1927) on Krivoarbatsky Lane in Moscow. The idea of a 'five-cylinder unit', wrote Melnikov later, 'came back to me in the marvellous duet of our house' (the house has two intersecting cylindrical towers).

In 1929 Melnikov took part in an international competition to design a lighthouse in Santo Domingo as a monument to Christopher Columbus. As well as the traditional techniques of monumental art, he incorporated kinetic elements, designed to be turned by the wind. The early 1930s were fateful years for Melnikov and the Russian avant-garde as a whole, as the Soviet authorities began an attack that led to all-out totalitarianism within the arts. His 'brilliant decade', as the architect referred to the years from 1923 to 1933, was at an end. The commissions dried up, and, after being subjected to scathing criticism by the first All-Union Congress of Soviet Architects in 1937 Melnikov lost his post as head of the seventh Mossoviet architectural studio, where he had worked since 1933. He also lost the right to teach at the Moscow Institute of Architecture.

The world-famous architect, one of only twelve international stars represented at the 1933 Milan Triennale, now sank into oblivion. Melnikov's life changed dramatically, as he sought and undertook commissions for portraits and official history

Rusakov workers' club, Moscow, 1927–29 – one of a series Melnikov produced in and around the capital. The three protruding seating areas could be converted into a single auditorium.

paintings, making good use of his painting diploma. His most important architectural works during these years were competition designs for the People's Commissariat for Heavy Industry on Red Square in Moscow (1934) and the USSR pavilion for the 1937 Paris Exhibition. The former produced two outstanding designs, by Melnikov and Ivan Leonidov – both recognized masters of 20th-century architecture who opened up new horizons for its growth and development. In the postwar years Melnikov submitted several competition designs in an attempt to get back into architecture. One of these, his design for the USSR pavilion at the 1964 New York World's Fair, proved that his ideas were as fresh as ever. His final work was a competition design for the children's cinema on Moscow's Arbat Street in 1967. In the last years of his life Melnikov worked on the manuscript of the autobiographical *Architecture of My Life*, which was published posthumously.

INVENTOR AND DISCOVERER

It is hard to fit Melnikov's work into the usual categories of 20th-century architecture, as it is not limited by the narrow bounds of a single style or trend. Nor is it easy to find the terminology for his formal language. Nonetheless, most critics agree that the architect possessed a unique and creative sense of invention that matched his powerful temperament and the sharp paradoxicality of his spatial, structural and artistic thinking. Melnikov was indeed a unique inventor, a discoverer of previously unknown forms and therefore comparable only with Pablo Picasso, who viewed the artist's studio as a laboratory for the invention of new forms. Melnikov valued the 'powerful spirit of the artist' above all else, and his inventiveness extended across the full range of architectural matters, from technical functionality and construction to aesthetic form and artistic composition. He could probably have patented many of his technical inventions, such as his system of latticed or honeycomb brickwork for the walls of his own house, his drive-in drive-out system for bus garages and car parks, his 'flexible room' system for altering the size and function of club rooms, his dynamic architecture of rotating floors for the *Leningrad Pravda* building or the blade-like wings of the Columbus monument design. Yet how could Melnikov's artistic and formal discoveries be patented, the poetic component of his architecture defined, its individual signature uniqueness recorded?

Most writers who have studied Melnikov's work describe the distinguishing features of his architecture as 'fresh', 'dynamic' and 'expressive'. These are qualities evident in almost all Melnikov's designs and structures: a novel, contrasting clash of spatial forms: multi-angled movement, vectors and forces. His work is full of inner tension, with shifts in form, deliberate breaks in symmetry and use of his beloved diagonals. The overall impression of interacting, geometrically varied forms is impermanent, mobile, close to a state of dynamic equilibrium. So how can this highly complex image be summarized? The answer may well lie in the words inscribed on the façade of the architect's own house: 'Konstantin Melnikov, architect'. They are both testimony to and symbolic of his matchless individuality. Throughout his life, Melnikov was a determined individualist who refused to subscribe to any one architectural movement. His architectural roots are to be found in the experiments of his predecessors, both at home and abroad. Yet he rejected the idea of imitation and vigorously defended the autonomy of his designs and ideas. Melnikov was endowed by nature with a unique inventiveness and bold imagination; with his architecture, as he himself put it, he pushed the bounds of the possible. He turned any architectural brief into a dynamic clash of forces, frozen for an instant before a wild leap into the unknown.

PIER LUIGI NERVI

Transfigurations of an engineer

1891–1979

WHENEVER HE SPOKE ABOUT HIS VOCATION, Pier Luigi Nervi remained faithful to a notion of building as an activity focused on achieving a given object with the highest possible performance – that is to say, obtaining maximum results using minimum means, according to a principle to be applied inexorably during each phase of the building process, from conception to realization. Though Nervi explicitly allowed also for aesthetic performance, and never saw this as a secondary value, his legacy lies in everything that exuberantly exceeded his rule of absolute technical and economic rigour: an inheritance of forms, that aspect of the builder's work that remains at the conclusion of a skilful design, and after the dismantling of a construction site organized with supreme rationality. This inheritance of forms, widely applauded by architectural critics and historians, and also admired by popular taste, accorded this Italian engineer legendary status while still in his prime.

Nervi was born in Sondrio, a small town in northern Italy, and in 1913 he graduated from the school of engineering of the University of Bologna. His autonomous professional activity began in 1923 in Rome, where he founded the first of two jointly owned construction companies. Until the 1950s, Nervi's activity as a designer was strictly related to his work as a building contractor, and only rarely did he separate the two. By contrast, the final phase of Nervi's career, in the wake of growing international fame and status, was marked by numerous commissions solely as a structural designer or consultant, of notable professional importance and from around the globe.

THE TECHNICIAN–ARTIST

From the start Nervi concentrated on the design and construction of structures in reinforced concrete. His work suddenly acquired fame in the early 1930s, thanks to the admiration expressed by national and international critics of architecture for the new Municipal Stadium in Florence, designed and constructed by Nervi from 1930 to 1932. Architectural sensitivity towards engineering was undergoing a profound cultural shift, eroding the wall that artists, during the 19th century, had established

One of Nervi's aircraft hangars built at Orvieto, Orbetello and Torre del Lago Puccini in 1939–42. Photography documented the structure's pure forms before cladding was applied.

between themselves and the expressions of the industrial age. As the Modernist avant-garde wound down and some of its fundamental principles began to take root, works of engineering became the object of effective critical interventions from the world of architecture. Nervi was fully involved in this cultural phenomenon. After the success of the Florence stadium, new constructions confirmed and consolidated his presence on the architectural stage. For his part, Nervi designed and wrote pursuing a twofold participation in the fields of technique and formal creation. In international terms, Nervi was thus the first engineer to acquire an identity as a technician–artist, an engineer–architect, simultaneously with the development of his work.

After the Florence stadium, with its famous elements (the roof canopy over the main stands, the Maratona tower and, above all, the three helicoidal staircases to the open-air seating), Nervi's profile began to define itself with two groups of military aircraft hangars in central Italy, the first in Orvieto (1935–38), and the second in Orvieto, Orbetello and Torre del Lago Puccini, from 1939 to 1942 (all destr. 1944). The success of these hangars – once again professional, critical and in the media – presaged the height of Nervi's maturity during the postwar period, when he confirmed his role as a highly original master of roof structures. Moreover, he took a decisive step between the first and second group of hangars. Although both were based on a geodesic structure of criss-crossing arches that meet at right angles, the first were monolithic constructions in site-cast reinforced concrete, while in the others the majority of the arches were obtained by assembling prefabricated truss elements. The construction principle that would guide Nervi's future work had thus been defined: structural prefabrication became his instrument for pursuing maximum economy.

THE LEGENDARY BUILDER

In reality, as Nervi himself pointed out, prefabrication offered numerous and diverse advantages, overcoming both the economic obstacles and formal restrictions of wooden formwork. In fact, it was possible to mass-produce building elements and significantly reduce construction times (often a determinant factor), as well as obtain 'great richness of form, delicate refinement of surfaces, and close rhythms, by the repetition of equal elements'. Nervi's postwar career, in which he became a legendary hero of construction, confirmed this dual reality: the majority of his works that are recognized as masterpieces were the result of building processes and construction sites that were organized with extraordinary efficiency (in other words, masterpieces in their own right).

Prefabrication was based on the use of a variation of reinforced concrete, developed and patented by Nervi himself during the Second World War, which he named 'ferro-cemento' (ferroconcrete). This material is obtained from the dense overlapping of layers of steel mesh made from small-diameter wire, incorporating this lightweight armature within a concrete-rich mortar. The resulting material is highly elastic and resistant to cracking. Ferroconcrete, used in different ways, would be a determining factor in Nervi's later career. In general, his research was concentrated on the structural design of the intrados of roof structures, for the most part typologically traditional: slabs, simple vaults and domes. To these typologies, as well as other less common ones, Nervi applied three categories of preferred formal solutions. In the case of floor slabs, the surfaces are traversed by an articulated pattern of ribs based on the isostatic curves of primary moments. Site-cast concrete could trace such complex curves only using ferroconcrete formwork (in turn modelled using plaster casts, and reused as modules in the different identical sections of the slabs). An early example is the underground warehouse for the Gatti Wool Mill in Rome (1951). Vaults and domes were instead based primarily either on a pattern of structural intersections in the form of lozenges or on corrugated surfaces whose capacity for resistance was enhanced by a densely undulating profile. In both cases, the roofs were made from precast ferroconcrete elements, jointed together after installation using reinforced-concrete ribs incorporated in particular sections of the prefabricated elements. Nervi's two halls of the Turin Exhibition (1947–48 and 1949–50) and the two sporting halls for the 1960 Rome Olympics are famous examples.

Equally famous, from the moment of their completion, are other roof structures and constructions that, for various reasons, constitute exceptions to the homogeneous groups described above. These include the UNESCO headquarters in Paris (1952–58; designed with Marcel Breuer and Bernard Zehrfuss), the structure for the Pirelli Tower in Milan (1955–60; architectural design by Gio Ponti), the Flaminio Stadium and the Corso Francia Viaduct for the Rome Olympics, the Palazzo del Lavoro in Turin (one of the buildings constructed for 'Italia 61', the centenary celebration of Italian unity) and the Burgo Paper Mill in Mantua (1961–63).

A symbolic apex marked the formidable rise of Nervi's career. In 1964 he was selected by Pope Paul VI to design the fan-shaped Papal Audience Hall in Vatican City. Nervi was asked to work in a context extraordinarily dense with historic and artistic value: the construction site was located in close proximity to St Peter's Basilica, in an area with a glimpse of Bernini's colonnade and in the shadow of Michelangelo's

Underground warehouse for the Gatti Wool Mill, Rome, 1951.

The dome of the Palazzetto dello Sport, Rome, under construction, 1956–57. As they enter the roof, the buttresses are transformed into slender ribs that divide the prefabricated elements.

cupola. As the pope stated during his inaugural address on 30 June 1971, Nervi was the 'architect' encouraged to dare in the face of these presences, possessing the 'genius and virtue' to do so. These words, and this commission, reflect a powerful yet accessible master. The pragmatic genius, the inventor of building systems and the hero of immense construction sites was also the creator of forms that were almost always easy to comprehend, and sometimes conventionally fascinating. All these factors, while determining Nervi's grandeur, were also the essence of a concept of building that would end with the death of its creator.

NEW VISIONS

B y 1970 the great masters of the Modern Movement were dead – including Mies van der Rohe and Le Corbusier (both born in the 1880s) and Frank Lloyd Wright (who was born in 1867 and lived to the age of ninety-one) – and much of the agenda of Modernism in architecture and town planning was being openly questioned, at least in Western countries. But American confidence and energy gave modern architecture a new sense of purpose. The work of Eero Saarinen, the great Finnish–American architect, and Oscar Niemeyer in Brazil pointed the way to a new freedom and expressiveness. Saarinen died in 1961, shortly after his fifty-first birthday, just as Niemeyer's exploration of the aesthetic possibilities of concrete were being unveiled to spectacular effect in the new capital of Brasília (1956–64); the Brazilian (born in 1907) remained active into the 21st century. Louis Kahn, arguably the greatest American architect of the 20th century after Wright, died in 1974, having created buildings of unique tectonic power. His definition of 'served and servant spaces' influenced Norman Foster's 'High Tech' generation of architects and reflected the increasingly significant issue of how mechanical services should be handled in large buildings. In Japan, utopian visions of the city held sway for a time: one proponent was Kenzo Tange, who forged a new Japanese Modernism from a marriage of Le Corbusier and indigenous tradition.

The second half of the 20th century saw architecture reinvigorated by a renewed dialogue with the engineers, who were increasingly liberated from their roles as mere facilitators. Indeed, it would be hard to apply that description to someone like Ove Arup, raised in Germany by Scandinavian parents and educated in Denmark, who founded a multidisciplinary global design empire based in London. Arup's role in realizing the extraordinary designs for the Sydney Opera House (1956–73) by the unknown Danish architect Jørn Utzon was as fundamental as it was controversial. The blurring of old boundaries between architecture and engineering was everywhere apparent, as reflected in the careers of several figures who are not easily categorized. One of these was Jean Prouvé, an engineer by training who pioneered new techniques of prefabricated building and explored new ways of using materials, notably in his extraordinarily innovative glazed façades. Content to be known as a 'constructor', he lectured at the Conservatoire National des Arts et Métiers in Paris through the 1960s and was an inspiration to the new generation of architects working in the High Tech mould, among them the Anglo-Italian Richard Rogers (born in Florence in 1933) and Renzo Piano (born in Genoa in 1937), winners of the competition for the Pompidou Centre in Paris (1971–77), for which Prouvé chaired the jury. Another influence on High Tech, and particularly on Norman Foster, was Richard Buckminster Fuller, best known for his geodesic domes but more significantly a prophet of sustainable design and a visionary environmentalist. Foster himself was to build on an unprecedented scale, establishing a global practice in the aftermath of his Hongkong & Shanghai Bank project (1981–85) in Hong Kong. He produced one of the most renowned structures of the recent past in the Millau Viaduct (2004) in southern France, designed in collaboration with the French engineer Michel Virlogeux.

The torch of expressionism, borne by Saarinen and Niemeyer, was taken up by Frank Gehry, whose highly sculptural buildings, including (in the late 1990s) the Bilbao Guggenheim and the Walt Disney Concert Hall in Los Angeles, depended on a sophisticated engineering input, itself made possible by a device unknown to previous generations: the computer. Though sometimes associated with deconstructivist theories of design, Gehry's work was at heart an imaginative exploration of the possibilities of concrete and steel. The architecture of Gehry, and also of younger architects such as the American Daniel Libeskind (born in Poland in 1946) and the Iraqi Zaha Hadid (born in Baghdad in 1950), depended on the skills of engineers. Another member of this younger generation whose sculptural approach to design has dismayed narrow rationalists is the Spanish architect–engineer Santiago Calatrava, whose reputation was forged with the design of memorable bridges, but whose imprint was later to be seen on opera houses, railway stations and museums across the world. Spanning the professions to an equal extent, the German architect–engineer Frei Otto has been linked in particular with the development of lightweight tensile and membrane structures, used to spectacular effect in the stadium for the 1972 Munich Olympics. But Otto has been just as happy to work with more basic materials, including timber and even cardboard. The environmental crisis of the late 20th century posed new challenges for everyone in the world of construction. Traditional ways of building have been re-examined, and adaptability, economy and flexibility have gained new significance: Kengo Kuma, for example, has reinterpreted Japanese building traditions for a new era in which the use of natural materials is much more than a mere fashion. The continuing challenge of sustainable design is one that the builders of the 21st century must address urgently.

R. BUCKMINSTER FULLER

Design for the future

1895–1983

R. BUCKMINSTER FULLER DESCRIBED HIMSELF as a comprehensive anticipatory designer: a person who uses contemporary technology to design in anticipation of future needs. Just how successful he was at designing for the future is debatable, but his ability to use engineering principles and technology as design tools is not. He was a successful inventor and received numerous patents for items as diverse as a prefabricated bathroom, a new type of map, rowing needles and the octet truss. He was also a businessman, writer, visionary, mathematician, professor and architect. Fuller disliked being considered an architect. He dismissed architects as exterior decorators tied to tradition and stylistic criteria, although he was pleased to accept the American Institute of Architecture's gold medal in 1970. The gold medal is a lifetime achievement award given to those who make significant contributions to architecture, and Fuller received it both for his architectural work, in particular for the development of the geodesic dome, and for his humanitarian work, especially his desire to make people successful in the universe. His other achievements included multiple designs for mass-produced houses, a three-wheeled car and the World Game, which tracks the earth's resources and reflects Fuller's concern for the future.

Fuller did not start out with such lofty goals. He performed well enough at Milton Academy, a private preparatory school in Massachusetts, to gain entry into Harvard University but then squandered the opportunity. Harvard expelled him for the first time in 1913, for skipping exams. He was sent to work in a textile mill in Canada, which proved to be more inspiration than punishment. While there, he began to take his facility with machines and inventiveness seriously. This was not the lesson he was supposed to learn: his family hoped that gritty factory work would encourage him to succeed at Harvard. It did not, and after his second expulsion in 1914 a family friend helped him secure a job as a cashier at Armour & Company, a meat processor. He left

Fuller at Black Mountain College, North Carolina, where he taught in 1948 and 1949.

Armour to join the US Naval Reserves in 1917, eventually enrolling in a special offi-cers' training programme. This was the only formal training Fuller received after leaving high school. Most of his later education and training was like that at the textile mill: on-the-job and intuitive adaptation of existing forms and systems. After the First World War he drifted for a while: he went back to Armour, worked for a short time selling trucks and then returned to the Naval Reserves. Aside from his reservist duties, he was unemployed in 1922 when his father-in-law, the architect James Monroe Hewlett, asked Fuller to start a new company, the Stockade Building System, with him. Thus Hewlett not only provided Fuller with a job, but, by introducing him to industrial processes, helped to lay the foundation for his life's work.

THE DYMAXION PROJECTS

Mass production became one of the driving forces behind Fuller's housing designs. He believed it was the most efficient way to combine industrial processes and engi-neering principles to do 'more with less', achieving the most while using the least amount of resources. Hewlett introduced this concept to his son-in-law during the founding of Stockade, which was a building-material and construction company based on a lightweight, economical, sturdy, mass-produced fibrous concrete block Hewlett had invented during the First World War. These same attributes figure in varying degrees in Fuller's designs for mass-produced houses from his first independ-ent project, the Dymaxion House (1927–29), through the Dymaxion Deployment Unit (1940) and the Dymaxion Dwelling Machine (Wichita House, 1945–46), to the geodesic dome (1945–49).

The Stockade company mass-produced blocks from which to build a house. Fuller began to work on the idea of mass-producing an entire house, the project that became the Dymaxion House, even before he was forced out of Stockade in 1927. Dymaxion, coined as an amalgam of dynamism, maximum and ions, was developed to give a sense of the underlying philosophy of the house, and the word became synonymous with Fuller. The Dymaxion House differed from other models of mass-produced houses on the market because it was to be fully equipped, much like a contemporary mobile home or modular house. More conventional models included those by Howard Fisher who, like Fuller, wanted to manufacture houses in the same manner as automobiles, and those sold by Sears Roebuck & Company, who basically provided internal framing and a shell. The Dymaxion House never went into produc-tion, nor did it turn its inventor into an entrepreneur, but it did launch Fuller's career. He used the media attention it generated to attract support for his later projects.

At the start of the 1930s his sphere of influence was limited primarily to Chicago and Manhattan, but by the end of the decade he had gained prominence on the national stage, and by the 1950s he was a figure of international importance.

The road to international fame was bumpy and plagued by false starts and problems. Fuller designed a one-piece metal bathroom (1937) that was produced in an edition of twelve. His three-wheeled car, the Dymaxion Transportation Unit, was a very promising project until an unfortunate accident near the entrance to the 1933 Chicago World's Fair and the bad press that followed prevented the car from going into production. He purchased the magazine *T-Square*, renaming it *Shelter*, and used it to promote the role that he felt standardization and mass production should play in architecture, mainly through a series of articles called 'Universal Architecture'. *Shelter* was short-lived, but Fuller continued to argue for the application of industrial processes to architecture and railed against the aesthetics of International Style in his lectures. For example, he called the Dymaxion House a 'machine for living', while Le Corbusier called his Villa Savoye (1929–31) 'a machine for living in' (*machine à*

Fuller's design for the experimental Dymaxion House, 1927–29 – a mass-produced single-storey hexagonal unit suspended by cables from a central mast.

habiter). Both were looking for an expression of the Machine Age, but Fuller wanted to put machines at the service of people, whereas Le Corbusier wanted to use machines to achieve an artistic ideal. In an ironic twist, the designs of Fuller's houses parallel developments by International Style architects: the Dymaxion House draws upon Le Corbusier's 'Five Points of a New Architecture' (1926), while a geodesic dome such as the Woods Hole restaurant (1954) is like a hemispherical version of the orthogonal metal and glass structures of 1950s Modernism, exemplified by Mies van der Rohe's Farnsworth House (1945–50).

However, Fuller's Dymaxion Deployment Unit, or Grain Bin House, the first house he successfully patented and mass-produced, did not follow this pattern. It was based on round corrugated metal grain bins made by the Butler Manufacturing Company, perhaps a wry comment on the American grain bins that had so inspired Walter Gropius in the early part of the 20th century. They were small, single-family houses, basically grain bins modified to serve as houses or, more appropriately, as shelter. After the United States entered the Second World War in 1941 they were used as housing for the military, but their production was limited because of wartime restrictions on the use of steel.

Another of Fuller's housing designs that was produced in limited numbers was the Dymaxion Dwelling Machine. He began work on it towards the end of the war and hoped it would provide a way to keep factories running after hostilities ceased and to give jobs to returning servicemen. Fuller retooled a Beech Aircraft Corporation factory in Wichita, Kansas, to mass-produce houses instead of airplanes. This house, popularly known as the Wichita House, was an updated version of the first Dymaxion House. Like the original, it was made of metal with a strip window and non-load-bearing walls and was supported by a central mast. But it was round instead of hexagonal, did not have a roof deck and was only slightly elevated off the ground, rather than raised a full storey to provide parking space below the house. Only two models were manufactured: these were purchased by the Air Force, which then sold them back to Fuller's company. William Graham bought the prototypes, joined them together and essentially grounded the houses by setting them on a foundation. Today, the restored Wichita House is at the Henry Ford Museum in Dearborn, Michigan. There is debate about why the house did not go into production. One explanation is that Fuller was too afraid of failing again to go forward with full-scale production, and another is that there were problems with funding. Although the Wichita House saw only limited production, like the first Dymaxion House, it helped Fuller to move on with his other more successful projects, such as the geodesic dome.

THE GEODESIC DOME

One of the most important architectural innovations of the 20th century, the geodesic dome is a covered, self-supporting hemisphere consisting of tetrahedronal mass-produced components. Since it is without interior supports, the geodesic dome provides the greatest possible amount of interior space in proportion to the area of the exterior. It is basically a structure without limiting dimensions. It was based on Fuller's observation of a directionally orientated (vectorial) system of forces, providing maximum strength with minimal structure, within the nested tetrahedron lattices of some organic compounds. He was also influenced by the work of Walther Bauersfeld in Germany, whose Zeiss I Planetarium (1923) in Jena predated Fuller's conception of the geodesic dome by more than twenty-five years; Fuller received a patent on his design in 1954.

Union Tank Car Company Dome, Baton Rouge, Louisiana, 1958 (destr. 2007). This opaque one-storey unit enclosed an area of some 10,770 square metres (115,900 square feet).

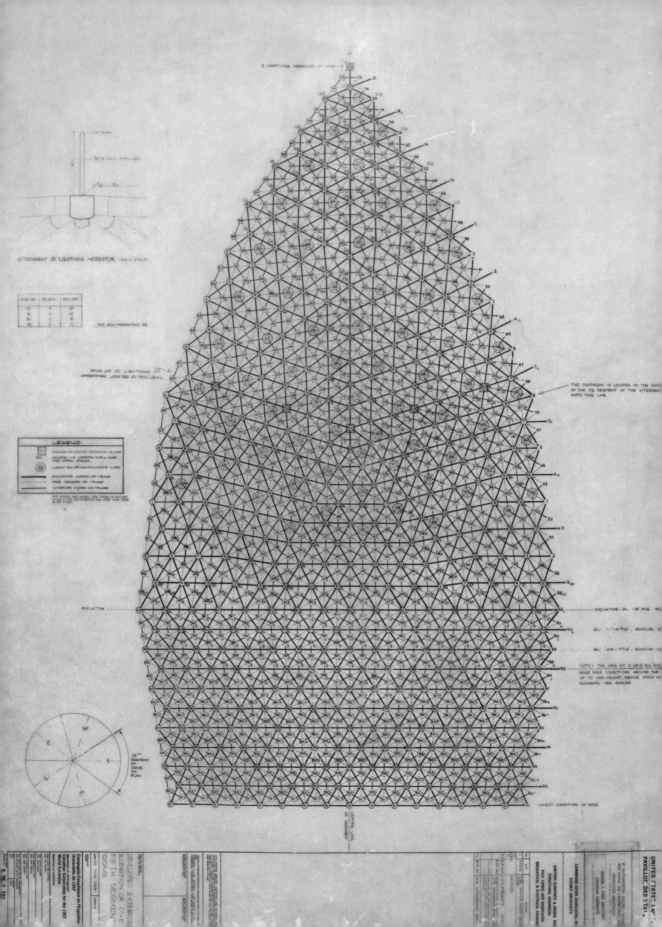

The geodesic dome covering the United States Pavilion at Expo '67, Montreal.
Drawing of a dome segment for the United States Pavilion. The finished structure comprised a space frame of steel pipes holding nearly 2,000 moulded acrylic panels.

Fuller began work on the geodesic dome while he was teaching at Black Mountain College in North Carolina in the summer of 1948, experimenting with materials – strips of cardboard or plastic or plywood, not usually associated with self-supporting structures – that could be used to construct his domes. The preferred materials were aluminium and plastic, as used in the Woods Hole restaurant dome. Fuller also experimented with structure and designed a collapsible dome with flexible joints, the 1948 Necklace Dome. Geodesic domes could cover great expanses of interior space, as did the demolished Union Tank Car Company Dome in Baton Rouge, Louisiana (1958). This one-storey dome had a diameter of 117 metres (384 feet) and a height of 38.1 metres (125 feet) to enclose an area of 10,770 square metres (115,900 square feet). Its covering was opaque, unlike that of the restored US Pavilion at Expo '67 in Montreal, which exhibited the transparency, openness and expressed structure characteristic of Modernist architecture.

There are variations of the geodesic dome, such as the Fly's Eye Dome (1965) and the plastic and fibreglass Radome (1954), but their structural systems are the same. Fuller also used the engineering principles underlying the geodesic dome to develop other structural systems. Tensegrity structures – skeletal structures whose tension rods are held together solely by members in compression – are related to geodesic domes and also to the work of the American sculptor Kenneth Snelson. Another example is

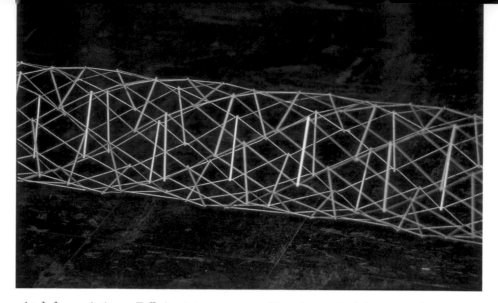

A tubular variation on Fuller's octet truss, patented in 1961 – a simple but extremely strong structural system based on interlocking octahedrons and tetrahedrons

the octet truss: a type of space frame Fuller patented in 1961. Despite its advantages, there is a major drawback to the geodesic dome. The hemispherical shape limits it primarily to industrial uses (Ford Rotunda, Dearborn, Michigan, 1953) and entertainment applications (Botanical Garden Climatron, St Louis, Missouri, 1960), although some, like Fuller, have found it suitable as housing (Fuller House, Carbondale, Illinois, 1960).

PHILOSOPHY AND SOCIAL AGENDA

Designing houses and shelters to be mass-produced was one component of Fuller's complex philosophy. His work shared the Modernist social agenda of making the world a better place through better design. He wanted to place technology at the service of humanity in order to do more with less. He also worked hard to make people realize that the earth is a closed system with limited resources. One aspect of this was not to generate waste when making buildings: Fuller believed industrial processes would make construction more efficient. To help clarify his ideas, Fuller lectured extensively and wrote more than fifteen books. His first, *4D Timelock* (1928), was a business prospectus and architectural treatise setting out many of the ideas that he would continue to develop throughout his life. His later books were more esoteric. For example, *Critical Path* (1981) outlined the various moral, economic and environmental crises facing the world, with suggestions for their solution. He also developed Synergetics (the geometry of thinking), a new type of maths based on the tetrahedron that was intended to help explain how the universe works. Ultimately, Buckminster Fuller wanted to redesign the built environment because he recognized he could not redesign people.

OVE ARUP

The outsider and the art of the impossible

1895–1988

O
VE ARUP BEGAN AND ENDED HIS ADULT LIFE AS A PHILOSOPHER: not an
academic philosopher exploring obscure interests in an opaque jargon, but
a relentlessly questioning, sceptical thinker who ranged across all the
moral, social and political issues of his time. Such philosophical questioning
informed his attitudes towards engineering problems, consultancies, business practices, architecture, design, taste and the environment. For fifty years
Arup typically published, in some form, 50,000 words a year. From
the 1920s onwards he argued that both the fundamental education
and the established practices, of architects and engineers alike, had
to be radically reformed. At the foundation level, engineers had to
be taught draughtsmanship, design and aesthetics; architects had
to be taught engineering, philosophy and self-critical communication skills. And, from the outset of any single commission, they
both had to learn to work together, and with their clients. He was
fiercely critical of architectural verbiage and deplored the self-
deceiving arrogance of architects who hid behind the mask of a
romantic artist. Equally, he deplored the philistine insensitivity and
social irresponsibility of engineers, and the professional narrowness
of their outlook and ambitions. In 1970 he summarized his views:
'The terms Architect, Engineer and Builder are beset with associa-
tions, from a bygone age … and they are inadequate to describe or
discuss the contemporary scene.' While part of his legacy, therefore,
is to be found in the shape of a successful and innovative global firm

of consultant structural engineers – Arup Associates – it can also be identified behind
radical changes that are gradually emerging within educational and professional
organizations.

Arup on the roof of Coventry Cathedral, where he acted as consultant engineer, 1951–62.

Berthold Lubetkin's Penguin Pool under construction at the London Zoological Gardens, 1934, for which Arup was structural consultant. He had met the architect several years earlier.

Arup held that the concepts and categories we devise to structure our thoughts unavoidably reflect our current beliefs, interests and goals, but that these are all, at different rates, becoming outdated, unwieldy or simply obstructive in new contexts. The disciplinary boundaries we erect can help us to focus but never to expand our vision. He was himself opposed to theories and ideologies of any kind – political, religious, artistic or scientific – because they too can be only provisional devices, and eventually inhibit critical thinking. Since we might be mistaken on any given occasion, the only justifiable approach is relentless self-critical enquiry. That is why he proclaimed that the ultimate immoral act is choosing not to think.

EDUCATION AND EARLY WORK

Ove Nyquist Arup was born in Newcastle upon Tyne, in England, to Johannes Arup, the Danish consular veterinarian, and his Norwegian second wife, Mathilde. Later that year the family was posted to Hamburg, where Ove spent his first twelve years, so his first language was German. He studied at Copenhagen University for nine years, initially reading philosophy, then mathematics and finally engineering. In 1922 Arup joined Christiani & Nielsen, a Danish firm specializing in reinforced-concrete design and construction, and was posted to Hamburg, transferring in 1924 as chief engineer to London. There, as a multilingual and highly cultured intellectual, Arup found himself an 'outsider' – a role he cultivated ever afterwards – in engineering circles. He first met and began to work with Berthold Lubetkin in the early 1930s, when he was engaged as consultant engineer on the Gorilla House and Penguin Pool (1934) for London's Zoological Gardens in Regent's Park, the Finsbury Health Centre (1935–38) and the block of apartments in Highgate, north London, known as 'Highpoint One' (1933–35).

From 1934 onwards Arup vigorously promoted the virtues of reinforced concrete, especially for massed housing: great economies of manufacture and construction could result from repeat forms, while also providing new freedoms for architectural design. He worked on designs for working-class flats, industrial silos and water towers, establishing a consultancy partnership with a London cousin. With war in Europe looming, in December 1937 the British government's Air-Raid Precautions Act required local authorities to undertake protection of life and property from aerial attack, and the London Borough of Finsbury commissioned Arup to design community shelters. He proposed double-helix underground shelters with entrance and exit ramps sufficiently shallow and wide that they could become car parks after the war. The principal means of construction was to employ his technique of climbing shuttering in reverse:

Ove's design for double-helix air-raid shelters in Finsbury (1938), which allowed for their later conversion into car parks.

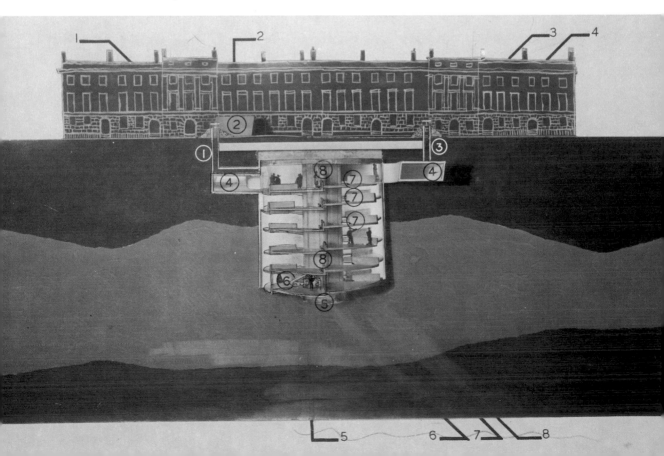

the shelter was a vast concrete drum, built into the ground by progressively deepening the hole and laying the concrete. The government rejected his proposal and none of his advanced public shelter designs was built. However, Arup was appointed to government committees on prefabricated housing and was also secretly commissioned to design and build the underground headquarters of Coastal Command near Harrow, and to design a protective fender for the floating jetties needed for D-Day in 1944. In addition he was involved in the Danish underground, delivering a remarkable address from the BBC's Broadcasting House in London.

INNOVATIVE CONSULTING PARTNERSHIP

In 1946, at the age of fifty-one, he established Ove N. Arup Consulting Engineers, with a staff of five. Their first-year turnover of £3,000 had risen to over £100 million by the time he died in 1988 and, as a global group, to almost £900 million by 2009 – with more than 10,000 full-time staff in ninety-two offices in thirty-seven countries. In the words of Sir Alan Harris, a fellow structural engineer and pioneer of prestressed concrete, in 1960: 'Those engineers who work with good architects in a spirit of harmony and common aims are really a new race, created by, and creating, a new sort of architecture and, thank God, a new sort of architect. The whole situation is almost the invention of one man, yourself.'

The firm's early buildings included large concrete shells such as bus garages, as well as domestic apartments constructed in reinforced concrete, but the project that

BELOW *Sketch of the Sydney Opera House (1956–73) by Jørn Utzon.* OPPOSITE *Precast concrete panels are assembled on the ribs of the Sydney Opera House, c. 1966. Arup's team used early computers to analyse the complex shell structures.*

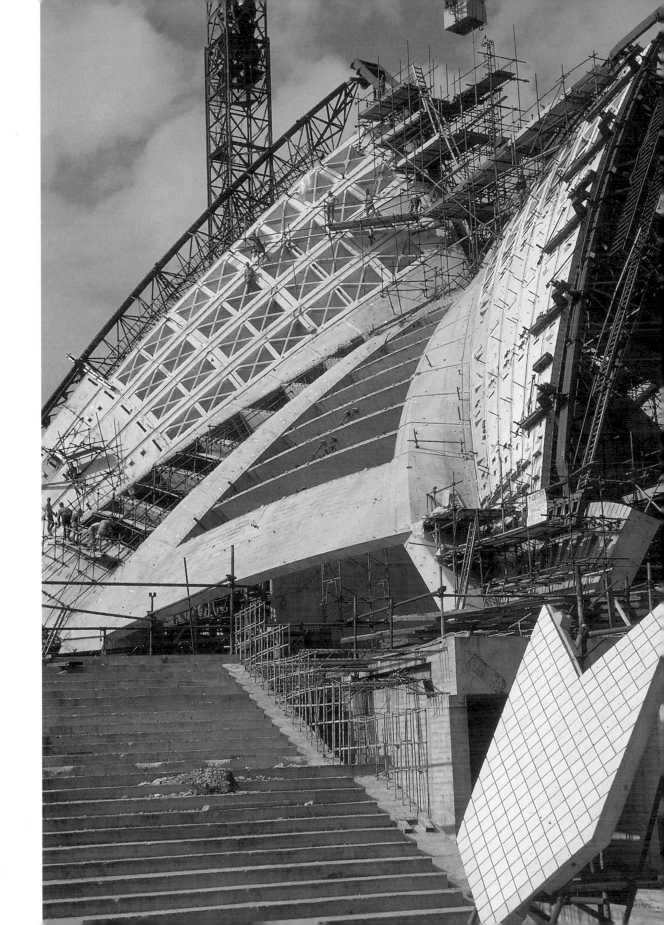

propelled the firm onto the global stage was an international competition in 1956 for a multipurpose concert hall, opera house and theatre in Sydney, Australia. The competition was won with beautiful pencil sketches by Jørn Utzon, an unknown Danish architect aged thirty-eight, who ultimately proved to be virtually illiterate mathematically, technically ignorant and without any knowledge of music (he had never been to an opera). Arup regarded Utzon as a conceptual genius, but the architect failed to submit measured drawings, details of scale, construction methods, interior configuration or costs, and Arup informed him within days that the shapes sketched in his freehand drawings could not be built using prestressed concrete. Other consultants reported that the design fell short of the client's seating requirements by almost a third. Utzon chose not to alert his clients, the New South Wales government, and as a result years of frustrating delays and arguments ensued, accompanied by huge cost increases. Utzon resigned from the Sydney Opera House project in 1966, and it was then discovered that there were almost no completed architectural drawings for the interior of the building, or for many of its other features. Another equally inexperienced team of architects struggled to complete the building, which was eventually opened by Queen Elizabeth II in 1973. It has since become a tourist and sculptural icon for Australia, but in spite of numerous modifications over fifty years its internal functions remain inadequate and its acoustics mediocre. The final cost, mostly borne by a state lottery, was A$102 million, against an unrealistic original speculation of A$7 million. Among the innovations employed in the construction of the building was Arup's extensive use of early computers in designing the complex geometries of the structure, for drawing three-dimensional shapes, and in setting out on site. The use of epoxy resin adhesives for jointing precast concrete was also unusual.

During the years of the Sydney saga Arup acted as consultant engineer for Coventry Cathedral (1951–62) and Sussex University (1960s), both designed by Basil Spence, but, aside from a footbridge in Durham (1961), he was not himself directly involved in any further projects. His ever-expanding firm, however, underook numerous prestigious structures – from the Pompidou Centre in Paris (1971–77), the new headquarters of the Hongkong & Shanghai Banking Corporation in Hong Kong (1981–85) and of Lloyds of London (1978–85) to the Millennium Bridge over the Thames (2000; reopened 2002), several airports and railway stations, the Channel Tunnel Rail Link (connecting Britain with continental Europe) and the 2008 Beijing Olympic stadiums. Among many other honours, Arup received a knighthood and the Gold Medal of the Royal Institute of British Architects: all sustained his enthusiasm to practise 'the art of the impossible'.

LOUIS I. KAHN

Architect of the poetics of action and construction

1901–1974

I T COULD BE ARGUED THAT THE WORKS OF LOUIS I. KAHN were the single greatest influence on world architecture during the second half of the 20th century. Kahn redefined modern architecture by re-establishing in the design of contemporary buildings both the relevance of human actions, as revealed in historical architecture, and the primacy of the art of construction. In the mid-20th century Kahn was one of many who believed that modern architecture had lost touch with its beginnings. Yet he stands virtually alone in having reconnected construction to its ethical imperatives and re-engaged space-making with its ancient origins.

Kahn was born on the Baltic island of Saaremaa, now in Estonia, and his family emigrated to the United States in 1906, settling in Philadelphia. Trained in the Beaux-Arts classical tradition by Paul Cret at the University of Pennsylvania, Kahn embraced the Modern Movement after graduating. Kahn's early works consisted almost exclusively of public housing designs and yet, by the Second World War, he had begun to question the capacity of the anti-monumental International Style to embody contemporary cultural meanings and social institutions. Kahn believed that monumentality in architecture was a spiritual quality conveying a sense of eternity – a quality embodied in the great monuments of the past. He also noted the critically important part played by structural perfection and material character in the creation of monumental architecture. These would prove to be the key themes of Kahn's career.

STRUCTURE, MASS AND SPACE

Kahn began teaching at Yale University in 1947 and was awarded an appointment at the American Academy in Rome in 1950. This brief period of historical rediscovery was pivotal in Kahn's development as one of the most important modern architects of his time. The eternal quality of heavy construction and the spaces shaped by massive masonry made a lasting impression on him and, after this year abroad, Kahn never again employed lightweight steel structures, building only with concrete and masonry. Upon his return from Rome, Kahn designed and built the Yale University

Art Gallery in New Haven (1951–53), his first significant work. His innovative floor structure was inspired by the geodesic domes of Buckminster Fuller, yet the triangular grid of cast-concrete beams, exposed in the ceilings below, is a powerful and heavy presence quite unlike the lightness idealized by Fuller. Incorporating the services within its massive depths, Kahn's articulate ceiling is also the opposite of the structurally and spatially neutral slab typical of International Style buildings. For Kahn, it was an ethical imperative to show how a building was made – the materials, joints and markings of construction being left exposed as the only ornament appropriate to modern architecture.

Kahn in the Yale University Art Gallery, New Haven, 1951–53.

The Bath House for the Jewish Community Center in Trenton, New Jersey (1954–58), was a small but important project with which, as he said, Kahn 'found himself as an architect'. The cruciform plan is composed of four pavilions forming at their centre a court, open to the sky, and each pavilion is made up of four heavy concrete block corner piers, upon which rests a light pyramidal roof of wood. The Bath House is at once modern, built of the most typical construction materials, and ancient, a place where earth and sky meet. While the larger Community Center was never built, the grid of individually roofed volumes demonstrated Kahn's conception that each inhabitational activity required its own clearly articulated room, with its own structure and light – the exact opposite of the 'free plan' typical of International Style Modernism.

In 1957 Kahn was appointed to teach at the University of Pennsylvania, and he began an association with two engineers: at the university, Robert Le Ricolais, a visionary poet of structure, and at his office, August Komendant, an expert on precast, post-tensioned concrete construction. The design of the Richards Medical Research Laboratories at the University of Pennsylvania (1957–65) is characterized by both expressed construction and articulated function. Each of the five laboratory towers, a square in plan, is constructed with a precast, post-tensioned concrete cantilevered structure, with structurally independent, load-bearing masonry service shafts located at the midpoints of each side, resulting in the laboratory floors being entirely free of structure or services. In this way, the building exemplifies Kahn's concept of 'served spaces' (primary functions) being formed by 'servant spaces' (services and structure).

INHABITATION, CONSTRUCTION AND LIGHT

In the First Unitarian Church of Rochester, New York (1959–69), Kahn fused the qualities of the light, diaphanous vaults of the Gothic cathedral and the heavy, shadowed walls of the medieval castle – all in an entirely modern construction. The sanctuary is a central, top-lit space, its solid, enclosing walls made of non-bearing concrete block, while its roof is a gently folded plane of cast concrete that rises to form large clerestory lights at the corners. The sanctuary is accessed from a perimeter ambulatory that is in turn surrounded by the classrooms, forming a thick protective outer layer around the inner sanctuary, their brick exterior walls folded to produce a deeply shadowed edge. This concept of surrounding primary spaces with shadow-giving walls, which Kahn described as 'wrapping ruins around buildings', is exemplified in his design for the Salk Institute at La Jolla, California (1959–65). The unrealized Meeting House was to be a series of independent room-buildings surrounding a central cubic hall, the outer range of rooms taking the form of hollow concrete shells wrapped around and shading glazed rooms within. The Salk Institute Laboratories consist of column-free laboratory floors alternating with service floors housing the concrete truss structure, the whole constructed of meticulously detailed cast concrete. Between the two laboratory buildings, where the scientists' studies are placed in towers, Kahn originally envisioned a garden, but he was convinced by the Mexican architect Luis Barragán to make instead a paved plaza, open to the sky and the ocean. Today this plaza, without any formal programme of use, remains one of the most powerful and deeply moving spaces ever built.

The Indian Institute of Management in Ahmedabad (1962–74) and the National Assembly Building for the capital of Bangladesh at Dhaka (1962–83) were the greatest built examples of Kahn's concept of 'the plan as a society of rooms', in which the spatial relationships between the rooms articulate their collective purpose. In addition 'the architecture of connection', as Kahn called the secondary spaces such as corridors, arcades, stairway landings and vestibules, are as important to the overall experience of these buildings as the primary spaces. Kahn understood that learning and decision-making occur not only in the classroom and assembly hall, but in the foyers, passageways, cafés and courtyards as well. In constructing these buildings Kahn 'made brick modern', as he said, using reinforced-concrete ties to restrain the outward thrust of load-bearing brick arches. In his design for the Phillips Exeter Academy Library in Exeter, New Hampshire (1965–72), Kahn turned the traditional programme of a library (central reading room surrounded by book stacks) inside out. It is a building-within-a-building: a brick outer shell containing the reading spaces surrounds the inner concrete book stacks. In this way, as Kahn said, one could 'take the book to the light' – from the protective darkness of the inner stacks to the natural light of the outer reading rooms. At the centre of the library is the most important room in the building, the entry hall, which goes from ground to sky, with giant circular concrete openings revealing the books – thereby celebrating the purpose of the building.

The Kimbell Art Museum in Fort Worth, Texas (1966–72), is rightly considered Kahn's greatest built work. The space is composed of a series of concrete vaulted roof forms, each spanning 30.5 metres (100 feet), split at their centres to allow light to flow in, bouncing off aluminium deflectors to spray the underside of the vaults with an ethereal silver light. Without question Kahn's most beautiful space, the Kimbell is

The promenade of the National Assembly Building, Dhaka, 1962–83. The assembly hall is to the left and offices to the right, linked by the full-height, naturally lit space of 'connection'.

also the most rigorously resolved example of his concept of the relation between light and structure, the interior spaces receiving natural light in ways that precisely articulate the structural elements. The Kimbell is also Kahn's most elegant built example of landscape planning, its entry sequence taking us past sunken sculpture gardens, under a vaulted loggia, past sheets of cascading water, through a gravel-floored courtyard filled with a grid of trees and then, quietly, into the very heart of the gallery itself. Kahn actually realized only a third of his designs, and many of his greatest works were never built: these include the Trenton Jewish Community Center, the Salk Institute Meeting House, the US embassy in Angola, the Mikveh Israel Synagogue, the Dominican Motherhouse, the Palazzo dei Congressi and the Hurva Synagogue. Taken together, these unbuilt designs constitute one of the most significant contributions to 20th-century architecture.

Entry gallery of the Kimbell Art Museum, Fort Worth, 1966–72. This 'ideal museum' comprises a series of naturally lit spaces given precise form by the concrete ceiling vaults and open, flexible floor plan.

JEAN PROUVÉ

The constructive imagination

1901–1984

A SPINE-LIKE FRAMEWORK – WITH THE STRENGTH, resistance and flexibility of a skeleton – and a skin: this was Jean Prouvé's concept of construction. Over years of designing and planning in his workshops, he created a whole series of basic 'skeletons' (portal frames, shells, props, load-bearing cores, stools) and skins to cover them, in the form of curtain walls that could be flexible, moveable, solid or glazed, in wood, neoprene or metal, fixed to the structural framework. This was the pragmatic and very personal path that he continued to follow as the 20th century progressed.

Jean Prouvé was a self-taught architect, born into a family of artists: his father Victor was a painter, sculptor and, alongside Émile Gallé, a founder of the Art Nouveau movement known as the School of Nancy. On Gallé's death in 1904, Victor Prouvé became the guiding force: his goal was to bring artists together with crafts and businesspeople to create an alliance of art and industry that could deliver the best to the masses. Health problems and the First World War prevented Jean from training as an engineer, as he had hoped. Nonetheless, he believed that the

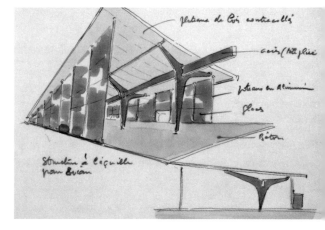

'greatest stroke of luck in his life' was to have 'become a worker so quickly'. He became an apprentice metalworker under Émile Robert and then under Adalbert Szabo, both in Paris, where he lodged with the art critic André Fontaine, a friend of his father. At Fontaine's home he met other intellectuals who were familiar with the philosophy of the school of Nancy, the idea that 'man was put on earth to create', and that the work of others should never be copied.

The supporting structure of the Evian pump room, which Prouvé produced for the architect Maurice Novarina in 1956–57 (the drawing dates from 1982).

INDUSTRIALIZATION AS A GOAL

Three major stages marked Jean Prouvé's progress towards his goal of industrialization. In 1924 he opened his first metal workshop in Nancy, where a hammer, anvil and forge were his basic tools. He quickly became interested in stainless steel, took on staff and then acquired high-performance equipment, including presses, that allowed him to fold thin sheet metal and thus strengthen it. 'I'm nothing but a twister of metal,' he used to say jokingly. By the end of the 1920s, after having used stainless steel to produce items such as lighting fixtures and stair rails, he had begun to make folded metal furniture. He dared to knock on the door of the architect Robert Mallet-Stevens, showed his drawings and received a commission for an entrance grille for a private mansion (1926); this encouraged him to leave 'artistic metalwork' behind and develop his ideas on architecture. In 1931 he became aware that his creative process required a different kind of tool. Aiming to work on an industrial scale, he needed to expand his premises to accommodate new machinery and take on more staff. In order to establish a working structure that could meet these new demands, he formed a company – the Ateliers Jean Prouvé – and it was under this name that he marketed his designs and took out several patents. Following his own code of social ethics, he set up a system of joint management that gave his employees more responsibility, allowed them to suggest improvements and gave them a share of the profits.

Passionate about all things mechanical, Prouvé admired the continuous improvements being made to cars and aircraft, and this led him to the question: why does no one devote the same attention to housing? 'If planes were built in the same way that our homes are,' he said, 'they would not fly.' He wanted to employ the best aspects of industrialization in order to create the best possible living environment, paying attention to the use of materials and costs and showing respect for the natural world: his desire to leave the ground unscathed in case the building had to be removed later often led him to use pilotis (supporting columns). Throughout the 1930s his most important works showcase his skill at designing and building innovative structures. One such, in collaboration with the architects Eugène Beaudouin and Marcel Lods, was the Maison du Peuple in Clichy (1936–39), in which a metal supporting structure (incorporating moveable roof and floor elements) allowed the construction of a curtain wall – probably the first – from moveable metal panels. Frank Lloyd Wright came to see this building in 1939 and expressed his admiration.

In the early 1940s Jean Prouvé built houses that used a portal frame as a load-bearing element. Made of folded sheet metal, it supported a metal beam to which rivets could be fixed, allowing the attachment of different types of façade panels and creating a free plan within the construction: load-bearing walls were no longer required. All the elements needed for this type of construction were designed, tested and manufactured in Prouvé's workshops, transported to the site by lorry and could be assembled within a day. The portal frame could also be used for furniture, a field in which Prouvé retained a keen interest: 'It is as interesting to design a piece of furniture as a 300-metre-tall [985-foot-tall] tower.'

In 1947, still working under the name Ateliers Jean Prouvé, he set up new premises in Maxéville on the outskirts of Nancy, this time on a more industrial scale: they were soon employing a workforce of two hundred. Due to the shortage of steel in the years following the war, he looked into using aluminium. He revisited and improved the principle of the portal-frame house, with all the elements factory-made from metal, and designed prefabricated buildings to be sent out to Africa, transporting the component parts by plane. It was also during this period that he built shed roofs, followed by shell roofs, which provided a self-supporting structure similar to his façade panels. He produced several furniture designs as well, most notably for university buildings.

In 1952, however, aluminium manufacturers took a majority stake in Prouvé's business. Without experience in the world of building and wanting only to sell as much aluminium as possible, they clashed with the architect's desire to produce good work at low cost. Prouvé resigned and left the Maxéville factory with a heavy heart: 'I really believe that I have had an exceptional stroke of luck in my life: that of having

The covered market of the Maison du Peuple, Clichy, 1936–39, with its revolutionary curtain wall of metal panels.

my own manufacturing workshop … a tool of my own! I built up that workshop from nothing. I expanded it regularly until it became a sizeable factory, well equipped with modern machinery. Its employees, who numbered around two hundred in 1952, were all friends.'

THE FINAL STAGE

In 1956 Jean Prouvé began the third stage of his career, working in a design office in Paris without any direct contact with the manufacturing process, a loss that he would always regret. He immediately continued with his experimental work and designed the Aluminium Centenary Pavilion (1954) with a load-bearing structure of cast aluminium. This was followed by the Evian pump room (1956–57), the Villejuif School (1956–57), based on propped structures, and the Abbé Pierre House ('House for Better Days') with its load-bearing core that could be entirely prefabricated and transported to the site (1956). He was hired by the Compagnie Industrielle de Matériel

The bare framework of Prouvé's temporary Villejuif School, 1956–57, under construction.

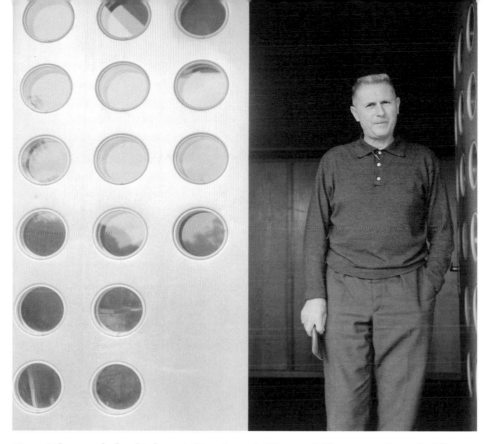

Prouvé photographed at his house in Rue Augustin-Hacquard, Nancy, in 1962 – a building in which he sought to demonstrate the possibilities offered by sheet-metal construction.

de Transport (CIMT), a firm that had foreseen the end of railway expansion and wanted to forge a place for themselves in the building industry. For the CIMT he designed many façade panels for schools, university buildings and Grenoble town hall (1964–68), as well as buildings for which he also designed the structure, including the Palais des Expositions in Grenoble (1967) and Total service stations. He also worked as a consultant on major projects, including the façades for the Centre National des Industries et des Techniques (CNIT) (1956) and the Tour Nobel (1968), both at La Défense in Paris, built on the principle of a central core and curtain walls with rounded corners.

His lectures at the Conservatoire National des Arts et Métiers (CNAM) in Paris (1957–70), in which he detailed several systems of construction, attracted many architects, both students and professionals. By the end of his life Prouvé was truly working on an industrial scale, something he had aimed to do since his earliest work, but he still missed having direct contact with the building process. When he was asked to appear in a dictionary of architects, his response was: 'I'm not an architect and I'm not an engineer. I am a factory man.'

OSCAR NIEMEYER

Radical critic of Modernist orthodoxies

BORN 1907

A S THE PRE-EMINENT FIGURE OF ONE OF THE MOST INNOVATIVE national interpretations of architectural Modernism and a radical critic of orthodox Modernist aesthetic formulae and moralizing ideologies, Oscar Niemeyer occupies a unique place in the pantheon of great builders. Tirelessly exploring the structural and formal possibilities of reinforced concrete over more than seven decades, and still in practice at over a hundred years old, Niemeyer has designed over six hundred buildings. Taking advantage of Brazil's advanced reinforced-concrete technology and working closely with highly committed structural engineers, Niemeyer found in concrete an ideal means to achieve what he refers to as an architecture of 'spectacle … plastic freedom and … inventiveness', rooted in Brazil's native traditions and tropical landscape, and challenging the dominance of clean white walls, straight lines and right angles, which, for him, 'issued from a European ethical tradition'. Conjugating architectural, structural and topographical events to achieve maximum fluidity, he prioritized the sensual reality of the architectural experience. Concrete, a material suited to the local economic and technological conditions, permitted Niemeyer to launch what he conceived as a 'new' and 'bolder architecture in the dimensions of Brazil', proclaiming the country's unequivocal modernity as well as its emancipation from Western prototypes.

BRAZILIAN ARCHITECTURAL MODERNISM

Born Oscar Ribeiro de Almeida de Niemeyer Soares Filho, in Rio de Janeiro, Niemeyer stresses his 'diverse ethnic roots', that is, his Brazilianness, in accordance with the national ideology of ethnic amalgamation. He studied at the Escola Nacional de Belas Artes from 1929 to 1934, where the patriarch of modern Brazilian architecture, Lúcio Costa, had added a 'Functional Course' and appointed as professor

Gregori Warchavchik, a pioneer of the Modern Movement in Latin America, with Affonso Eduardo Reidy as his assistant. The short-lived course provoked explosive opposition from the school's Beaux-Arts majority, but it was popular with the students Costa described as 'a purist battalion dedicated to the impassioned study of Walter Gropius, Ludwig Mies van der Rohe and especially Le Corbusier'. In 1936 Niemeyer joined the team of architects who designed the first state-sponsored Modernist skyscraper in the world, the Ministry of Education and Public Health in Rio de Janeiro (1936–44), under the leadership of Costa and later of Niemeyer, and with Le Corbusier acting as a consultant in 1936. The new headquarters for the ministry that had assumed the task of shaping the 'new man, Brazilian and modern' constitutes the first complete application of Le Corbusier's 'Five Points of a New Architecture'. But these were combined with local materials and techniques from historic colonial architecture, such as the hand-painted *azulejos*; allusions to the Brazilian landscape and Baroque monuments; sensuous curves; shading devices and bold colours related to the Moorish traditions of Portuguese architecture; the tropical gardens of Roberto Burle Marx, epitomizing the desire to transgress the rules of prosaic functionalism; and the integrated, specially commissioned works of Brazilian artists.

A symbol and manifesto of Brazilian modernity, the ministry building achieved the desired hybridity of nationalist rhetoric and was hailed by Philip L. Goodwin in the US as 'the most beautiful government building in the Western hemisphere'. It embraced all things revalorized and radicalized by the Brazilian Modernist artists of

OPPOSITE *Oscar Niemeyer in his studio in Rio de Janeiro, December 2007.*
BELOW *São Francisco de Assis, Pampulha, Belo Horizonte, 1940–43.*

the 1920s, whose Pau-Brasil and Antropofagia movements had conceived a strategy to unite the native with the foreign, infecting 'civilizing' imports with what was perceived as the tropical, irrational 'primitive'. The anticolonialist Antropofagist strategy of contaminating European Modernism with the Dionysian *espirito de brasilidade* was also employed by Costa and Niemeyer in the Brazilian Pavilion at the 1939 New York World's Fair. But it was Niemeyer's pioneering leisure complex on the shores of an artificial lake at Pampulha (1940–43), a new suburb of Belo Horizonte, that led *L'Architecture d'Aujourd'hui* to declare in 1946 that Niemeyer was moving away from 'the triumph of the straight line' and 'the monumental Cartesianism' of the Ministry and the 'Corbusian school', towards 'the affirmation of his own originality' in 'the triumph of the curve'.

CURVES OF TRANSGRESSION

Niemeyer speaks of his 'tropicalization' of all he learned from Le Corbusier and never tires of repeating: 'My architectural oeuvre began with Pampulha, which I designed in sensual and unexpected curves.' Commissioned by the then mayor of Belo Horizonte, Juscelino Kubitschek, the complex included a small church (Brazil's first listed Modern monument), an ingeniously planned casino with a lavish interior, a delightful dance hall and restaurant with a meandering concrete canopy, a yacht club, golf club and a hundred-room hotel (unbuilt). Spectacle and luxury, pleasure, beauty and sensuality were emphatically affirmed as legitimate pursuits in Niemeyer's complex at Pampulha, his personal architectural manifesto. A wilfully rich palette of fine materials and techniques, purposefully employed detailing and applied ornament were combined with Burle Marx's intensified images of tropical nature and fully integrated artworks to create a unique body of work, motivated by a vision for a modern national architecture with a repertoire of voluptuous curves and tropical motifs imagined as eminently Brazilian. If the Loosian figure of the English gentleman embodied 'the truly modern style' of Apollonian Europe, Niemeyer found in the eroticized figure of the Brazilian woman of African descent, the *mulata*, the incarnation of the Dionysian *espirito de brasilidade*: 'My work is not about "form follows function", but "form follows beauty" or, even better, "form follows feminine".

Working with structural engineer Joaquim Cardozo, at the Pampulha Church of São Francisco de Assis Niemeyer used structural parabolic vaults as form- and space-defining elements. Shell structures and variously configured vertical supports appear frequently in his mature projects that populated Brazil's rapidly growing urban centres in the 1950s. The freely undulating volume of his forty-storey Edifício

Edifício Liberdade, Belo Horizonte, 1954–60 (later renamed Edifício Niemeyer in honour of the architect's brother). Brises-soleil continue along the solid wall, which is clad with black-and-white cement tiles by Athos Bulcão.

COPAN (1951–66), with 5,000 residents, decidedly invaded the urban core of São Paulo, Latin America's premier industrial and financial centre, contesting the dichotomy between the private, feminine world of home and pleasure, and the public, vertical and hard-edged, masculine world of work and power, and challenging the gender polarities of the American city. As at the COPAN, the dynamism of Niemeyer's Edifício Liberdade (1954–60) in Belo Horizonte was accentuated by continuous, horizontal, concrete *brises-soleil*, which function as sunshades on the glazed part of the façade but continue along the tile-clad wall, underscoring aesthetic concerns that transgress the original utilitarian intent of the device.

The *Architectural Review* of October 1954 reported that Niemeyer's new house in Rio de Janeiro was at 'the centre of discussion' among foreign visitors at the 1953 São Paulo Art Biennale, who failed to appreciate the simultaneous rhythms of its polymetric architecture. Niemeyer's domestic masterpiece, the Casa das Canoas (1952–53), appears to consist of no more than a concrete, free-form canopy with a pool amid a

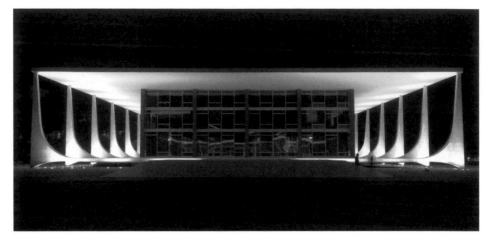

Supreme Court, Praça dos Três Poderes, Brasília, 1958–60.

tropical garden that merges seamlessly with a fantastic landscape. At this house in 1956, the ebullient president Juscelino Kubitschek recruited Niemeyer's help for the realization of his most ambitious scheme: the building of Brasília, a city uncompromisingly modern, which would herald 'the New Age of Brazil'.

TOWARDS A MORE DEMOCRATIC ARCHITECTURE

Inaugurated on 21 April 1960, the new federal capital was conceived as a symbol of national unity. The choice of Niemeyer represented the choice of the style in which 20th-century architects and politicians had sought to imagine the nation – Brazilian *and* modern. On the country's central plateau, away from the coastal tropical paradise that embodied the European legacy, Niemeyer's architecture for the 'real Brazil' of the hinterland entered into a dialogue with the landmarks of architectural history in order to affirm the autonomy of Brazilian architecture and 'create … the past of tomorrow'. The desire for monumentality informed Lúcio Costa's masterplan as well as Niemeyer's civic architecture for 'the acropolis of the new Brazil'. But rather than mass, solidity and weight, Brasília's colonnaded ceremonial buildings proposed lightness, elegance and grace, underscoring the individuality of their constituent parts – the white marble-clad columns – yet subordinating the individuality of equals to the synthesis of the whole, representing the democratic polis.

During the years that Niemeyer was forced into exile by Brazil's military dictatorship, which came to power in 1964, he exploited advanced Brazilian engineering and Europe's technology and skilled labour force to produce buildings that were both aesthetically challenging and structurally daring. The precisely patterned, exposed-concrete arcades of the Mondadori headquarters in Segrate, near Milan (1968–75), resemble those of Brasília's Palácio do Itamaraty (Ministry of Foreign Affairs, 1962–70), but at Segrate Niemeyer incorporated a random aspect into the design. On each elevation, the twenty-two parabolic arches of variable width and curvature are united by a single parametric equation. Niemeyer's 'modern version of the Greek temple' ranks among his greatest achievements.

Driven by a desire to invent ever new ways to address the relation between the individual building and the city, in France and later in Brazil following the return of democracy in the 1980s, Niemeyer gradually moved beyond the idea of an architecture that is merely beautiful towards an architecture that is more consciously democratic, prioritizing urban public space as fundamental for the enactment of the rights of citizenship. In a classic Niemeyer inversion of conventional hierarchies of space and use, his late civic landmarks, such as the Museum of Contemporary Art in Niterói (1991–96) and the NovoMuseu (2001–2) in Curitiba, are dominated by ramps that transgress functional requirements and invite the public to appropriate them as promenades. Underlining the public nature of the buildings, these long, languorously unfolding ramps serve as an architectural metaphor for Brazil's legendary beach, a space onto which Niemeyer projects his ideal of a good life.

Museum of Contemporary Art, Niterói, 1991–96.

EERO SAARINEN

Exuberance and technological innovation

1910–1961

URING HIS SHORT BUT PROLIFIC CAREER EERO SAARINEN managed to design half a dozen major corporate campuses, numerous innovative college buildings, a highly original skyscraper, an experimental theatre, two unusual American embassies, several influential churches and three thrilling airports – making technological breakthroughs of different kinds in all of them. Ten major buildings were underway when he died of a brain tumour in 1961.

He was born in Helsinki and moved to the US in 1923 with his parents, the early modern architect Eliel Saarinen and the sculptor and weaver Loja Saarinen. Although his first commissions came through the family firm, Eero's independent victory in the 1947–48 competition to design the St Louis Gateway Arch suddenly made him the most sought-after American architect of his generation. The parabolic arch – 192 metres (630 feet) tall, the height of a 62-storey building – was designed in collaboration with engineer Fred Severud and has a triangular profile. Its stainless-steel skin helps support the concrete structure underneath and the steel scaffolding further inside that was used to erect the arch. It was not completed until 1965.

TECHNICAL INVENTIVENESS

After winning the Arch competition, Eero took charge of the family firm's commission for the General Motors Technical Center near Detroit (1948–56), a project of 900 acres and twenty-five buildings with a budget of $100 million. Instead of the original Art Deco design that had proved too costly, Eero developed an International Style scheme, influenced by the work of Mies van der Rohe at the Illinois Institute of Technology, but with lighter framing, a shiny, stainless-steel, hemispherical Styling Dome, and a large reflective water tower in an enormous pool. He introduced numerous technical innovations, some inspired by the automobile industry, such as neoprene gasket weather seals (similar to those used for windscreens) to hold uniquely thin sandwich panels

Although Saarinen won the competition to design the St Louis Gateway Arch in 1948, it was not completed for another seventeen years, with the help of engineer Fred Severud.

Saarinen stands over a model of Morse and Stiles Colleges, Yale University, 1958–62, whose concrete fabric was embedded with stones to help them relate to earlier buildings.

of fixed glass and porcelain enamel to their aluminium frames. These prefabricated exterior and interior walls were windproof and waterproof, and allowed the glass or panels to be 'zipped' out whenever the use of a building changed. End walls were covered with brightly coloured glazed brick. The drafting rooms had the first completely luminous ceilings with special modular plastic pans. As Saarinen later noted, 'All of these developments became part of the language of modern architecture.'

While the Technical Center was underway, Saarinen designed a cylindrical brick chapel surrounded by a moat, and the nearby Kresge Auditorium for the Massachusetts Institute of Technology (1950–55). Its thin-shell concrete dome consists of a single cutaway section – an eighth of a sphere – resting on its own three pendentive-like points, with very considerable abutments buried in the ground so that the dome seems to rise weightlessly. A few years later Saarinen created the even bolder David S. Ingalls Hockey Rink at his alma mater, Yale University (1956–59). This cable-hung structure has a tall, curved concrete spine running down the centre with a web of cables slung over it, like a blanket over a laundry line, and is covered with a rubberized coating and stabilized with concrete. For another commission at Yale, the dormitories of Morse and Stiles Colleges (1958–62), he devised a new kind of concrete embedded with large stones to give the surface a rough-hewn appearance compatible with Yale's older 'Collegiate Gothic' buildings, but in a new, modern and economical way.

Saarinen explored the reflective properties of steel and glass in various projects, but for the Bell Telephone Laboratories in Holmdel, New Jersey (1957–62), he developed the first fully mirrored glass to make the large boxy structure 'disappear' into the landscape. For the John Deere company's headquarters in Moline, Illinois (1956–64), he used self-sealing corrosion-resistant steel as an architectural material for the first time, with the help of his partner John Dinkeloo, a technical genius who worked on many of the firm's innovations. Saarinen's skyscraper for the headquarters of the Columbia Broadcasting System (CBS) in New York (1960–65) departed radically from the Miesian model predominant at the time. Sheathed in black granite, it was supported at the core and around the edges by reinforced-concrete columns instead of a uniform structural grid of steel ones like those in other New York skyscrapers. Its outer walls have an angular pleated profile, and the tower seems to grow out of the ground and soar straight up to the sky.

MASTERPIECES OF AIRPORT DESIGN

The architect's masterpieces, however, were the TWA Terminal, on a prominent wedge-shaped site across from the entrance to Idlewild (now John F. Kennedy) Airport in New York (1956–62), and the sprawling Dulles International Airport in Chantilly,

Saarinen's sketch of the David S. Ingalls Hockey Rink at Yale University, 1956–59, which conveys the fluid character of the cable-hung structure he envisioned.

Virginia, near Washington, DC (1958–63). Both were designed with Ammann & Whitney engineers, who also worked with Saarinen on Athens airport (1960–69) in Greece. The dramatic Dulles concourse has one gigantic open space covered by a cable-hung roof deck slung between two rows of eight rib-shaped concrete columns that slope outwards to counteract the pull of the cables. A curved entablature curls around the ends, forming a marquee and shading the huge expanses of glass that have rounded corners like airplane windows. Since the height of the columns varies from 19.8 metres (65 feet) in the front and only 12.2 metres (40 feet) in the back, the concourse has an asymmetrical profile, giving the interior a lively shape. The first airport built solely for jets, Dulles introduced a new idea: mobile lounges that bring passengers to the planes to save them a walk to gates that are nearly a kilometre (half a mile) away.

TWA's innovations had more impact on airport design. At the entrance, outgoing passengers parted with their baggage, which travelled to the planes on the ground level, while they took moving sidewalks through tubular tunnels in elevated bridges to the boarding areas in protruding 'fingers' 38 metres (125 feet) away. They departed through one wing while incoming passengers arrived in another and retrieved their luggage from the first moving carousels, and everyone gathered in the exuberant, vaulted, two-storey lobby. It was this completely curved space, with floors that bend up to form walls and walls that turn into ceilings – fitted with swooping benches, rounded counters, even circular floor tiles – that made the terminal one of the most exciting and beloved buildings in the US. The TWA Terminal, which resembles a bird in flight, is composed of four double-curved reinforced concrete shells, supported at three points. They are connected by two curvilinear buttresses 15.5 metres (51 feet) tall, joined at the centre by a plate that holds them in mutual equilibrium. The clear distance between the buttresses varies between 36.6 metres (120 feet) and 61 metres (200 feet), and the longest unsupported distance between the tips of the shells is about 95 metres (310 feet). The lightweight, umbrella-vault, reinforced concrete roof ranges in thickness from about 18 centimetres (7 inches) at the edges to about 100 centimetres (40 inches) where the wings meet the concrete, which is nearly a metre (3 feet) thick. The cantilevers extend 25 metres (82 feet).

With the TWA Terminal, Saarinen managed to create a building that expresses the excitement of travel rather than a static, enclosed place, but it was not easy. His office spent 5,500 man hours preparing detailed drawings – contour maps of the building's

The bold interior of the TWA Terminal at John F. Kennedy Airport in New York, 1956–62, is composed completely of curvilinear forms.

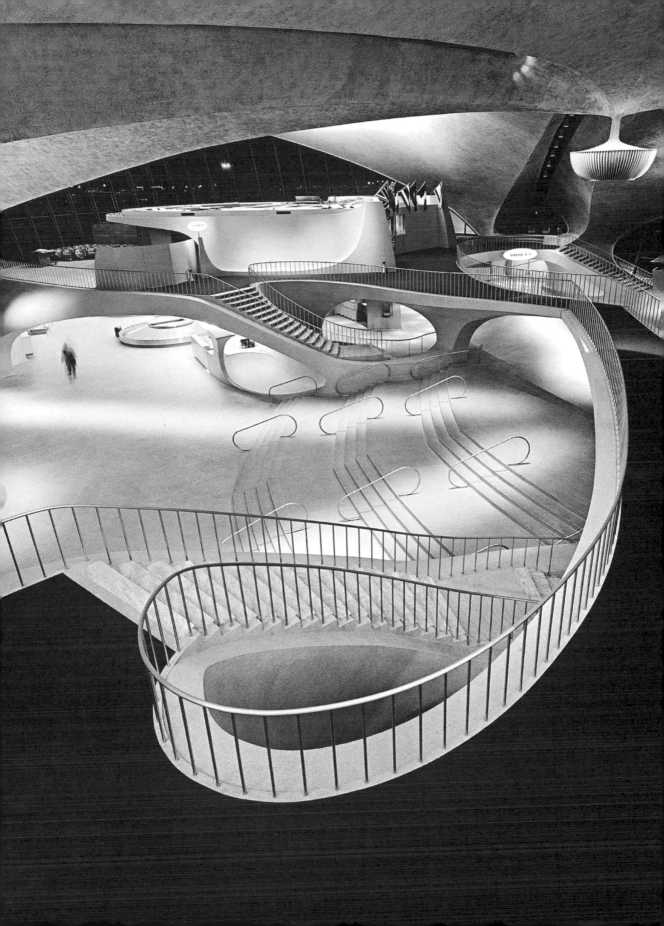

The concrete cable-hung roof of Dulles International Airport, 1958–63, designed in partnership with Ammann & Whitney engineers, is slung between outward-sloping colonnades of different heights.

major elements – and coordinating their efforts with engineer Abba Tor at every turn. The contractors had to develop drawings of each rib and connection for the formwork that shaped the concrete. Some of those calculations were checked by computer, but there was no computer-aided design at the time. Calculations for the geometry and the structural design of the thin shells and buttresses were made manually.

Every building Saarinen created was different: each one was designed for a particular client and site, so he never developed a recognizable style. His work was therefore difficult to classify, which was one reason he was ignored soon after his death. Another was that his work so aptly expressed the spirit of its time that when times changed, it lost some of its meaning. Although he was only interested in creating architecture that rose to the level of art, he was so committed to serving clients that he would redesign projects as many as half a dozen times, reworking them even after they started construction. Saarinen showed the same loyalty to the people in his office, where sixty talented architects from all over the world worked extraordinary hours when nine to five was the norm, because, as one employee put it, 'He never, simply never, let you down.' Happily, in recent years, interest in Saarinen has resurfaced, and their extraordinary efforts are appreciated once more.

FREI OTTO

Innovator of tensile and membrane structures

BORN 1925

FREI OTTO WAS BORN IN SAXONY IN GERMANY, the son of a stonemason and sculptor. His mother gave him the unusual first name Frei, meaning 'free', and the demands of this adjective later became a theme for his life. As a young man he experienced the cult of Nazism, with its heavy monumental buildings, and flew aircraft over burning cities. These experiences had a major influence on him; throughout his life he has aimed to create lightweight, natural and adaptable architecture for a democratic society.

Otto with a model of his 'City in the Arctic' project, 1970. He proposed a vast cable-net roof that would protect a city of up to 40,000 inhabitants from the extreme climate.

Construction of the cable-net roof for the German Federal Republic pavilion, Expo '67, Montreal.

SUSPENDED ROOFS

As an architecture student at the Technische Universität in Berlin, Otto received a grant in 1950 that allowed him to travel to the United States, where he saw the work of some of the great masters of modern architecture, including Frank Lloyd Wright and Erich Mendelsohn. He was particularly intrigued by Matthew Nowicki's design for a sports arena in Raleigh, North Carolina, which included a roof supported by steel cables, and this stimulated his interest in building large-scale roofs. His studies were published in 1954 in a dissertation called *Das hängende Dach* ('The Suspended Roof'), in which he explored the brand-new architectural potential of tent structures, which had until this point been viewed as short-lived, cheap and unstable. Beginning with the four-point canopy that he designed as a bandstand for the 1955 Federal Garden Exhibition in Kassel, with its two high and two low boundary points creating a stable saddle shape, Otto spent the following decades turning tensile architecture into an established and powerful style of building with great formal qualities.

In many tensile structures based on the forms of saddles, points, arches and waves, Otto explored the potential of this architectural field and established that membranes cannot be freely sketched but should be allowed to take their own shape within a given space, through a natural optimization process called 'form-finding'. From 1958 his research was carried out at the Entwicklungsstätte für den Leichtbau (Development Centre for Lightweight Construction, known as the EL) in Berlin-Zehlendorf, which he himself founded. Since the span and load-bearing capacity of a membrane are both limited, Otto went on to develop wide-span lightweight structures formed from large, curving, saddle-shaped cable nets. His first cable-net roofs were designed for the Swiss National Exhibition in Lausanne in 1964. In the same year Fritz Leonhardt offered Otto a position in Stuttgart, where he worked as director of the newly founded Institut für Leichte Flächentragwerke (Institute of Lightweight Structures, known as the IL) until he was made emeritus professor in 1991. Unlike any other institution in the world, the IL is a laboratory carrying out research into the basic principles that underlie the entire field of architecture and engineering. The IL's numerous publications, conferences and experiments generated a huge amount of material, and the many participants took Frei Otto's ideas around the world.

Research into the technique and potential of cable-net structures was also carried out at the IL, and when Frei Otto, together with Rolf Gutbrod, won the competition to design the German Federal Republic pavilion for Expo '67 in Montreal, he produced a test version of the planned cable-net design in the form of an experimental building on the Stuttgart University campus, which was later turned into the home of the IL. The tensile pavilion in Montreal, which was seen as a demonstration of the new, open and democratic Germany, brought him international recognition and influenced the architect Günter Behnisch in his design for the tent roofs over the stadium buildings in the Munich Olympic Park; Otto then collaborated on the construction (1968–72).

ADAPTABLE BUILDINGS

As early as 1959 Otto published a manifesto on 'adaptable buildings', and this went on to become a central theme in his work. His experiments with membranes and cable nets took him deeper into the fundamentals of a lightweight and adaptable form of

Tent roofs over the Munich Olympic Park stadium buildings, designed in collaboration with Günter Behnisch, 1968–72.

building. In contrast to conventional building methods, which are almost always concerned with producing buildings that are long-lasting and reliable but that can be altered only with difficulty or not at all, Otto saw a demand for continually changing architecture and for building methods that could make this possible. He therefore sought architectural forms that could be easily altered or dismantled if their users or intended use changed.

One of the central aspects of adaptable building was convertible roofs that could react to changes in the weather and create sheltered spaces within a short period of time. Otto was one of the first architects to reawaken interest in retractable roofs, a structural form known since antiquity. His first large-scale, electrically operated, moveable roof was designed in 1965 for an open-air theatre in Cannes, and he created a similar roof shortly afterwards for another theatre in a ruined church in Bad Hersfeld in Hessen (1967–68); this was followed by retractable membranes over swimming pools in Paris, Lyon and Regensburg. The supporting mechanism used the same principle as an umbrella or parasol. Frei Otto turned this type of device into a new architectural form and has continued to expand it in new directions since the early 1970s.

Alongside the further development of membrane and cable-net structures, in the 1960s Otto moved on to the theme of grid shells, with construction methods based on the inversion principle and the distortion of a lattice-like grid into a double-curved shell. The inversion principle is based on the fact that hanging cables, chains or nets find their own form according to the laws of physics. By inverting these hanging forms, which are in pure tension, it is possible to create shapes for arches, vaults and

Umbrella roofs for the Federal Garden Show, Cologne, 1971. The supporting structure is positioned above the tensile fabric, which can be extended pneumatically.

The Japanese Pavilion at Expo 2000, Hanover, devised by Shigeru Ban in collaboration with Otto. The latticework structure consisted of rigid paper tubes.

domes whose own weight is supported by pure compression. The second construction principle of grid shells is closely related to the building process: a flat lattice made of thin laths can be shaped into a double-curved form as long as all the grid intersections are flexible. When the grid has reached its intended shape, the structure can be made into a rigid shell by fixing the nodes and edges in position. After the first grid shells at the University of California in Berkeley (1962) and at the 1962 DEUBAU construction fair in Essen, Otto worked in collaboration with Carlfried Mutschler on the Multihalle exhibition space in Mannheim (1975), a building with a roof area of 9,500 square metres (102,257 square feet), whose powerful design and simple construction are comparable to Otto's cable-net structures in Montreal and Munich.

In 1962, in his book *Zugbeanspruchte Konstruktionen* ('Tensile Structures'), Frei Otto referred to air as the lightest of all building materials: the use of air as a supporting element is the ultimate in lightweight building. Working with the firm Stromeyer, he created his first pneumatic building in 1966 for a technology firm in Cologne. He subsequently produced many designs based on pneumatic principles, including roofs for swimming pools, storage containers, airships and large-scale enclosures for extreme climates, such as the 'City in the Arctic' project (1970) with Kenzo Tange.

Long before the current ecology movement, Frei Otto was concerned with environmental issues and the impact of people on existing ecological systems, and he carried out theoretical research in this area. His endeavours in the field of what is now called passive solar building design date back to the early 1950s. At first he researched the possibility of heating buildings using only sunlight. In 1967, in collaboration with Rob Krier, he built himself a house and workshop in Warmbronn that became Germany's first passive solar house. This was followed in 1987 by the 'eco-houses' in the Berlin Tiergarten, built for the International Building Exhibition. To Otto, ecological building meant improving the environment, raising the quality of living by including gardens, and making living areas versatile and adaptable, as well as saving energy in all its forms. He wanted to use natural constructions to create an architecture that could sustainably meet people's needs and have as little damaging impact on the environment as possible.

Frei Otto has engaged in interdisciplinary research throughout his life, in a way that few others have emulated. When asked how he should be professionally categorized, he once answered: 'Many people call me an engineer. At heart I am a seeker of design and sometimes also a finder of design, who is aware of the imperfection of what he does and produces ... I try to understand nature, even though I have realized that nature can never be understood by a living creature who is part of nature himself. "Less is more" is a saying that fascinates me: needing fewer houses, fewer materials, less concrete and less energy, but building humanely, using the elements that are available: earth, water, air. Building close to nature and making a lot out of a little, observing things critically and thinking them through before putting pen to paper. It's better to hardly build at all than to build too much!'

Otto has certainly not built too much, but his work has nonetheless had an impact on architecture and structural design that few 20th-century architects can rival.

FRANK GEHRY

Designer of expressively iconic buildings

BORN 1929

O F ALL THE LEADING AMERICAN ARCHITECTS WORKING IN THE LAST decades of the 20th and the first years of the 21st centuries, none has achieved a global reputation to match that of Frank Gehry. Canadian by birth but a resident of Los Angeles since early adulthood, Gehry has combined a relentless pursuit of technical and structural innovation with a sometimes playful but essentially serious regard for the American vernacular, a combination that echoes the work of the greatest American architect of the first half of the 20th century, Frank Lloyd Wright.

Gehry was born (as Frank Goldberg) in Toronto, moving with his parents to Los Angeles in 1947, where he studied architecture at the University of Southern California before working for a series of local practices. He opened his own office in Santa Monica in 1962. Gehry's early work reflected the influence of Frank Lloyd Wright and of iconic Californian Modernists including Richard Neutra, Rudolph Schindler and Raphael Soriano, but by the late 1960s his architecture had turned in a new direction. This was reflected in projects such as the O'Neill hay barn at San Juan Capistrano and the Davis house and studio at Malibu; the latter was commissioned by the painter Ron

Davis, who was part of a coterie of West Coast artists with whom Gehry socialized and exchanged ideas. Both buildings made extensive use of cheap components, timber and corrugated metal, and the Malibu project featured a plan form that gently prefigured the free planning and rejection of the orthogonal seen in Gehry's later, iconic projects. The expressive spirit that Gehry admired in the work of Alvar Aalto and Hans Scharoun thus found an outlet in his own work.

Frank Gehry (left) at work in his Los Angeles studio, where the first sketches and cardboard models are made.

Gehry's home in Santa Monica. He extended and remodelled it in 1977–78, after which it became an iconic modern house and a place of pilgrimage for architects.

The project that made Gehry famous, however, was the Santa Monica house he built – or rather extended – for his own occupation in 1977–78. 'The house that built Gehry', as one critic has described it, was, in the architect's own words, 'just a dumb little house', a typical middle-class dwelling of the sort long despised by the Modernist establishment but rediscovered in the writings of Robert Venturi and Denise Scott Brown. The house was radically transformed by 'cutting away from it, exposing some parts and covering up others'. It was wrapped in an outer skin of corrugated metal and chain-link fencing, pierced by large glazed openings set at eccentric angles. Internal spaces were reconfigured and the timber frame exposed. The house attracted international interest.

Concurrently, Gehry was working on a straightforwardly commercial project, the Santa Monica Place shopping mall, where he 'realized the limits of my interest in trying to please the marketplace'. His work for Loyola Law School, extending over more than two decades from 1978, showed a strong response to the environment of downtown Los Angeles, with oblique references to classical architecture that could be seen as a commentary on the Postmodernist fashions of the period. The project included the renovation of some existing buildings – a significant theme in Gehry's work, and reflected in his successful conversion of a warehouse as a temporary home for the Los Angeles Museum of Contemporary Art (1983). The 1980s saw Gehry working across a wide spectrum: spectacular houses (including the opulent Schnabel Residence in Brentwood); the design of furniture in bent wood and cardboard, and of fish lamps (fish were to become a persistent motif in his work); the headquarters of the Chiat Day advertising agency in Venice, Los Angeles; and offices for the Disney Corporation in Anaheim.

INNOVATION IN COMPUTER-AIDED DESIGN

Already recognized as the leader of a new school of West Coast design, Gehry broke out of California with his offices and showrooms for the Vitra furniture company in Weil am Rhein, Germany, commissioned in 1988. Whereas his earlier buildings had played with the juxtaposition of contrasting geometries, using materials derived from the America of the urban strip and farmstead, the Vitra project saw Gehry emerging as a consciously sculptural designer, moulding a building out of white render and metal cladding in a way that contained echoes of Le Corbusier's chapel at Ronchamp. The project impacted on the working methods of Gehry's expanding office, where the design process had always depended heavily on drawing and physical modelling, but this new direction in his architecture drove the practice towards an extensive use of computer-aided design (CAD), employing innovative techniques developed in the US during the 1980s, and towards a new strategy for working with

Vitra International Manufacturing Facility and Design Museum, Weil am Rhein, 1987–89.

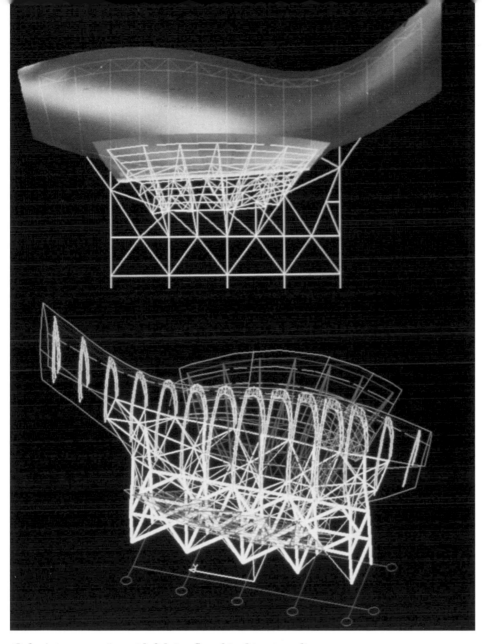

Gehry's preoccupation with fish is reflected in this extraordinary structure, 54 metres (177 feet) long, located on Barcelona's waterfront. It was commissioned as part of the regeneration of the city's rundown port area for the 1992 Olympic Games.

structural engineers and contractors. Gehry argues that this system restored the primacy of the architect in the design process: 'it makes the architect more the parent and the contractor more the child – the reverse of the 20th-century system'. CAD drawings could be used by manufacturers to produce custom-made building components, from steel frames to cladding panels.

Indeed, Gehry's office was pioneering in its use of computers, which became fundamental to the future development of his architecture. It gave him a freedom to create forms that Jørn Utzon, for example, had sought when designing the Sydney Opera House, but that were denied by the limited technologies of the mid-20th century. The practice's first fully fledged exercise in CAD design – involving the use of an advanced technique initially developed for the aerospace industry, which allowed it to computer-model buildings in three dimensions – was the giant fish sculpture commissioned for the 1992 Barcelona Olympics. For Gehry, however, the process of design still begins with the sketch and the physical model; the computer does not generate forms but enables them to be realized.

THE RISE OF 'ICONIC' ARCHITECTURE

During the early 1990s Gehry's work was briefly categorized as 'deconstructivist' and corralled into a school of design linked to a philosophical agenda that Gehry – a pragmatist and intuitive designer who does not subscribe to the theoretical concerns of architects such as Bernard Tschumi, Daniel Libeskind and Peter Eisenman – did not share. Nonetheless, the sculptural character of his architecture made him a leading figure in the rise of 'iconic' architecture, creating buildings in which, rationalist critics argued, the pursuit of memorable form became more significant than the response to a practical brief. Gehry has been fortunate to secure the support of a series of courageous clients for projects that created their own sense of place. One of these clients was Thomas Krens of the Guggenheim Foundation, which commissioned Gehry to design the Guggenheim Museum in Bilbao, a building that played a major part in the regeneration of the Basque city and has attracted millions of visitors since its opening in 1997. Clad in titanium, the museum provided the fullest expression to date of the liberation of architecture provided by the computer. The central atrium, 50.3 metres (165 feet) tall, evokes the drama of Wright's atrium in the Manhattan Guggenheim. The Walt Disney Concert Hall in Los Angeles, commissioned in 1988 but not opened until 2003, was part of the regeneration of the city's Bunker Hill district. Some inspiration for the project came from Scharoun's Philharmonic concert hall in Berlin (1956–63), but the extraordinary juxtaposition of forms, in this case clad in stainless steel, is pure Gehry.

The abandonment (in 2002) of a spectacular project for a new Guggenheim in Lower Manhattan was a major disappointment for Gehry, as was the cancellation of a

The Guggenheim Museum in Bilbao, opened in 1997, is probably Gehry's best-known project. Clad in titanium, the building is located on a riverside site close to the historic centre.

$1 billion stadium project for Brooklyn. Instead, Gehry had to content himself with building New York's tallest residential building, the 76-storey Beekman Tower (2011), close to Brooklyn Bridge. A further honour was his selection as the designer of a national memorial to President Dwight D. Eisenhower, planned for a site in Washington, DC. At the age of eighty he was still engaged in cultural and educational projects worldwide. The New World Symphony Hall in Miami, completed in 2010, appears to mark a further change of direction in Gehry's work, away from the sculptural towards a calmer aesthetic – even if its external projection wall is a dramatic gesture. Had Gehry built little apart from the Bilbao Guggenheim – one of the few recent buildings to impact on the popular consciousness globally – he would still merit recognition as a great builder. But Gehry has been a consistent innovator in terms of building design and technology over half a century of practice and the creator of a succession of extraordinary buildings. He is unquestionably the most celebrated and influential American architect of the present age.

The New World Symphony Hall, Miami, 2010. The exterior lacks Gehry's trademark structural gymnastics, but the building's innovative features include a multi-storey screen on the façade that relays performances taking place inside the hall.

KENZO TANGE

The architect of megastructures

1913–2005

KENZO TANGE EMERGED AS ONE OF JAPAN'S MOST PROMINENT architects during the postwar reconstruction era, in which he played a prominent role as both an architect and urban designer. In 1949 he won the national competition for the Hiroshima Peace Centre where, in addition to the entire Peace Park, he designed and completed his well-known Hiroshima Peace Memorial Museum in 1955. Fashioned in rough reinforced concrete, the design reflected the influence not only of Le Corbusier, but also some elements of traditional Japanese architecture. The building established Tange's reputation at home as well as internationally. Boldly displaying the tectonic purity of its structure, the museum introduced a movement in Japan of which the motto was 'concrete is ours'. Reinforced concrete is well suited to resist both the earthquakes and fires that frequently plague the country. Along with the growing significance of modern architecture's predilection for structural rationality, this launched an architecture in Japan in which structural and engineering considerations played important roles.

Tange was born in Osaka and pursued his architectural education in the engineering department of the University of Tokyo from 1935 to 1938, after which he worked for four years in the office of Kunio Maekawa, who was a disciple of Le Corbusier. In 1942 Tange returned to the university for graduate studies and received his degree in 1946, becoming an assistant professor and in 1963 a full professor in the same university. While an academic he started practising in the design laboratory he established at the university, and just as he had benefited from his experiences in Maekawa's studio, so did many young Japanese architects in his Tange Laboratory, which he reorganized in 1961 as Kenzo Tange and URTEC. Among his students and initial collaborators were Arata Isozaki, Kisho Kurokawa and Fumihiko Maki, who all became leading internationally renowned architects.

Tange's architecture was significantly shaped by the circumstances in which he started his career and grew as an architect. An enormous amount of reconstruction was needed after the devastations of the war. Entire cities and the whole infrastructure of the country needed to be rebuilt. The shortages of material and financial means in the postwar era also dictated the economy of building and the rationality of architecture. This was conducive to the spread of modern architecture, which advocated restrained and even minimalist designs. Contemporary modern architecture also gained special momentum in the 1960s, when Japan emerged from the postwar period and its economy began to soar exponentially. In this unparalleled progress, known as the 'Japanese economic miracle', industrial technology too showed tremendous advances and was to be a significant force in conceiving architecture as well as urban design.

URBAN PLANNING AND DESIGN

Tange became interested in urban planning and design while still a student, and all his architectural works were designed with a strong reference to this larger public realm. His first noted Hiroshima project already had an urban design dimension, as it had to address a larger area of the city. Tange's numerous city hall projects, produced within a government programme to promote new democratic institutions in the country, are further examples. These include the Tokyo Metropolitan Government Office (1957), the Kagawa Prefectural Government Office in Takamatsu (1958) and the Kurashiki City Hall (1960). In addition to creating a powerful and easily identifiable core for each city, these buildings showed new approaches to both tectonic and spatial articulation. While carrying the imprint of the post-and-beam constructional logic of Japanese wooden architecture, they developed this logic further in the dimensions of large and (with the Kurashiki building) increasingly monumental concrete structures.

The rapid industrialization and fast-growing economy of the country also meant explosive urbanization as people rushed to cities – the productive centres of the economy, best represented by Tokyo. The unchecked urbanization resulted in congestion that far surpassed the traditionally tightly woven urban fabric of Japanese cities and produced serious environmental problems – air, water and noise pollution – leading to the impoverishment of urban life. Kenzo Tange and the young architects working with him were acutely aware of these predicaments and sought innovative solutions. They believed that, while reckless industrialization brought Japanese cities to the brink of environmental collapse, industrial technology, if properly applied in architecture and urban design, could also alleviate many of the problems. With this in mind, a group of these young architects launched the Metabolist movement in 1960, which aimed at flexibility as well as easy and ordered expansion of the built environment. Tange strongly influenced and promoted their work and was in turn inspired by their ideas.

In 1960 Tange, assisted by some of his disciples, devised a monumental new urban scheme, his famous 'A Plan for Tokyo', which he envisioned as built partially over the existing urban fabric and partially over the water of Tokyo Bay. This plan was conceived as a megastructural system stretching in linear fashion over a distance of some 30 kilometres (18½ miles). In this extensive scheme all public facilities were arranged between the huge parallel, looped bridges serving as the infrastructure of urban circulation, while residential areas branched out of it. Tange designed both the public and residential units as enormous megastructures, effectively blurring the distinction between architecture and the new city proper. The remarkable detailing of Tange's solution was displayed in the form of a large and impressive physical model.

Kurashiki City Hall, 1960. Cast in reinforced concrete, with details reminiscent of Le Corbusier, the massive building is an early example of Tange's architecture of megastructures.

Tange before his famous 'A Plan for Tokyo' (1960). The unrealized scheme for Tokyo Bay consisted of enormous bridge structures for circulation, and huge buildings over pilotis.

Although 'A Plan for Tokyo' was not built, the experience Tange gained helped him implement many of its inherent ideas within his architectural work. Some of the buildings in the Plan, jointly developed by Tange and Isozaki, were elevated above the ground by means of structural shafts. These served both as the sole vertical support and for the provision of services, including vertical circulation, in the buildings. This solution, in which cylindrical service shafts acted as posts or columns in greatly expanded size and hollowed-out form, became a model for numerous subsequent designs. The 1966 Yamanashi Press and Broadcasting Centre in Kofu is perhaps the best example of Tange's application of this system. The monumental building is elevated and supported by sixteen vertical concrete service shafts of different heights, among which floors, in the form of closed spatial units, stretch like bridges in a way that leaves many gaps and cavities in the overall volume. This porous matrix of megastructural systems, with its remarkable flexibility that could accommodate internal expansion, was the revolutionary realization of a quasi 'city in the air'. Tange also used this model in projects such as his much smaller Shizuoka Press and Broadcasting Centre of 1967 and the

Supported by only sixteen cylindrical shafts, the Yamanashi Press and Broadcasting Centre in Kofu, completed 1966, is the quintessential model of megastructures.

Tange's National Gymnasiums for the 1964 Tokyo Olympic Games. Representing the peak of his most creative period, they were designed with large and unique suspension structures, resulting in highly impressive interiors.

1970 Kuwait Embassy and Chancellery, both in Tokyo. Moreover, the three-dimensional structural matrix returns, in a somewhat modified form, in one of Tange's more recent works, the 1996 Fuji Television Headquarters Building in Tokyo.

PUBLIC SHOWCASES FOR MAJOR NATIONAL EVENTS

The early 1960s gave Tange an opportunity to explore a different kind of structural solution when he was commissioned to design the main facilities of the 1964 Tokyo Olympic Games, the famous National Gymnasiums. Here he applied a system of suspension structures, wherein clusters of steel cables support and comprise the roofs of the two arenas. Working with the talented structural engineer Yoshikatsu Tsuboi, Tange designed the larger arena with two pylons of reinforced concrete 126 metres (413 feet) apart and with two primary cable systems stretched between them, anchored in the ground at both ends. Secondary structures connected these main cables to the concrete compression 'drum' that served as the upper edge of the

266

spectators' grandstands. He defined the smaller arena with a single concrete pylon from which the main cable spiralled out by way of steel supporting rods. Shaped entirely with novel and impressive curvilinear geometry that was also vaguely reminiscent of gently curving Buddhist temple roofs, this magnificent complex of structures – the largest of its kind in the world at the time – is justly regarded today as one of the most important landmarks in 20th-century modern architecture.

The opportunity for Tange to build his largest and arguably most significant megastructural achievement was provided by another major Japanese event, the Osaka Expo in 1970. He was entrusted with the masterplan of the entire site and the design of its infrastructure, including the central Festival Plaza. The Expo was a major showcase for Japan's technological progress in the 1960s, so Tange, once again with the assistance of Tsuboi, designed the Plaza with a colossal steel space-frame structure as its 'roof' – a feat of technological and engineering bravura of unparalleled dimensions. The frame measured some 108 by 292 metres (355 by 958 feet) in plan and was supported by six massive steel-lattice pylons at a height of 30 metres (100 feet). Assembled entirely on the ground, the huge structure was then hoisted into place by hydraulic jacks. Tange designed this megastructure to accommodate several experimental prefabricated capsule houses on display within the frame, thus alluding to his initial vision of a 'city in the air'.

The space-frame roof covering the Festival Plaza at the Osaka Expo, 1970. With its gigantic dimensions, it alluded to a visionary 'city in the air'.

NORMAN FOSTER

Invention and innovation in structure and materials

BORN 1935

THE MONUMENT TO CHRISTOPHER WREN inside St Paul's Cathedral in London is famously inscribed 'Si monumentum requiris, circumspice': if you seek his monument, look around you. It is hard to imagine where such a memorial could be located to commemorate Norman Foster, who stands alongside Wren and Edwin Lutyens as a towering presence in the history of British architecture. In contrast to both his illustrious predecessors, however, Foster's architectural imprint has been global: he has built in more than thirty countries, including China, Japan, the United States, Australia, the Middle East and throughout Europe. Structural invention, the innovative use of materials, the pursuit of memorable but essentially rational form and, increasingly, the search for low-energy, sustainable approaches to building are the key characteristics of Foster's work.

Norman Foster was born to working-class parents in Stockport, Greater Manchester. His upbringing in inner-city Manchester led to employment, at the age of sixteen, as a clerk in the city's town hall, but following national service in the Royal Air Force Foster was able to enter the school of architecture at the University of Manchester. After graduation he secured a fellowship to study for a master's degree at Yale, where Paul Rudolph was the charismatic head and Vincent Scully and Serge Chermayeff were teaching. His experience of America, where he studied and worked between 1961 and 1963, was formative: Foster was inspired by the energy and optimism of the United States and by seeing at first hand the buildings of Frank Lloyd Wright, Mies van der Rohe and Louis Kahn. At Yale he also met Richard Rogers, with whom, on their return to England, he formed the Team 4 Architects practice (the other partners were Foster's future wife Wendy Cheesman and her sister Georgie). In the four years of its existence, Team 4 saw both Foster's and Rogers's approach to architecture transformed, away from traditional 'wet' construction to lightweight building in steel and glass; American precursors, including the West Coast Case Study houses and the work of Mies, were a major influence on this fundamental transition.

Perhaps the most significant product of the Team 4 years was the Reliance Controls factory at Swindon (completed 1966, demolished 1991), a flexible, open-plan container that prefigured the future direction of Foster's architecture. Foster's work at Team 4 and the major projects undertaken by the practice he launched with Wendy Foster in 1967, Foster Associates, were designed in collaboration with the structural engineer Anthony Hunt. Foremost among these were the Willis Faber & Dumas offices (1974) in Ipswich and the Sainsbury Centre for Visual Arts (1977) at the University of East Anglia campus outside Norwich. The latter was a prime example of the integrated enclosure, the 'sleek shed', which he premiered at Reliance Controls and further developed in the 1980s for the terminal building at London's Stansted Airport (opened 1991). The skilful integration of services was a key feature of these projects, as was the manipulation of daylight, a perennial concern of Foster's (who has admitted 'a particular passion for natural light').

The Sainsbury Centre at the University of East Anglia, Norwich, 1977. It offered a radical view of the art museum as a place where paintings, sculpture and other media could be viewed in an informal setting, as well as including teaching space.

GOING GLOBAL

Foster was to work with Hunt on other projects, but with the Hongkong & Shanghai Banking Corporation (HSBC) headquarters in Hong Kong, won in competition in 1979, he began a long collaboration with Ove Arup. Arup was a global operation and Foster's practice itself moved onto a global platform with the Hong Kong project; completed in 1985, it was widely described as 'the most expensive building in history'. Most of Foster's partners moved to Hong Kong, though he remained in London and

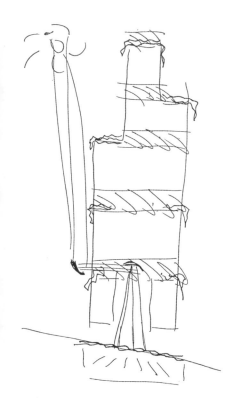

built the foundations there for a continuing practice. The cancellation of an outstanding scheme for a BBC Radio headquarters in central London was a bitter disappointment, but the HSBC building had established Foster as a leading international architect. It was also the first stage in what has since been seen as his reinvention of the tall building, with the flexible working spaces of Willis Faber & Dumas now stacked vertically to create nearly 100,000 square metres (1 million square feet) of offices, with a soaring ten-storey atrium topped by the 'sun scoop' that directs controlled natural light into the heart of the building.

Equally innovative, but with a rather different agenda, was the Commerzbank tower in Frankfurt, a project won in competition in 1991, which featured 'sky gardens' as part of a services strategy that made the structure a pioneer in the use of natural ventilation for tall office buildings. Some of the lessons of the Commerzbank project were applied in the tall office tower for Swiss Re at St Mary Axe in the City of London. Completed in 2004, the 'Gherkin', as it is popularly known, has become a symbol of London to rival Big Ben and St Paul's Cathedral. Foster's belief in building high remains undented, despite the abandonment of the visionary Millennium Tower projects designed respectively for Tokyo Bay and the City of London (the London site eventually housed the Gherkin). He was selected in 2006 to design a 78-storey tower on the Ground Zero site in Manhattan; construction was in abeyance for several years, and Foster had to content himself with the more modest Hearst Tower).

ABOVE *This sketch for the Hongkong & Shanghai Bank (1981–85) shows the 'coat hanger' structural solution that gives the building much of its distinctive character.* OPPOSITE *Although now surrounded by later high-rises, the bank remains a prominent presence on the Hong Kong skyline and is one of the key landmarks of late 20th-century world architecture.*

Although Foster did not complete a major building in London until 1991, his international success led to the award of the Royal Gold Medal for Architecture in 1983, followed by a knighthood (1990), the Order of Merit (1997) and finally a life peerage (1999). A string of international honours includes the Pritzker Prize in 1999. Since the early 1990s Foster's practice (now Foster + Partners) has built extensively in London, including commercial work that reflects the scale of its operations: by 2009

Not merely highly distinctive in shape, Foster's building for Swiss Re at St Mary Axe, London, completed in 2004, is notable as an example of low-energy design.

there were twenty-five offices (some temporary) around the world, and a total payroll of 1,400. In forty years, Foster's practice had evolved from a leading-edge experimental studio to an international business. Inevitably, not all the commercial projects undertaken by the practice reflect the hand of a leading world architect – the HSBC tower at Canary Wharf in London's Docklands (completed 2002), an impressive example of the loyalty of Foster's clients, has none of the innovative features of its predecessor in Hong Kong, though it is characteristically better detailed than most of the buildings in the development. Norman Foster has personally been more involved in those London projects that involved the transformation of public space, including the Millennium Bridge linking the City with Southwark (2000; reopened 2002), the British Museum Great Court (2000) and the reconstruction of Trafalgar Square (2001–4). A particularly significant project was the Sackler Galleries (1985–91) at the Royal Academy of Arts, where Foster added a new gallery and circulation spaces in the interstices between historic buildings.

RECONSTRUCTION AND INFRASTRUCTURE

This experience was put to good use in the reconstruction of the Reichstag building in Berlin as the seat of the parliament of the reunified Germany. For a foreign architect to win the commission to recreate this symbol of German identity was a remarkable achievement, but Foster's first proposal for the Reichstag – making the restored building the focus of a great public space within a huge steel and glass enclosure – was considered too radical. It was also too costly. As built (completed 1999), the scheme includes a restored version of the lost Reichstag dome, which could be seen as a concession to those who wanted the building reinstated much as it was before its ruination in 1945. Yet Foster's dome (or 'cupola', as he prefers to call it) is not an empty symbol: he has argued that it is 'a sign to show that something has changed'. The dome incorporates a public route to the summit of the building, which has become one of the most popular visitor attractions in Berlin. Internally, it incorporates another 'sun scoop' to channel controlled daylight into the debating chamber below. Reinvigorating and extending historic buildings has become an important element in Foster's work: the Royal Academy and British Museum projects have been followed by major schemes, drawing on the British Museum and the Reichstag, for the Museum of Fine Arts in Boston and the Smithsonian Institution in Washington, DC. Foster's lean, minimal approach has become an established way of building in tune with history – the Carré d'Art (1993), for example, sits happily in Nîmes alongside the Maison Carrée, the best preserved of all Roman temples.

ABOVE *Foster at work on the Reichstag project, 1995: success in the competition cemented his international standing.* BELOW *Reichstag, Berlin: cross-sectional drawing of the dome. The completed project represents a classic marriage of old and new.*

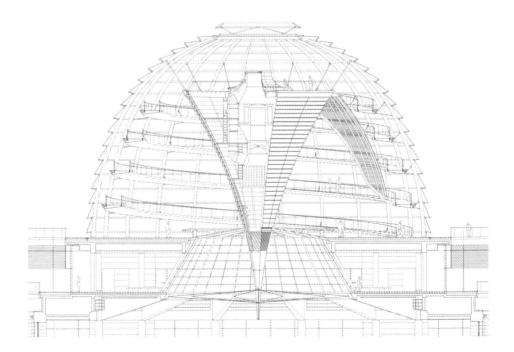

Germany has been a significant focus for Foster's work, both in the field of environmentally progressive design – seen, for example, in a series of office buildings in Duisburg (1991–2003) – and in that of infrastructure. The reconstruction of Dresden's main railway station (completed 2005), burnt out by wartime bombs, is one of a number of major Foster projects in this sector, which also include the spectacular underground station at Canary Wharf (completed 2000) in London and the stations for the metro system in Bilbao (1988–97), some with memorable 'Fosterito' entrance canopies. Foster has always had a passion for flying, and three major airport terminals have followed on from the success of Stansted. Chek Lap Kok in Hong Kong, designed in collaboration with Arup, opened in 1998. Its great roof is formed of 122 steel lattice shells, each covering 1,300 square metres (13,993 square feet) – a 'kit of parts' structure on a huge scale and arguably the finest of Foster's airports. The terminal at Beijing Airport, constructed in only two years by a workforce of 50,000 and opened in time for the 2008 Olympics, is the world's largest airport building (and possibly the world's largest building), notable not only for its size, but also for the refinement and elegance of its structure. The new Queen Alia Airport in Jordan is currently under construction.

Chek Lap Kok Airport, Hong Kong, completed in 1998. With its uncluttered interior and plentiful natural light, it is one of Foster's most successful airport designs.

At the heart of Foster's success over nearly half a century of practice has been his creative and genuinely collaborative relationship with engineers – initially Anthony Hunt, and for many years a succession of leading figures at Arup. It is often difficult, and usually pointless, to seek to unravel the relative contributions of architect and engineer; and many of the most remarkable structural solutions in Foster's oeuvre were driven by his own quest for efficiency and elegance of form. One of the most renowned of recent Foster projects is the Millau Viaduct (completed 2004), which carries the A75 autoroute 270 metres (890 feet) above the river Tarn in southern France. The structural engineering of the bridge, the world's tallest, is by the French engineer Michel Virlogeux, but the extreme elegance of the structure reflects Foster's input.

CONTINUING INNOVATION

The Foster office is not only the base for a highly successful global practice, but also a centre for research and innovation; Foster himself has always declined to do the obvious. Back in the 1970s he jettisoned designs for the Sainsbury Centre just as the building was about to go out to tender. Years later, persuading the client to back his instincts, he suddenly abandoned plans for a masted roof for the new Wembley Stadium (completed 2007) in favour of one suspended from a great arch, which has since become another of his London landmarks. In recent years a strong interest in sustainable design, which has characterized the practice from the 1970s on, has become ever more central to its work. The most spectacular product to date is the new city of Masdar (ongoing) in Abu Dhabi, designed by Foster + Partners as a carbon-neutral settlement covering six square kilometres (over two square miles) with a projected future population of 50,000.

In 2010 Norman Foster celebrated his seventy-fifth birthday. Though largely resident abroad, he has remained an active figurehead for his London-based practice. The extent of his achievements, not least the part he has played in making London a global architectural capital, is indisputable. He has been responsible for a number of masterly projects among more than a thousand undertaken by his office since the 1960s, including nearly 250 completed buildings. Foster's own personality and the influence he has maintained over the work of his international practice have set the output of his practice apart from that of its rivals, confirming his own place in architectural history.

Foster's masterplan for the new city of Masdar, Abu Dhabi, is a blueprint for a sustainable urban future. Housing up to 50,000 people, the city will use renewable energy sources.

SANTIAGO CALATRAVA

A universal designer

BORN 1951

TODAY, IN A TIME DOMINATED BY SPECIALIZATION and the consequent fragmentation of knowledge, there are very few designers who can be called universal, but Santiago Calatrava is one of these few. He has designed, with seemingly equal ease and success, a huge range of projects large and small, from bridges, buildings and urban complexes to furniture, ceramics and sculpture. Not only can he produce dream-like sensual and visual analogies: he also employs cutting-edge technology and scientific analytical tools. Based on this holistic approach, Calatrava has succeeded in demonstrating that newly built infrastructure does not have to be solely an expensive necessity, psychologically dull and environmentally disruptive. He has shown that these constructions can also be culturally significant and even poetic, enhancing the sense of identity and community.

Santiago Calatrava Valls was born in 1951 in the village of Benimamet, now part of Valencia. His childhood years were spent in a declining agrarian society under the shadow of Franco's oppressive political regime, but it was also an environment of natural beauty with a rich architectural heritage. He studied at the School of Architecture as well as the School of Arts and Crafts in Valencia and, soon after graduating in 1975, he went to Zurich to study engineering at the Swiss Federal Institute of Technology (ETH). His doctoral thesis, 'On the Foldability of Space Frames' (1981), was an interdisciplinary investigation involving topology, mechanical and civil

Foldable frame structure, from Calatrava's thesis 'On the Foldability of Space Frames', 1981.

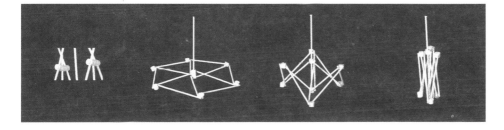

engineering. He wanted to solve a practical problem: how to fold three-dimensional umbrella-like spatial structures, which ultimately would be used to span a large area, by first transforming them into flat planar surfaces, or even into a linear 'stick' like a shut umbrella. The inspiration and implications were clearly technological: the US space agency NASA was already asking this question regarding complex devices that had to be stored compactly for transit in space capsules and then opened up once in space. From the architectural point of view, the answer could be used to develop roofs that would open and close as needed, providing flexible dividers to accommodate a variety of uses. There was also an aesthetic aspect, already discussed by the Futurists and Constructivists, associated with the desire to capture the idea of mobility, the dynamic continuum of space, in the form of iconic structures. In his thesis Calatrava tried to answer this question through analysis, developing a systematic method for constructing such structures from the simple to the more complex. The practical applications of his work were limited but the pragmatic implications were enormous, endowing him with the powerful capacity to envision new structures that moved, that accommodated movement or that represented movement.

During his final years at the ETH and the first few years after he had set up his practice in Zurich, Calatrava became involved with a series of theoretical bridge projects named after their location: the Alpine bridges. Again the idea was to use rational thinking to investigate the form and function of the basic elements that make up a bridge and to explore alternative ways of combining them. It was while engaged in this enquiry, however, that Calatrava began to think that analytical methods were not enough and that they had to be complemented with imagination, analogy and metaphor, based on growing plants, flying birds or the moving human body. He began applying his new approach to a variety of commissions involving the design of parts of buildings and structural components: folding roofs, moving doors and mobile enclosure walls, beams, columns, balconies and small-scale buildings. This led to the emergence of the 'Calatrava style' – a way of thinking, rather than a formal language.

THE 'CALATRAVA STYLE'

Commissioned in 1983 to design the Ernsting Warehouse in Coesfeld, Germany, a distribution centre for a casual-wear retailer, Calatrava proposed cladding the new building in a single material – untreated aluminium – and shaping it to produce different effects of texture and light that would create an image suggesting the ripple effect of textiles. The most effective part of the scheme was in the doors of the loading bays, constructed out of vertical slats hinged along a curved line and connected at their lower points to a horizontal frame that could be raised or lowered. When the frame was raised, the vertical slats left the plane of the façade and, thanks to the differentiated triple-jointing of each U-shaped extruded profile, offered a graceful cantilevered roof resembling the drapery and folds of a creased cloth. Despite being protected by a patent, the design has been replicated around the world ever since.

Calatrava experimented further with the relation between structure and movement in his first major project, the Stadelhofen railway station in Zurich (1983–90), for which he won a competition. The site was challenging, squeezed into a dense urban area next to a hill that had once been a bastion of the city's fortifications. Calatrava carved an open platform while respecting the slope of the terrain, retaining the hill with a concrete box-beam. Above the box-beam, running its full length, is a promenade, enhanced by a cable trellis to create a transparent green 'canopy' that softens the station's intrusion into its environment and relates to the green area behind. From this promenade, travellers reach the platforms via stairs and a lift, or cross over bridges that span the tracks to the lower side. Driven by the articulation and representation of movement, the overall scheme is a compact, 'finely woven' complex of conduits at multiple levels, different interlocking scales and qualities of movement: the effect is accentuated by the flow of light penetrating all levels through the glass roof and the glass blocks of the walkways.

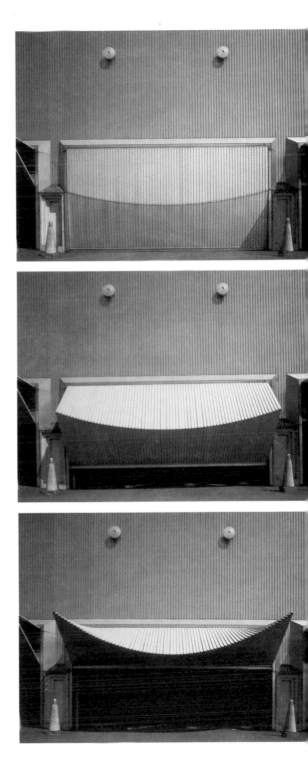

The loading bays of the Ernsting Warehouse in Coesfeld (1983–85), constructed of sinuous aluminium slats.

pestico 1   pestico 2   puente de Sevilla

en ste capitulo se explora la analogía y el
cambio de escala

el mismo personaje
difiere según a realidad
i que de ella suma
etapa definitiva

definición del proyecto del puente de Sevilla

THE POETICS OF MOVEMENT IN STRUCTURES

Equally dedicated to the celebration of the poetics of movement in structures is the Alamillo Bridge and Cartuja Viaduct in Seville (1987–92), built for the Universal Expo. In contrast to the complexity and compactness of the Zurich station scheme, the Seville bridge is serene and lean, but not static. Reflecting the intricacies of the programme and the site, movement is both functionally accommodated and subtly represented. The Alamillo Bridge confounds the assumption that bridges are static structures, by definition symmetrical and rigid, made up exclusively of compression or tension elements calculated in order to offer the maximum span through the minimum of materials. By contrast, it shows that bridges can be seen instead as complex objects that carry out multiple functions in the face of irregular and unexpected constraints. They must resist wind, rain and seismic forces, and most of the time they rest on uneven ground and fit into irregular sites. As well as being conduits for vehicles, bridges are social places for looking at the view, contemplation and meeting.

Designing the Alamillo Bridge, Calatrava paid particular attention to the totality of these requirements, including small but significant details from the human point of view, such as the provision of shade and light for the pedestrians. The complex scheme of the bridge – its strange configuration, leaning asymmetrical pylon, hexagonal steel box-beam spine deck supported by cantilevered steel wings, the unprecedented elimination of back stays to support the leaning pylon (the weight of the deck is sufficient to counterbalance the pylon's forces) – comes from a refusal to reduce and suppress as well as a desire to include and enrich, fusing all these functions into a single 'well-formed whole'. In addition, the paradoxical shape of the structure, looking as if it is ready to collapse in the state of being raised, implies what has been called a 'pregnant moment': a narrative of movement, catastrophe and rebirth. The basic concept of the back-leaning pylon can be traced back to earlier Calatrava sculptures consisting of an inclined stack of marble cubes balanced by a tensioned wire. As with his scientific investigations, making sculpture is not an autonomous activity. It is integral to the overall process of design thinking dedicated to the construction of concrete spatial–sensual hypotheses – as opposed to the abstract explorations of folding frames seen in his dissertation. Even if the sculptural configurations are extreme and paradoxical, as with his Suspended Void or Discerning Eye (1993), they are still potentially instructive for structures yet to come.

Preliminary sketches by Calatrava for the Alamillo Bridge, built for the Universal Expo in Seville, 1987–92.

Although most Calatrava projects are linked to special events or sites, his repertoire is not confined to 'star' situations. In contrast to the suspended serenity of Alamillo Bridge, emerging out of a vast open plain, the Puerto Bridge in Ondarroa, Spain (1989–95), is intricate and dramatic without being offensive or exhibitionistic. Despite its idiosyncratic configuration, the bridge shares a profound relationship with its surroundings, echoing attributes of the site. Its curved shape, snugly fitting into the curve of the port, reflects the forms of the anchored boats and gentle slopes of the surrounding hills, while its hard-edged white colour and geometry emphasize the unique qualities of the site and define its identity.

Chords Bridge for the Jerusalem Light Rail tramway, 2002–11.

Calatrava's projected World Trade Center PATH Terminal, New York City, begun 2003.

SITES DEFINED BY CRISIS AND CONFLICT

Many Calatrava infrastructure projects, especially bridges, are in socially challenging areas, confronting environments in a state of crisis, neighbourhoods undergoing economic decline, forgotten communities, obsolescent industrial sites, or renowned sites torn by tension and conflict. The Chords Bridge for the new Jerusalem Light Rail tramway (2002–11), at the junction of Jaffa Road, was a chaotic and degraded site, despite its history and significance: in ancient times, this was the road that connected the Old City of Jerusalem with Jaffa on the Mediterranean, and today it links Jerusalem with Ben Gurion Airport and Tel Aviv. Calatrava's cable-stayed scheme, with one inclined pylon and a deck in curved alignment, is intended to act as a modern landmark and gateway to the city. The inclined pylon consists of a triangular steel box that diminishes towards the top. The cables are arranged in a reverted alignment, generating a parabolic shape that appears to evolve three-dimensionally, and the pylon seems to jump out of this configuration like a huge flame blown by the desert wind, or like a massive tilting mast that announces Jerusalem as 'a port on the shore of eternity', the 'Venice of God'.

Equally important in terms of function and meaning is one of Calatrava's most recent works, the permanent World Trade Center PATH Terminal in New York City, due to open in 2014. Commissioned by the Port Authority of New York and New Jersey, the complex serves both commuter and subway trains, offers a potential rail link to the airport, and is part of the renewal project following the 9/11 terrorist attack in 2001. It is intended not only to replace what the September 11th tragedy destroyed, but also to act as a catalyst in bringing back to the area around-the-clock urban activities and new hope to the traumatized neighbourhood. The aim is to recapture not only the vitality of the district before 9/11 but also a spirit that has been lost in New York since the 1930s: the commitment to large-scale, public urban and infrastructure projects that serve and celebrate the community in the manner of Penn Station, Grand Central Terminal, the Brooklyn Bridge and Central Park. Once again movement, real and virtual, dominates Calatrava's scheme. In addition to the fluid geometry, the dynamic interpenetration of solids and voids, provision is made for daylight to flood into the underground space at all levels up to the train platform, approximately 21 metres (70 feet) below the street. At night the direction of light is reversed, the source located in the underground area 'serving as a lantern' for the neighbourhood above. In addition, a bird-like mobile structure marks the entrance to the underground facility.

Calatrava used a similar structure for his first completed American project, the Quadracci Pavilion at the Milwaukee Art Museum (1994–2001). Opening and closing its wings like a gigantic bird hovering majestically alongside the shore of Lake Michigan, ready to take off, it serves as a shading device but also to signal museum events. When the wings open, their sides parallel the inclined pylon that holds a cable-stayed footbridge connecting the exhibition pavilion to the city, symbolically suggesting the link between art and everyday life. In the case of the World Trade Center Terminal, the winged structure evokes a dove and a phoenix, indicating the victory of life over death and intelligence over brute force. The hub could be said to summarize Calatrava's oeuvre and the ideals behind it – opening up pathways where once there were natural or man-made barriers, enabling dialogue and offering, both physically and symbolically, the freedom needed for creativity and vice versa.

The mobile brise-soleil *of the Quadracci Pavilion, Milwaukee Art Museum, 1994–2001.*

KENGO KUMA

An architecture of materiality and immateriality

BORN 1954

SINCE THE EARLY 1990s KENGO KUMA HAS EMERGED as one of the most significant representatives of Japanese architecture in the 'post-bubble' era. Establishing his office (Kengo Kuma & Associates) in Tokyo in 1990, he has produced a large and fast-increasing number of major projects that have attracted the attention and admiration of a wide range of audiences including the public, fellow architects and critics, as well as clients all over the world. His works have won many prestigious awards and prizes, and have been exhibited in well-known galleries and museums in Japan, China, France, Italy, Germany, Poland, Finland, the UK and the US. With interest in his architecture growing, Kuma's designs are now sought after both in Japan and beyond: over half his commissions come from abroad and, with branch offices in Paris and Beijing, he has completed works in France, China, Korea, Italy, Germany, the UK and the US.

Kuma was born in Yokohama, receiving his master's degree in architecture from the University of Tokyo in 1979. He then spent a year as a visiting scholar in the Graduate School of Architecture at Columbia University, New York City, from 1985 to 1986. Kuma's ideas and understanding of architecture have been shaped by diverse experiences and influences. The first of these was the traditional Japanese wooden house, with its deep shadowy interiors, where he lived as a child. Later, the newly constructed National Gymnasiums in Tokyo, designed by Kenzo Tange, had a lasting impact on the ten year old, influencing his decision to become an architect. In the late 1970s Kuma studied under Hiroshi Hara at the University of Tokyo, and his mentor's interest in domestic and vernacular architectures drew his attention to these areas at a time when they were not sources of inspiration for most architects. Similarly, he was attracted to the 'floating world' of Hara's sensual designs, in which reality and illusion were seamlessly blended. Yet Kuma differed from his mentor in that he favoured a less decorative interpretation of traditional models – which, in addition to those of Japan, included for him many examples of native African architecture, drawn from his extensive travels there in 1979, as a member of Hara's university research group.

BLENDING ARCHITECTURE INTO ITS ENVIRONMENT

After some brief initial ventures into Postmodern classicism that proved less than successful, Kuma radically changed the direction of his architecture in the early 1990s. He redefined his modus operandi in order to better achieve his goal, as stated in his famous motto: 'I want to erase architecture.' With this strong determination to blend his architecture into its environment, his first strategy was to bury buildings, as much as possible, underground. Among these projects are the remarkable small Kirosan Observatory (Yoshiumi-cho, Oshima Island, 1994) and the Kitakami Canal Museum (Ishinomaki, 1999). However, as opportunities for such a mode of building are rather limited, he expanded his range with a sharp focus on materials, learning from the techniques of traditional Japanese architecture, which was conceived in natural materials as an integral part of the surroundings rather than a stand-alone monument. Lessons drawn from the timeless example of *sukiya* (tearoom) style residences have also helped him foster an ecological and environmentally friendly architecture, which since the mid-1990s has become increasingly important under the new and more restrictive conditions of severe economic recession and limited energy sources. Yet Kuma's architecture is not limited to mere pragmatic considerations.

While Kuma's work is minimalist in response to the new sobering realities in Japan and now also beyond, it is not devoid of human significance; on the contrary, it richly rewards both users and keen observers with its refined, quiet beauty and strong sense of 'less is more'. His designs, with their understatement and simplicity of architectural form or volume, display a welcome anonymity. For example, the Hiroshige Museum of Art (Bato, Nakagawa-machi, 2000) is a simple extended one-storey pitched-roof glass building covered completely by dense wooden slats. The Plastic House (Tokyo, 2002), the LVMH Group headquarters (Shinsaibashi, Osaka, 2004), and even the large Nagasaki Prefectural Art Museum (2005) and Asahi Broadcasting Corporation building (Osaka, 2008) are shaped as straightforward geometric compositions, placating rather than adding to the chaos of their volatile urban settings.

Guided by a renewed Japanese sensibility towards the built environment, Kuma's approach is a clear rejection of the overly flamboyant and excessively decorative formal designs that characterized much, if not all, of the architecture built in Japan during the 'bubble era' of the 1980s and early 1990s. It also testifies to his refusal to participate in the now widespread fashion, encouraged by Frank Gehry's 'Bilbao effect', of producing twisted, contorted and seductive – yet too often empty – architectural images. As the architectural historian William Curtis has observed: 'Architecture today is in danger of degenerating into a game played with over-complicated forms and

Entrance to the Hiroshige Museum of Art, Bato, 2000. The building is a simple glass space enveloped in delicate screens made of densely spaced wooden slats.

computer-generated images ... [which demonstrates] an obsession with willful imagery, excessive visual rhetoric and vapid form-making for its own sake.'

HYPNOTIC AND SENSORY ARCHITECTURE

Indeed, Kuma's intention is not the creation of strong idiosyncratic forms or architecture as visual spectacle, so he does not rely on arbitrary structural or technological bravado. Rather, he concentrates unfailingly on the totality of architectural experience which, though involving the visual attributes of the built work, yet transcends them by extending that experience to all the faculties of human perception, especially tactility and movement. In our accelerated age of commodification and instant gratification, his almost hypnotic sensory architecture – with its sophisticated spatial articulation, vibrant and sensuous surfaces, subtle details and shifting patterns of light and transparency – heightens our perceptive sensibilities and invites us to slow down and take our time within it. Only through such intimate interaction with his buildings can we as observers discover and fully appreciate the value and richness invested in them.

Many of these qualities in Kuma's designs derive from his strong and particular emphasis on architecture's materiality, as well as the craftsmanship of its construction and tectonic precision. Kuma experiments with the broadest possible range of materials: from the natural, including wood, bamboo, paper, vines and other plants and stone, to the manufactured, such as plastic, synthetic fabric, vinyl, metals and glass. However, rather than relying on the substantiality, bulk and weight of these materials, Kuma aims to render them as ethereal matter by 'breaking' them down or using their smallest units in 'infinitely' repetitive matrices, light textures and delicate veils. He

applies this strategy, which he calls 'particlization', especially when the material (i.e. wood or stone) is bulky and heavy, as can be seen in the Stone Plaza and Museum (Nasu, 2000). Whatever the material, Kuma is intent on finding a way to turn it into permeable membranes and screens that lightly and ambiguously envelop, rather than solidly and clearly demarcate, the boundaries of his buildings or spaces, thereby filtering light and the environment into the realm of architecture.

Although Kuma's designs are patently contemporary, one might even say modern, they unfailingly reveal a close relation to the attributes of traditional Japanese architecture. Like their historic counterparts, his works (which he often calls 'weak architecture') tend to be light and fragile, appearing to gently 'dissolve' into their surrounding natural or urban landscape. Examples include, among many others, the Lotus House (Zushi, 2005), the Ginzan Onsen Fujiya Ryokan (Obanazawa, 2006), the Chokkura Plaza and Shelter (Takenazawa, 2006), the Yien East/Archipelago (Kyoto, 2007) and the Garden Terrace Hotel (Nagasaki, 2009). His growing number of teahouse projects also attest to this relationship. Each of these small structures is constructed with a different material and an innovative technique that uses, as always, various 'soft technologies'. Kuma is thus set to redefine the essence of this well-known historic type of architecture. Altogether Kuma's work demonstrates that he is committed as much to modernity as to Japanese traditions, without mimicking either of them.

ABOVE *Lobby of the Ginzan Onsen Fujiya Ryokan, Obanazawa, 2006. The tall screens are made of bamboo strips 4 mm (⅛ in.) thin.* OPPOSITE ABOVE *Roof terrace of the Garden Terrace Hotel, Nagasaki, 2009.* OPPOSITE BELOW *The Lotus House, Zushi (2005), is designed with a perforated stone curtain, offering both privacy and an intimate relationship with the garden.*

CONTRIBUTORS

SUSSAN BABAIE is an art historian specializing in the Islamic world, especially Persian architecture and manuscript production in the 17th and 18th centuries. She has taught at Ludwig Maximilian University, Munich, and at the University of Michigan, and has been a visiting scholar at the Getty Research Institute in Los Angeles. Her publications include *Isfahan and its Palaces: Statecraft, Shi'ism and the Architecture of Conviviality in Early Modern Iran* (2008).

TIM BENTON is Professor of Art History at the Open University (Emeritus), England. His publications include *The Villas of Le Corbusier and Pierre Jeanneret: 1920–1930* (new edn 2007) and *Le Corbusier conférencier* (2007), and he has written numerous chapters and articles on the subjects of Modernism in architecture, Le Corbusier, and Italian architecture of the 1920s and 1930s. He has also co-curated several exhibitions on the prewar period, such as *Art and Power: Europe Under the Dictators 1930–1945* (1995), *Art Deco* (2003) and *Modernism: Designing a New World* (2006).

BOTOND BOGNAR is Professor and Edgar A. Tafel Chair in Architecture at the University of Illinois Urbana-Champaign. For the past thirty-five years he has investigated various aspects of Japanese architecture and urbanism, publishing numerous books, essays and articles on the topic. Among his latest works are *Beyond the Bubble: The New Japanese Architecture* (2008) and *Material Immaterial: The New Work of Kengo Kuma* (2009).

MARTIN BRESSANI is an architect and architectural historian teaching at McGill University's School of Architecture in Montreal. He has published in many of the topical forums for architectural debates, including *Assemblage, Any Magazine* and *Log*, and has contributed essays to many books and scholarly journals. His specialized area of research is French 19th-century architecture, and he is currently completing a monograph on the French architect and theoretician Eugène-Emmanuel Viollet-le-Duc.

STEVEN BRINDLE works as a historian in the Properties Presentation Department of English Heritage, having previously been an Inspector of Ancient Monuments. He has published

extensively on the history of architecture and engineering, including the books *Paddington Station: Its History and Architecture* (2004), *Brunel: The Man Who Built the World* (2005) and *Shot from Above: Aerial Aspects of London* (2006).

TIMOTHY BRITTAIN-CATLIN is the author of *The English Parsonage in the Early Nineteenth Century* (2008) and *Leonard Manasseh and Partners* (2010). An architect and a regular contributor to *The World of Interiors* for more than twenty years, he is also Senior Lecturer at the Kent School of Architecture, University of Kent, and editor of *True Principles*, the journal of the Pugin Society.

KARLA CAVARRA BRITTON is a lecturer at the Yale School of Architecture, where she teaches the history of architecture and urbanism. Her writings include the monograph *Auguste Perret* (2001) and, with Dean Sakamoto, *Hawaiian Modern: The Architecture of Vladimir Ossipoff* (2007). She was also editor of *Constructing the Ineffable: Contemporary Sacred Architecture* (2010).

JAMES CAMPBELL is Fellow in Architecture and History of Art at Queens' College, Cambridge, and a fellow of the Society of Antiquaries. An architect and architectural historian, he is the author of *Building St Paul's* (2007) and has contributed numerous articles on Wren to academic journals.

MIKE CHRIMES has worked as Librarian at the Institution of Civil Engineers, London, for over thirty years. As well as overseeing major computerization projects, he has used his life-long interest in history to promote the institution's historical collections and to develop a better understanding of engineering history. His publications include *Civil Engineering 1839–1889: A Photographic History* (1991) and, as editor, the first two volumes of the *Biographical Dictionary of Civil Engineers in Great Britain and Ireland* (2002, 2007).

GWENAËL DELHUMEAU, an architectural historian, teaches at the École Nationale Supérieure d'Architecture de Versailles. His research focuses on the role of technology in the production of innovative materials and techniques by manufacturers, contractors and inventors. His thesis, *L'invention du béton armé: Hennebique 1890–1914* (1999), was published in 1999 and won the Prix du Livre d'Architecture.

EDWARD DIESTELKAMP is the Building Design Adviser for the National Trust and secretary to its architectural panel, which advises on the conservation, adaptation and design of the Trust's properties throughout England, Wales and Northern Ireland. He has published articles on the history of technology in the building industry and particularly on the use of iron in building construction during the late 18th and 19th centuries.

RICCARDO DIRINDIN received his doctorate in the history of architecture and town planning at the University of Florence and currently works in the Department of Visual Arts at the University of Bologna. His research focuses on Modernism, and in particular on the issues of technology, pleasure and space. He is author of *Lo stile dell'ingegneria: Architettura e identità della tecnica tra il primo modernismo e Pier Luigi Nervi* (2010).

DAVID DUNSTER is a former Roscoe Professor of Architecture at the University of Liverpool, and has taught at Kingston University, University College London, and Rice University, Houston. He has lectured worldwide and written on a wide variety of architectural and urban topics. His publications include *Key Buildings of the Twentieth Century: Volume 1, Houses 1900–1944*, and *Volume 2: Houses 1945–1989* (1985, 1990).

SABINE FROMMEL is director of studies in Renaissance art history at the École Pratique des Hautes Études, Sorbonne. Her specialized field of research is the history of architecture from the 15th to the early 19th centuries, and the relationship between France and Italy. She is the author and editor of many books and articles, including monographs on Sebastiano Serlio and Primaticcio.

CAROL GAYLE is Associate Professor of History at Lake Forest College, Illinois. She is the author (with Margot Gayle) of *Cast-Iron Architecture in America: The Significance of James Bogardus* (1998)

and has published numerous articles on cast-iron architecture for academic journals.

ANDREI GOZAK is an architect, architectural writer and teacher based in Moscow. He is a frequent lecturer at the Moscow Institute of Architecture and at institutions worldwide. Among his publications are monographs on Alvar Aalto and Ivan Leonidov, and a study of the Melnikov House in Moscow.

REHA GÜNAY is an architectural historian who teaches at the Mimar Sinan Fine Arts University and at Yeditepe University, both in Istanbul. His main topics of interest are the preservation of historic buildings, and architectural photography. He has published widely on Turkish architecture and on Sinan, including *Sinan: The Architect and his Works* (2002) and *A Guide to the Works of Sinan the Architect in Istanbul* (2006).

PETER JONES is Emeritus Professor of Philosophy and a former director of the Institute for Advanced Studies in the Humanities at the University of Edinburgh. His research interests focus on the Scottish Enlightenment. He is the author of *Ove Arup: Masterbuilder of the Twentieth Century* (2006), based on exclusive access to Arup's private archive.

EBBA KOCH is a professor of Asian art at the Institute of Art History, Vienna University, and a senior researcher at the Austrian Academy of Sciences. Since 2001 she has been the architectural adviser to the Taj Mahal Conservation Collaborative. Her research interests are Mughal art and architecture, and the artistic connections the Mughals shared with their neighbours and with Europe. Among her publications are *Mughal Architecture* (1991), *Mughal Art and Imperial Ideology* (2001) and *The Complete Taj Mahal* (2006).

GERALD R. LARSON is a professor of architecture at the University of Cincinnati. He has lectured and written widely, and has a particular interest in the history of the skyscraper. He is currently completing a comprehensive study to be titled *Chicago and the Skyscraper, 1832–1891.*

BERTRAND LEMOINE, an architect and engineer, is currently Research Director of the Centre National de la Recherche Scientifique, Paris, and Director of the Atelier International du Grand Paris. He has published over forty books and numerous articles on architecture and construction history, especially on iron and steel constructions such as the Eiffel Tower.

LORETTA LORANCE is an architectural historian who teaches in the School of Visual Arts in New York. Her most recent publication is *Becoming Bucky Fuller* (2009), which re-examines the architect's early career and describes how he constructed for himself the persona of a visionary and forward-looking sage.

ROBERT MCCARTER is an architect and author, and is currently the Ruth and Norman Moore Professor of Architecture at Washington University in St Louis. Among his many books are *Fallingwater: Frank Lloyd Wright* (1994), *Frank Lloyd Wright* (1997), *Louis I. Kahn* (2005) and *Frank Lloyd Wright: Critical Lives* (2006). He is currently preparing books on Alvar Aalto and Carlo Scarpa, and *Architecture as Experience*, a general primer co-authored with Juhani Pallasmaa.

JAYNE MERKEL is an architectural historian and critic, and the author of the monograph *Eero Saarinen* (2005). She is also a contributing editor for *Architectural Design* magazine and *Architectural Record*. Her writing has appeared in *Art in America, Artforum, Harvard Design Magazine* and the *Journal of the Society of Architectural Historians*.

WINFRIED NERDINGER is Professor of Architectural History and Director of the Architectural Museum at the Technical University of Munich. He has curated numerous exhibitions and written many books on the architecture of the 19th and 20th centuries, including monographs on Gottfried Semper and Walter Gropius, and surveys on the architecture of the Weimar Republic and the Nazi era. He is the author of *Frei Otto Complete Works: Lightweight Construction, Natural Design* (2005).

JORDI OLIVERAS teaches architectural theory and criticism at the Universitat Politècnica de Catalunya, and has been a visiting professor at Columbia University, New York, the University of California, Los Angeles, and SIAL at Royal Melbourne University. His current research focuses on modern architecture as a practice of concepts and ideas.

STYLIANE PHILIPPOU is an architect and architectural historian. She has practised in Athens, Edinburgh, London and Paris, and has taught architectural design, history and theory at the universities of Edinburgh and Plymouth. She has lectured internationally on aspects of Brazilian Modernism. Her book *Oscar Niemeyer: Curves of Irreverence* was published in 2008.

PIERRE PINON is an architect and historian. He currently teaches at the École Nationale Supérieure d'Architecture de Paris-Belleville and is a research associate at the Institut National d'Histoire de l'Art, Paris. He has written several works on the history of Paris, including *Paris: Biographie d'une capitale* (1999) and the *Atlas du Paris haussmannien* (2002), and on the history of architecture in the 18th and 19th centuries.

KENNETH POWELL is an architectural historian, critic and consultant based in London. He has written extensively on 20th-century and contemporary British architecture, and is the author of books on the work of Norman Foster, Richard Rogers and other major British architects. He is an honorary fellow of the Royal Institute of British Architects and has served on the Council of the Architectural Association.

PHILIPPE PROST is an architect and planner who teaches at the École Nationale Supérieure d'Architecture de Paris-Belleville. He has published numerous articles and books on military architecture, including *Vauban, le style de l'intelligence: Une oeuvre source pour l'architecture contemporaine* (2008). In addition, he has directed the restoration of a number of Vauban's fortresses and is currently working on a scheme to transform the Monnaie de Paris.

CATHERINE DROUIN-PROUVÉ is a writer and art historian. Together with other members of her family, she is a director of the Société Jean Prouvé, which oversees the conservation of her father's archives. She has contributed numerous articles on Prouvé to journals and exhibition catalogues.

FRANCISCO SANIN is a practising architect and currently Professor and Chair of Graduate Programs at Syracuse University, New York. His research is centred on the relationships between architecture and urban form. He has taught at Princeton University, the Architectural Association in London, Kingston University, and at various institutions around the world.

ORNELLA SELVAFOLTA is Professor of Architectural History at the Politecnico di Milano. Her scholarly fields of interest are the history of landscape, engineering, architecture and applied arts from the 18th to the 20th centuries. She has organized exhibitions on these subjects, participated in international symposiums and published extensively. Her latest writings include 'Milano e la Lombardia', in *Storia dell'architettura italiana. L'Ottocento* (2005) and *Milano 1906: L'Esposizione Internazionale del Sempione e le arti decorative* (2009).

MARTIN STEFFENS is a Berlin-based art historian, writer and curator. He has been editor and co-editor of several architectural history and scientific publications, and also curates exhibitions on the history of art and culture. Since 2008 he has managed '48 Stunden Neukölln', one of the biggest art festivals in Berlin. His book on Schinkel, *Karl Friedrich Schinkel: An Architect in the Service of Beauty*, was published in 2003.

ROBERT TWOMBLY teaches architectural history at the City College of New York. He is the author of *Louis Sullivan: His Life and Work* (1987), editor of *Louis Sullivan: The Public Papers* (1988) and, with Narciso Menocal, co-author of *Louis Sullivan: The Poetry of Architecture* (2000).

ALEXANDER TZONIS is Professor of Architectural Theory at Tsinghua University, Beijing, and Professor Emeritus at Delft University of Technology. He was educated at Yale University, taught at Harvard, and has been visiting professor in many universities worldwide. Among his many titles are *Santiago Calatrava: The Poetics of Movement* (1999), *Le Corbusier: The Poetics of Machine and Metaphor* (2001), and *Santiago Calatrava: The Complete Works* (2004).

SELECT BIBLIOGRAPHY

PIONEERS OF STRUCTURE

FILIPPO BRUNELLESCHI

Bartoli, Lando, *La Rete Magica di Filippo Brunelleschi* (Florence: 1977)

Battisti, Eugenio, *Filippo Brunelleschi* (Milan: 1976)

Boraso, Stefano, *Brunelleschi 1420, Il Paradigma prospetico di Filippo di ser Brunellesco: Il caso delle tavole sperimentali ottico-prospettiche* (Padua: 1999)

Fanelli, Giovanni, *Brunelleschi* (Florence: 1980)

Filippo Brunelleschi nella Firenze del '3-'400 (Florence: 1977)

Filippo Brunelleschi, La sua opera e il suo tempo (Florence: 1977, 1980)

Klotz, Henrich, *Filippo Brunelleschi: The Early Works and the Medieval Tradition* (New York: 1990)

Manetti, Antonio di Tucci, *The Life of Brunelleschi*, intro. Howard Saalman (University Park, PA: 1970)

Ruschi, Pietro, Bomby, Carla and Tarassi, Massimo, *La Città del Brunelleschi* (Florence: 1979–80)

Saalman, Howard, *Filippo Brunelleschi: The Buildings* (London and University Park, PA: 1993)

Saalman, Howard, *Filippo Brunelleschi: The Cupola of Santa Maria del Fiore* (London: 1980)

Trachtenberg, Marvin, *The Dominion of the Eye* (Cambridge: 1997)

Vasari, G., *Lives of the Most Eminent Painters, Sculptors and Architects*, trans. G. du C. de Vere, 10 vols (London: 1912–15; rev edn New York: 1979)

Vescovini, Graziella Federici, 'La Prospettiva del Brunelleschi, Alhazen e Biagio Pelacani a Firenze', in *Filippo Brunelleschi, La sua opera e il suo tempo* (Florence: 1977, 1980), 333–48

QAVAM AL-DIN SHIRAZI

Golombek, Lisa, *The Timurid Shrine at Gazur Gah* (Toronto: 1969)

Golombek, Lisa and Wilber, Donald, *The Timurid Architecture of Iran and Turan*, 2 vols (Princeton: 1988)

O'Kane, Bernard, *Timurid Architecture in Khurasan* (Costa Mesa, CA: 1987)

Wilber, Donald, 'Qavam al-Din ibn Zayn al-Din Shirazi: A Fifteenth Century Timurid Architect', *Architectural History* 30 (1987), 31–44

SINAN

Günay, Reha, *Sinan: The Architect and his Works* (Istanbul: 2009)

Kuran, Abdullah, *Mimar Sinan* (Istanbul: 1986)

Necipoglu, Gülru, *The Age of Sinan: Architectural Culture in the Ottoman Empire* (Princeton and London: 2005)

SHAH JAHAN

Begley, Wayne and Desai, Z. A., *Taj Mahal: The Illumined Tomb: An Anthology of Seventeenth-Century Mughal and European Documentary Sources* (Cambridge, MA: 1989)

Begley, Wayne and Desai, Z. A., 'Ustad Ahmad', in *Macmillan Encyclopedia of Architects* (London: 1982), vol. 1, 39–42

Koch, Ebba, *The Complete Taj Mahal and the Riverfront Gardens of Agra* (London: 2006)

Koch, Ebba, *Mughal Architecture: An Outline of Its History and Development (1526–1858)* (Munich: 1991; 2nd edn New Delhi: 2002)

Nicoll, Fergus, *Shah Jahan: Rise and Fall of the Mughal Emperor* (London: 2009)

Qaisar, A. J., *Building Construction in Mughal India, The Evidence from Painting* (New Delhi: 1988)

CHRISTOPHER WREN

Campbell, James W. P., *Building St Paul's* (London: 2007)

Colvin, Sir Howard, *A Biographical Dictionary of British Architects 1600–1840* (London: 4th edn 2008)

Davies, C. S. L., 'The Youth and Education of Christopher Wren', *English Historical Review*, vol. CXXIII, no. 501 (2008), 300–301

Geraghty, Anthony, *The Architectural Drawings of Sir Christopher Wren at All Souls College, Oxford: A Complete Catalogue* (London: 2007)

Jardine, Lisa, *On a Grander Scale* (London: 2002)

Summerson, John, 'Christopher Wren: Why architecture', in *The Unromantic Castle* (London: 1990), 63–68

SÉBASTIEN LE PRESTRE DE VAUBAN

Blanchard, Anne, *Vauban* (Paris: 1996)

Faucherre, Nicolas and Prost, Philippe (eds), *Le Triomphe de la méthode: le traité de l'attaque des places de M. de Vauban ingénieur du roi* (Paris: 1992)

Monsaingeon, Guillaume, *Vauban un militaire très civil, lettres* (Tours: 2007)

Prost, Philippe, *Vauban le style de l'intelligence* (Paris: 2007)

Virol, Michèle (ed.), *Les Oisivetés de M. de Vauban* (Seyssel: 2007)

THE AGE OF IRON

THOMAS TELFORD

Gibb, A., *The Story of Telford* (London: 1935)

Hadfield, C., *Thomas Telford's Temptation* (Cleobury Mortimer: 1993)

Institution of Civil Engineers, *A Collection of Works of Art and Objects of Historical Interest* (London: 1950)

Maclean, A., *Telford's Highland Churches* (Argyll: 1989)

Paxton, R. A., 'The early development of the long span suspension bridge in Britain', in *Proceedings of an International Conference on Historic Bridges* (Wheeling, WV: 1999)

Paxton, R. A., 'Review of *Thomas Telford's Temptation*', The Institution of Civil Engineers Panel for Historical Engineering Works *Newsletter*, no. 60 (December 1993), 6–7

Penfold, A. E. (ed.), *Thomas Telford: Engineer* (London: 1980)

Rolt, L. T. C., *Thomas Telford* (London: 1958)

Ruddock, T., *Arch Bridges and their Builders, 1735–1835* (Cambridge: 1979)

Smiles, S., *Lives of the Engineers*, vol. II (London: 1861)

Southey, R., *Journal of a Tour in Scotland in 1819* (London: 1929)

Southey, R., 'Review of *The Life of Thomas Telford*', *Quarterly Review*, January–March 1839

Telford, T., *The Life of Thomas Telford, Civil Engineer, Written by Himself*, ed. J. Rickman (London: 1838)

KARL FRIEDRICH SCHINKEL

Bergdoll, Barry, *Karl Friedrich Schinkel: An Architect for Prussia* (New York: 1991)

Haupt, Andreas, *Karl Friedrich Schinkel als Künstler. Annäherung und Kommentar* (Munich and Berlin: 2001)

Schinkel, Karl Friedrich, *Sammlung architektonischer Entwürfe (Collection of Architectural Designs)* (Chicago: repr. 1981)

Snodin, Michael (ed.), *Karl Friedrich Schinkel: A Universal Man* (New Haven: 1991)

Steffens, Martin, *Karl Friedrich Schinkel 1781–1841: An Architect in the Service of Beauty* (Cologne: 2003)

JAMES BOGARDUS

Badger's Illustrated Catalogue of Cast-Iron Architecture [1865], intro. Margot Gayle (New York: 1981)

Bannister, Turpin, 'Bogardus Revisited', Parts I and II, *Journal of the Society of Architectural Historians*, vol. 15, no. 4 (Winter 1956), 12–22, and vol. 16, no. 1 (March 1957), 11–19

Bogardus, James [with Thomson, John W.], *Cast Iron Buildings: Their Construction and Advantages* (New York: 1856, repr. 1858); repr. in Gifford, Don (ed.), *The Literature of Architecture* (New York: 1966), 359–70, and in *The Origins of Cast Iron Architecture in America*, intro. W. Knight Sturges (New York: 1970) [n.p.]

Gayle, Margot and Gayle, Carol, *Cast-Iron Architecture in America: The Significance of James Bogardus* (New York: 1998)

Waite, John G., 'The Edgar Laing Stores (1849)', in Waite, John G. (ed.), *Iron Architecture in New York City* (Albany, NY: 1972), 1–21

Wright, David G., 'The Sun Iron Building', in Dilts, James D. and Black, Catharine G. (eds), *Baltimore's Cast-iron Buildings and Architectural Ironwork* (Centreville, MD: 1991), 22–32

JOSEPH PAXTON

Bird, Anthony, *Paxton's Palace* (London: 1976)

Chadwick, George F., *The Works of Sir Joseph Paxton 1803–1865* (London: 1961)

Colquhoun, Kate, *A Thing in Disguise: The Visionary Life of Joseph Paxton* (London and New York: 2003)

McKean, John, *The Crystal Palace, Joseph Paxton and Charles Fox* (London: 1994)

Piggott, Jan, *Palace of the People: The Crystal Palace of Sydenham 1854–1936* (London: 2004)

Thorne, Robert, 'Paxton and Prefabrication', in Walker, D. (ed.), *The Great Engineers: The Art of British Engineers 1837–1937* (London: 1987), pp. 52–69

VICTOR BALTARD

Delaborde, H., 'Architectes contemporains: Victor Baltard', *Revue des Deux-Mondes*, n. s. 2, II (15 April 1874), 788–811

Garnier, C., 'Notice sur Victor Baltard', *Séance publique annuelle de l'Institut de France* (Paris: 1874)

Lemoine, Bertrand, *Les Halles de Paris. L'histoire d'un lieu, les péripéties d'une reconstruction, la succession des projets, l'architecture d'un monument, l'enjeu d'une cité* (Paris: 1980)

Magne, A., '"Nécrologie" de V. Baltard', *Revue Générale de l'Architecture*, XXXI (1874), columns 86–88

Pinon, Pierre, *Louis-Pierre et Victor Baltard* (Paris: 2005)

Sédille, P., 'Victor Baltard, architecte', *Gazette des Beaux-Arts*, IX (May 1874), 484–96

ISAMBARD KINGDOM BRUNEL

Brindle, Steven, *Brunel – the Man who Built the World* (London: 2005)

Brunel, Isambard, *The Life of Isambard Kingdom Brunel, Civil Engineer* (London: 1870; new edn Stroud: 2006)

Buchanan, Angus, *The Life and Times of Isambard Kingdom Brunel* (London: 2002)

Rolt, L. T. C., *Isambard Kingdom Brunel* (London: 1957)

A. W. N. PUGIN

Atterbury, Paul (ed.), *Pugin: Master of Gothic Revival* (New Haven and London: 1995)

Atterbury, Paul and Wainwright, Clive (eds), *Pugin: A gothic passion* (New Haven and London: 1994)

Hill, Rosemary, *God's Architect* (London: 2007)

Pugin, A. W. N., *Contrasts* (Salisbury: 1836; London: 1841; facsimile edn Reading: 2003)

Pugin, A. W. N., *True Principles* (London: 1841; facsimile edn Reading: 2003)

Stanton, Phoebe, *Pugin* (London: 1971)

EUGÈNE-EMMANUEL VIOLLET-LE-DUC

Auzas, Pierre-Marie (ed.), *Actes du colloque international Viollet-le-Duc, Paris 1980* (Paris: 1980)

Baridon, Laurent, *L'imaginaire scientifique de Viollet-le-Duc* (Paris: 1996)

Bergdoll, Barry (intro.), *The Foundations of Architecture: Selections from the 'Dictionnaire raisonné'* (New York: 1990)

Camille, Michael, *The Gargoyles of Notre-Dame: Medievalism and the Monsters of Modernity* (Chicago and London: 2009)

Damish, Hubert (intro.), *L'architecture raisonnée, extraits du Dictionnaire de l'architecture française* (Paris: 1964), 9–26

Foucart, Bruno (ed.), *Viollet-le-Duc* (Paris: 1980)

Leniaud, Jean-Michel, *Viollet-le-Duc ou les délires du système* (Paris: 1994)

Summerson, John, 'Viollet-le-Duc and the Rational Point of View' [1947], in *Heavenly Mansions and other Essays* (New York: 1998), 135–58

JOHN FOWLER

Chrimes, M. M., 'Sir John Fowler – engineer or manager', *Institution of Civil Engineers Proceedings: Civil Engineering*, 97 (1993), 135–43

Engineering, 4 (1867), 556–59

Humber, W. (ed.), *A Record of the Progress of Modern Engineering*, 4 (1866)

Lee, R., *Colonial Engineer: John Whitton 1819–1898 and the Building of Australia's Railways* (Sydney: 2000)

Mackay, T., *Life of Sir John Fowler* (London: 1900)

Paxton, R. A. (ed.), *100 Years of the Forth Bridge* (London: 1990)

Westhofen, W., *The Forth Bridge* (London: 1890), 64–69

CONCRETE AND STEEL

GIUSEPPE MENGONI

Chizzolini, Gerolamo and Poggi, Felice, 'Piazza del Duomo e Galleria Vittorio Emanuele', in *Milano tecnica dal 1859 al 1884* (Milan: 1885), 195–220

Flory, Massimiliano Finazzer and Paoli, Silvia, *La Galleria di Milano: lo spazio e l'immagine* (Milan: 2003)

Fontana, Vincenzo and Pirazzoli, Nullo, *Giuseppe Mengoni, 1829–1877: un architetto di successo* (Ravenna: 1987)

Gioeni, Laura, *L'affaire Mengoni. La piazza Duomo e la Galleria Vittorio Emanuele di Milano. I concorsi, la realizzazione, i restauri* (Milan: 1995)

Guadet, Julien, *Eléments et théorie de l'architecture*, vol. IV, *Les éléments de la composition* (Paris: 1880), 85–87

Guccini, Anna Maria, 'Giuseppe Mengoni: formazione e professione dai disegni dell'Archivio di Fontanelice', in Guccini, Anna Maria (ed.), *La memoria disegnata. Atti delle Giornate di Studi Mengoniani* (Bologna: 2004), 145–56

Jorini, F. A., 'La cupola della Galleria Vittorio Emanuele', *L'Edilizia Moderna* (1892), 4–6

Ricci, Giulio, *La vita e le opere dell'architetto Giuseppe Mengoni* (Bologna: 1930)

Selvafolta, Ornella, 'Il contratto di costruzione della Galleria Vittorio Emanuele II', in *Il modo di costruire* (Rome: 1990), 433–46

Selvafolta, Ornella, 'La Galleria Vittorio Emanuele II di Milano', in Castellano, Aldo and Selvafolta, Ornella (eds), *Costruire in Lombardia. Aspetti e problemi di storia edilizia* (Milan: 1983), 221–65

WILLIAM LE BARON JENNEY

Condit, Carl, *The Chicago School of Architecture* (Chicago: 1975)

Larson, Gerald R., 'Toward a Better Understanding of the Evolution of the Iron Skeleton Frame in Chicago', *Journal of the*

Society of Architectural Historians, vol. XLVI
(March 1987), 39–48
Turak, Theodore, *William Le Baron Jenney:
A Pioneer of Modern Architecture* (Ann Arbor,
MI: 1986)
Zukowski, John (ed.), *Birth of a Metropolis*
(Chicago: 1987)

GUSTAVE EIFFEL
Bermond, D., *Gustave Eiffel* (Paris: 2002)
Carmona, M., *Eiffel* (Paris: 2002)
Deschodt, E., *Gustave Eiffel: Un illustre inconnu*
(Paris: 2003)
Eiffel, G., *La Tour de trois cents metres* (Paris: 1900;
rev edn, 2 vols, ed. B. Lemoine, Cologne:
2006)
Lemoine, B., *Gustave Eiffel* (Paris: 1984)
Lemoine, B., *La Tour de Monsieur Eiffel* (Paris:
1989)
Loyrette, H., *Gustave Eiffel* (Paris: 1986)
Marrey, B., *La Vie et l'œuvre extraordinaire de
Monsieur Gustave Eiffel ingénieur* (Paris: 1984)
Mathieu, C. (ed.), *Gustave Eiffel: Le Magicien du fer*
(Paris: 2009)
Poncetton, F., *Eiffel: Le Magicien du fer* (Paris:
1939)

FRANÇOIS HENNEBIQUE
Collins, P., *Concrete: The Vision of a New
Architecture* (London: 1959)
Cusack, P., 'Architects and the reinforced concrete
specialist in Britain, 1905–08', *Architectural
History*, vol. XXIX (1986), pp. 183–96
Delhumeau, Gwenaël, *L'invention du Béton Armé:
Hennebique, 1890–1914* (Paris: 1999)
Gubler, J., 'Les beautés du béton armé', in Gubler,
J., *Motion, emotions: Thèmes d'histoire et
d'architecture* (Gollion: 2003)
Simonnet, Cyrille, *Le Béton: Histoire d'un matériau*
(Marseilles: 2005)

ANTONI GAUDÍ
Collins, G. R., *Antonio Gaudí* (New York: 1960)
Collins, G. R., Bassegoda i Nonell, J. and Alex,
W., *Antonio Gaudí: Designs and Drawings*
(New York: 1968)
De Solà-Morales, I. and Català Roca, F., *Gaudí*
(Stuttgart: 1983)
Lahuerta, J. J., *Antoni Gaudí 1852–1926:
Architecture, Ideology and Politics* (Milan: 2003)
Martinell, C., *Gaudí: His Life, His Theories,
His Work* (Barcelona: 1975)
Sert, J. L. and Sweeney, J. J., *Antoni Gaudí*
(London: 1960)

LOUIS H. SULLIVAN
De Wit, Wim (ed.), *Louis H. Sullivan: The Function
of Ornament* (New York: 1986)
Schmitt, Ronald E., *Sullivanesque: Urban
Architecture and Ornamentation* (Chicago: 2002)
Twombly, Robert, *Louis Sullivan: His Life and
Works* (New York: 1986)
Twombly, Robert (ed.), *Louis Sullivan: The Public
Papers* (Chicago: 1988)
Weingarden, Lauren S., *Louis H. Sullivan:
The Banks* (Cambridge, MA: 1987)

FRANK LLOYD WRIGHT
Levine, Neil, *Frank Lloyd Wright, Architect*
(Princeton: 1997)
Lipman, Jonathan, *Frank Lloyd Wright and the
Johnson Wax Buildings* (New York: 1986)
McCarter, Robert, *Frank Lloyd Wright* (London:
1997)
McCarter, Robert (ed.), *On and By Frank Lloyd
Wright: A Primer of Architectural Principles*
(London: 2005)
Riley, Terrence (ed.), *Frank Lloyd Wright, Architect*
(New York: 1994)
Sergeant, John, *Frank Lloyd Wright's Usonian
Houses* (New York: 1976)

AUGUSTE PERRET
Britton, Karla, *Auguste Perret* (London: 2001)
Cohen, Jean-Louis, Abram, Joseph and Lambert,
Guy, *Encyclopédie Perret* (Paris: 2002)
Collins, Peter, *Concrete: The Vision of a New
Architecture* (London: 1959)
Culot, Maurice et al., *Les Frères Perret: L'oeuvre
complete* (Paris: 2000)
Frampton, Kenneth, *Studies in Tectonic Culture*
(Cambridge, MA: 1995)
Gargiani, Roberto, *Auguste Perret, 1874–1954*
(Milan: 1993)

MIES VAN DER ROHE
Banham, Reyner, *Design by Choice* (London: 1981)
Carter, Peter, *Mies van der Rohe at Work* (London:
1999)
Mertins, Detlef (ed.), *The Presence of Mies*
(Princeton: 1996)
Neumeyer, Fritz, *The Artless Word: Mies van der
Rohe on the Building Art*, trans. Mark
Jarzombek (Cambridge, MA: 1994)
Oechslin, Werner et al., *Mies van der Rohe in
America* (New York: 2001)
Schulze, Franz, *Mies van der Rohe: A Critical
Biography* (Chicago: 1995)
Spaeth, David, *Mies van der Rohe* (London and
New York: 1985)

LE CORBUSIER

Benton, T., *The Villas of Le Corbusier and Pierre Jeanneret 1920–1930* (Basel and Boston: 2007)

Curtis, W., *Le Corbusier: Ideas and Forms* (London: 1986)

Le Corbusier, Cohen, J.-L. et al., *Toward an Architecture* (Los Angeles: 2007)

Moos, S. von, *Le Corbusier: Elements of a synthesis* (Rotterdam: 2009)

Samuel, F., *Le Corbusier in Detail* (Amsterdam, Boston and London: 2007)

KONSTANTIN MELNIKOV

Khan-Magomedov, S., *Konstantin Melnikov* (Stroyizdat: 1990)

Lukhmanov, N., *Club Architecture* (Moscow: 1930)

Pallasmaa, Juhani with Gozak, Andrei, *The Melnikov House* (London: 1996)

Starr, F., *Melnikov: Solo Architect in a Mass Society* (Princeton: 1978)

Strigalev, A. and Kokkinaki, I., *Konstantin Stepanovich Melnikov: World of the Artist* (Moscow: 1985)

PIER LUIGI NERVI

Dirindin, Riccardo, *Lo stile dell'ingegneria. Architettura e identità della tecnica tra il primo modernismo e Pier Luigi Nervi* (Venice: 2010)

Huxtable, Ada Louise, *Pier Luigi Nervi* (New York, London and Milan: 1960)

Nervi, Pier Luigi, *Aesthetics and Technology in Building* (Cambridge, MA: 1965)

Nervi, Pier Luigi, *Costruire correttamente. Caratteristiche e possibilità delle strutture cementizie armate* (Milan: 1955, 2nd edn 1965; New York: 1956)

Olmo, Carlo and Chiorino, Cristiana (eds), *Pier Luigi Nervi. Architecture as Challenge* (Cinisello Balsamo [Milan]: 2010)

NEW VISIONS

R. BUCKMINSTER FULLER

Baldwin, J., *BuckyWorks* (New York: 1997)

Chu, Hsiao-Yun and Trujillo, Roberto, *New Views on Buckminster Fuller* (Stanford, CA: 2009)

Fuller, R. B. with Marks, R. W., *The Dymaxion World of Buckminster Fuller* (New York: 1963, repr. 1973)

Gorman, Michael John, *Designing for Mobility* (Milan and New York: 2005)

Lorance, Loretta, *Becoming Bucky Fuller* (Cambridge, MA: 2009)

Zung, Thomas T. K., *Buckminster Fuller: Anthology for a New Millennium* (New York: 2002)

OVE ARUP

Drew, Philip, *The Masterpiece: Jørn Utzon, A Secret Life* (Melbourne: 1999)

Francis, A. J., *The Cement Industry, 1796–1914: A History* (Newton Abbot: 1977)

Hoggett, Peter (ed.), 'Ove Arup's 90th Birthday Issue', *The Arup Journal*, vol. 20, 1 (Spring 1985)

Jones, Peter, *Ove Arup, Masterbuilder of the Twentieth Century* (New Haven and London: 2006)

Morreau, Patrick (ed.), *Ove Arup 1895–1988* (London: 1988)

Saint, Andrew, *Architect and Engineer: A Study in Sibling Rivalry* (New Haven and London: 2007)

Sommer, Degenhard, Stöcher, Herbert and Weisser, Lutz, *Ove Arup & Partners* (Basel: 1994)

LOUIS I. KAHN

Brownlee, David and De Long, David, *Louis I. Kahn: In the Realm of Architecture* (New York: 1991)

Gast, Klaus-Peter, *Louis I. Kahn: The Idea of Order* (Basel: 1998)

Giurgola, R., *Louis I. Kahn* (Boulder, CO: 1975)

Latour, Alessandra (ed.), *Louis I. Kahn: Writings, Lectures, Interviews* (New York: 1991)

Leslie, Thomas, *Louis. I. Kahn: Building Art, Building Science* (New York: 2005)

McCarter, Robert, *Louis I. Kahn* (London: 2005)

JEAN PROUVÉ

Archieri, Jean-François and Levasseur, Jean-Pierre, *Jean Prouvé, cours du CNAM/1957–1970* (Liège: 1990)

Jean Prouvé, La poétique de l'objet technique (Weil am Rhein: 2004)

Lavalou, Armelle (ed.), *Jean Prouvé par lui-même* (Paris: 2001)

Peters, Nils, *Jean Prouvé* (Cologne: 2006)

Sulzer, Peter, *Jean Prouvé, Œuvre complète*, 4 vols (Basel: 1995–2008)

OSCAR NIEMEYER

Deckker, Zilah Quezado, *Brazil Built: The Architecture of the Modern Movement in Brazil* (New York: 2001)

Evenson, Norma, *Two Brazilian Capitals: Architecture and Urbanism in Rio de Janeiro and Brasília* (New Haven and London: 1973)

Niemeyer, Oscar, *The Curves of Time: The Memoirs of Oscar Niemeyer* (London: 2000)

Philippou, Styliane, *Oscar Niemeyer: Curves of Irreverence* (New Haven and London: 2008)

Schwartz, Jorge (ed.), *Brasil 1920–1950: De la Antropofagia a Brasília* (Valencia: 2000)

Vidal, Laurent, *De Nova Lisboa à Brasília: l'invention d'une capitale (XIXe–XXe siècles)* (Paris: 2002)

EERO SAARINEN

De Long, David G. and Peatross, C. Ford (eds), *Eero Saarinen: Buildings from the Balthazar Korab Archive* (New York: 2008)

Merkel, Jayne, *Eero Saarinen* (New York: 2005)

Nakamura, Toshio (ed.), 'Eero Saarinen', *Architecture and Urbanism*, extra cdn, no. A+U E8404 (April 1984)

Pelkonen, Eeva-Liisa and Albrecht, Donald (eds), *Eero Saarinen: Shaping the Future* (New Haven: 2006)

Román, Antonio, *Eero Saarinen: An Architecture of Multiplicity* (New York: 2003)

Saarinen, Aline (ed.), *Eero Saarinen on His Work* (London and New Haven: 1962)

Temko, Allan, *Eero Saarinen* (New York: 1962)

FREI OTTO

Burkhardt, Berthold (ed.), *Frei Otto: Schriften und Reden 1951–1983* (Braunschweig and Wiesbaden: 1984)

Mitteilungen des Instituts für Leichte Flächentragwerke, Universität Stuttgart, 40 vols (German and English) (Stuttgart: 1969–2004)

Nerdinger, Winfried (ed.), *Frei Otto Complete Works: Lightweight Construction, Natural Design* (Basel, Boston and Berlin: 2005)

Otto, Frei, *Das hängende Dach* (Berlin: 1954)

Otto, Frei and Rasch, Bodo, *Finding Form: Towards an Architecture of the Minimal* (Stuttgart: 1995)

Roland, Conrad, *Frei Otto Structures* (London: 1970)

Wilhelm, Karin, *Architekten heute: Portrait Frei Otto* (Berlin: 1985)

FRANK GEHRY

Dal Co, Francesco and Forster, Kurt W., *Frank O. Gehry: The Complete Works* (New York: 1998)

Friedman, Mildred, *Gehry Talks* (London: 2003)

Ragheb, J. Fiona (ed.), *Frank Gehry, Architect* (New York: 2001)

KENZO TANGE

Bettinotti, Massimo (ed.), *Kenzo Tange 1946–1996: Architecture and Urban Design* (Milan: 1996)

Bognar, Botond, *Contemporary Japanese Architecture* (New York: 1985)

Boyd, Robin, *Kenzo Tange* (New York: 1962)

Kulterman, Udo (ed.), *Kenzo Tange 1946–1969: Architecture and Urban Design* (London: 1970)

Sharp, Dennis, 'Kenzo Tange (1913–2005)', *The Architectural Review*, vol. 217 (May 2005), p. 36.

Stewart, David, *The Making of a Modern Japanese Architecture* (Tokyo and New York: 1987)

NORMAN FOSTER

Jenkins, David, *Foster Catalogue* (Munich, New York and London: 2008)

Jenkins, David (ed.), *Norman Foster, Works*, 5 vols (Munich, New York and London: 2003–)

Pawley, Martin, *Norman Foster: A Global Architecture* (London: 1999)

Sudjic, Deyan, *Norman Foster: A Life in Architecture* (London: 2010)

SANTIAGO CALATRAVA

Kent, Cheryl, *Santiago Calatrava* (New York: 2005)

Levin, Michael, *Santiago Calatrava: Artworks* (Basel: 2003)

Tzonis, Alexander, *Santiago Calatrava: The Complete Works* (New York: 2004, 2nd edn 2007)

Tzonis, Alexander, *Santiago Calatrava: The Poetics of Movement* (New York and London: 1999)

Tzonis, Alexander and Caso Donadei, Rebecca, *Calatrava: The Bridges* (New York and London: 2005)

Tzonis, Alexander and Lefaivre, Liane, *Santiago Calatrava: Creative Process*, 2 vols (Basel: 2001)

KENGO KUMA

Alini, Luigi, *Kengo Kuma: Works and Projects* (Milan: 2005)

Bognar, Botond, *Kengo Kuma: Selected Works* (New York: 2005)

Bognar, Botond, *Material Immaterial: The New Work of Kengo Kuma* (New York: 2009)

Futagawa, Yukio (ed.), *Kengo Kuma: Recent Projects* (Tokyo: 2009)

Houdart, Sophie and Chihiro, Minato, *Kuma Kengo. An unconventional monograph* (Paris: 2009)

Yoshida, Nobuyuki (ed.), 'Kengo Kuma', *The Japan Architect*, no. 38, special issue (Winter 2000)

SOURCES OF ILLUSTRATIONS

a = above; b = below; c = centre

1 Photo Scala, Florence – courtesy of the Ministero Beni e Att. Culturali; 2–3 National Media Museum/Science and Society Picture Library; 4–5 istockphoto.com; 6 Photo Will Pryce © Thames & Hudson Ltd, London; 7 Erich Lessing/akg-images; 8–9 British Library, London; 10 Photo Angelo Hornak; 11 British Library/akg-images; 12 Courtesy the Institution of Civil Engineers, London; 13 From *Dictionnaire raisonné de l'architecture française du XIe au XVIe siècle*, vol. 4 (Paris: 1859); 14 Chicago Architectural Photographing Company; 15 © Arcaid/Alamy; 17 Time Life Pictures/Getty Images; 18 © Edmund Sumner/VIEW; 23 Photo Scala, Florence – courtesy of Musei Civici Fiorentini; 24 Photo Scala, Florence – courtesy of the Ministero Beni e Att. Culturali; 26 Brancacci Chapel, Santa Maria del Carmine, Florence; 27 Alinari Archives, Florence; 30 © B. O'Kane/Alamy; 31 © Corbis; 33 © Sheila Blair and Jonathan Bloom. Courtesy of the Aga Khan Visual Archive, MIT; 34 Rijksmuseum, Amsterdam; 35 Photo Scala, Florence; 36 Museo Nazionale del Bargello, on loan to the Piccolo Museo, Palazzo Strozzi, Florence; 37 Alinari Archives, Florence; 39 Photo Scala, Florence – courtesy of the Ministero Beni e Att. Culturali; 41 Jon Arnold/awl-images; 42 © Reha Günay; 43 Gérard Degeorge/akg-images; 44 © Reha Günay; 46 Freer Gallery of Art, Washington, DC (39.49);; 49, 50 © Ebba Koch; 51 From *Royal Society Register Book Original*, II, pp. 321–22, dated 4 December 1663; 53, 54 The Warden and Fellows of All Souls College, Oxford; 55 Sir John Soane's Museum, London; 57 © Chris Andrews/Oxford Picture Library; 58 Master and Fellows of Trinity College, Cambridge; 59 Bodleian Library, Oxford; 61 Guillo/Archives CDA/akg-images; 62 École Supérieure et d'Application du Génie, Angers/Giraudon/Bridgeman Art Library; 63 Guillo/Archives CDA/akg-images; 64 Georg Gerster/Panos Pictures; 65 Collection du ministère de la défense, Service Historique de la Défense, Département de l'armée de terre, France; 68, 69, 70 Courtesy the Institution of Civil Engineers, London; 71 Photo Stefan Schaffer; 72, 73 Courtesy the Institution of Civil Engineers, London; 75, 77 Nationalgalerie, Staatliche Museen zu Berlin; 78 SSG Potsdam-Sanssouci; 80 Nationalgalerie, Staatliche Museen zu Berlin; 81 Courtesy the Newington-Cropsey Foundation; 83 Mary Evans Picture Library; 84 Courtesy the Baltimore Sun Company, Inc. All Rights Reserved; 85 from Bogardus, J., *Cast Iron Buildings* (1856). Courtesy Peabody Essex Museum, Salem, Massachusetts; 86 Collection of Wayne Colwell; 87 RIBA Drawings Photographs Collection, London; 88 Liverpool Record Office, Liverpool Libraries; 89 © Country Life; 90–91 RIBA Library Drawings Collection, London; 93 V&A Images, Victoria and Albert Museum; 94 RIBA Library Drawings Collection, London; 95 Bibliothèque nationale de France, Paris; 96 Bibliothèque de l'Ecole nationale supérieure des beaux arts, Paris; 97 Patrick Müller © Centre des monuments nationaux; 98, 99 Bibliothèque historique de la Ville de Paris; 100 Science Museum Pictorial/Science and Society Picture Library; 101 © Robert Harding Picture Library Ltd/Alamy; 102 National Railway Museum/Science and Society Picture Library; 103 NRM – Pictorial Collection/Science and Society Picture Library; 104 Science and Society Picture Library; 106 With the permission of the University of Bristol Library Special Collections (ref. DM162/8/1/1/Sketchbook 1852–1854/f. 18); 107 Palace of Westminster, London; 108 V&A Images, Victoria and Albert Museum, London; 109 © Martin Charles; 111 RIBA Library Drawings Collection; 112 Courtesy The Landmark Trust; 113 From *Dictionnaire raisonné de l'architecture Française du XIe au XVIe siècle*, vol. 4 (Paris: 1859); 114 © Ministère de la Culture – Médiathèque de l'Architecture et du Patrimoine, Dist. RMN/photo RMN; 115 Alinari/Bridgeman Art Library; 116, 117 From *Entretiens sur l'architecture*, Paris, first issued in 1868; 118 © Ministère de la Culture – Médiathèque du Patrimoine, Dist. RMN/photo RMN; 119 from Mackay, T., *Life of J. Fowler* (London: 1900); 120, 122, 123 Courtesy The Institution of Civil Engineers, London; 125 PLA collection/Museum of London; 129 © Bettmann/Corbis; 130, 131 Achille Bertarelli Print Collection, Milan; 132 Biblioteca Trivulziana and Archivio Storico Civico, Milan; 133 Civico Archivio Fotografico, Milan; 134 Ryerson and Burnham Libraries Book Collection, Ryerson and Burnham Archives, The Art Institute of Chicago. Digital File No. DFRWCE.Port_Jenney; 135 Photo J.W. Taylor (Chicago), *c.* 1890s. HALIC, The Art Institute of Chicago. Digital File No. 16473; 136 From *Industrial Chicago* (Chicago: 1891); 137 Photo J. W. Taylor (Chicago), 1913. HALIC, The Art Institute of Chicago; 138 Library of Congress, Washington, DC; 139 Photo C. D. Arnold. World's Columbian Exposition Photographs by C. D. Arnold, The Art Institute of Chicago. Digital File No. 198902.03_067-104; 140 ND/Roger-Viollet/Topfoto; 143 © David Bagnall/Alamy; 144–45 Musée Carnavalet/Roger-Viollet/Topfoto; 146, 147 Roger-Viollet/Topfoto; 148 From Mollins, S. de, 'Le béton de ciment armé, procédé Hennebique', *Bulletin de la Société vaudoise des ingénieurs et des architectes*, 1893, pl. 22; 150 CNAM/SIAF/Cité de l'architecture et du patrimoine /Archives d'architecture du XXe siècle; 151 Courtesy Gwenaël Delhumeau; 152 CNAM/SIAF/Cité de l'architecture et du patrimoine/Archives d'architecture du XXe siècle; 154 Iberfoto/AISA; 155 Cátedra Gaudí Archives ETSAB-UPC; 156 J. Bedmar/Iberfoto/AISA; 158 Cátedra Gaudí Archives ETSAB-UPC; 159 Private collection; 160 © Jordi Camí/Alamy; 161 Ricatto/Iberfoto/AISA; 162 Sullivaniana Collection, The Art Institute of Chicago. Digital File No. 193101.080623-01; 163 J. W. Taylor (Chicago), *c.* 1890s. HALIC, The Art Institute of Chicago. Digital File No. 49666; 164 Photo Richard Nickel, courtesy John Vinci; 165 Chicago Architectural Photographing Company; 167, 168 Photo courtesy Robert Twombly; 171 Courtesy Special Collections Research Center, University of Chicago Library; 172 From *Frank Lloyd Wright: Ausgeführte Bauten* (Berlin: 1911); 173 © Richard A. Cooke/Corbis; 174 RIBA Library Photographs Collection; 176 Photograph David Heald © The Solomon R. Guggenheim Foundation, New York; 179 © Albert Harlingue/Roger-Viollet/Topfoto; 180, 181, 182 CNAM/SIAF/CAPA, Archives d'architecture du XXe siècle/Auguste Perret/UFSE/SAIF/année; 184 Bibliothèque de la Ville, La Chaux-de-Fonds, Switzerland, Fonds Le Corbusier; 185, 186 © FLC/ADAGP, Paris and DACS, London 2011; 187a © Bildarchiv Monheim GmbH/Alamy; 187b © Peter Cook/VIEW; 189 Franz Hubmann/Imagno/akg-images; 190, 191a Photo Tim Benton; 191b © Olivier Martin Gambier/Artedia/VIEW; 193 Hedrich Blessing/arcaidimages.com; 194 Digital image Mies van der Rohe/Gift of the Arch./MoMA/Scala. © 2011 The Museum of Modern Art, New York; 195 © Klaus Frahm/artur; 197 Martine Franck/Magnum Photos; 198 RIBA Library Photographs Collection, London; 199 Canadian Centre for Architecture, Montreal; 202, 204 Centro archivi MAXXI architettura, Rome; 205 RIBA Library Photographs Collection, London; 209, 211, 213, 214, 215, 216 Courtesy the Estate of R. Buckminster Fuller; 217, 218 © Arup; 219 RIBA Library Drawings Collection, London; 220 State Library of New South Wales. Courtesy Jan Utzon; 221 © Arup; 224 Louis I. Kahn Collection, The University of Pennsylvania and the Pennsylvania Historical and Museum Commission. Photo Lionel Freedman; 227 © Peter Cook/VIEW; 228 © Michel Denance/Artedia/VIEW; 229 © Collection Centre Pompidou, Dist. RMN/Jean-Claude Planchet/Georges Meguerditchian/photo RMN; 231 Fonds J. Prouvé. Bibliothèque Kandinsky, Centre Pompidou, MNAM, Paris; 232 © Lucien Hervé/Artedia/VIEW; 233 Fonds J. Prouvé. Bibliothèque Kandinsky, Centre Pompidou, MNAM, Paris; 234 © Marcelo Sayao/epa/Corbis; 235, 237, 238 © Styliane Philippou; 239 © Alan Weintraub/Arcaid/Corbis; 241 © Charles E. Rotkin/Corbis; 242, 243 Manuscripts and Archives, Yale University Library, New Haven; 245, 246 © Balthazar Korab Ltd; 247 © Bettmann/Corbis; 248 Architectural Press Archive/RIBA Library Photographs Collection; 250 Photolibrary; 251 RIBA Library Photographs Collection; 252 © Roland Halbe/artur; 254 © Douglas Kirkland/Corbis; 255 Photo T. Kitajima; 256 © Marie Velasco; 257 Image courtesy Gehry Partners, LLP; 258 © Luc Boegly/Artedia/VIEW; 260 www.studiom-miami.com; 263 Courtesy Tange Associates; 264 Photo Akio Kawasumi. Courtesy Tange Associates; 265 Photo courtesy Shinkenchiku-sha Co., Ltd; 266 Photo by Osamu Murai; 267 Photo courtesy Shinkenchiku-sha Co., Ltd; 269 Photo Will Pryce © Thames & Hudson Ltd, London; 270 © Norman Foster; 271 © Ian Lambot; 272 © Construction Photography/Corbis; 274a Photo © Rudi Meisel, Berlin; 274b Foster + Partners; 275 Photo Will Pryce © Thames & Hudson Ltd, London; 276 Foster + Partners; 277 Santiago Calatrava, Architect & Engineer; 279a, 279c, 279b Palladium Photodesign/Oliver Schuh – Barbara Burg. Courtesy Santiago Calatrava, Architect & Engineer; 280a, 280b Santiago Calatrava, Architect & Engineer; 282 Palladium Photodesign/Oliver Schuh – Barbara Burg. Courtesy Santiago Calatrava, Architect & Engineer; 283 Santiago Calatrava, Architect & Engineer; 284 Alan Karchmer. Courtesy Santiago Calatrava, Architect & Engineer; 287, 288, 289a, 289b © Botond Bognar

INDEX